British Art Now: An American Perspective

1980 Exxon International Exhibition

by Diane Waldman

This exhibition is sponsored by

Exxon Corporation

with the support of The British Council

The Solomon R. Guggenheim Museum,

New York

in association with

The American Federation of Arts and

The Royal Academy, London,

with the support of

Esso Petroleum Company, Limited

Artists in
the Exhibition

John Edwards

Alan Green

Tim Head

Keith Milow

David Nash

Hugh O'Donnell

Nicholas Pope

Simon Read

Published by

The Solomon R. Guggenheim Foundation, New York, 1979

ISBN: 0-89207-020-X

Library of Congress Card Catalogue Number: 79-89380

Lenders to
the Exhibition

Frits and Agnes Becht, Naarden, The Netherlands
Alan Green
David Nash
Hugh O'Donnell
Silas Rhodes

Annely Juda Fine Art, London
Rowan Gallery, London
Anthony Stokes Gallery, London

The Arts Council of Great Britain, London
The British Council, London
Leeds City Art Galleries, Leeds
The Solomon R. Guggenheim Museum, New York
Rijksmuseum Kröller-Müller, Otterlo, The Netherlands

4

Preface and Acknowledgements

British Art Now: An American Perspective may be said to have evolved from two exhibition traditions at the Guggenheim Museum. On the one hand, it is the first in a sequence of projected international counterparts of *Young American Artists,* shown here as the *1978 Exxon National Exhibition.** Simultaneously, however, it derives from the survey, *Younger European Painters: A Selection,* 1953, whose title is indicative of its scope, as well as from a series of Guggenheim Internationals presented under our aegis between 1956 and 1971. When the encyclopedic premise of the latter became strained, these shows were abandoned in favor of investigations of regional developments. *Amsterdam-Paris-Dusseldorf,* 1972, was the first of these presentations. All of these events devoted to international art form the background for the *Exxon International Exhibitions* which alternate biennially with the *Exxon National Exhibitions.* Thus, *British Art Now* fulfills two of the Guggenheim Museum's longstanding commitments. The first is to younger artists whose work has not yet reached a wide audience; the second, to artists from abroad and thus to internationalism.

Long experience with national and international surveys has convinced us of the futility of committees for such purposes. Since 1964, therefore, a single curator has been responsible for the selection of these shows; it has been our policy, however, to rotate curators to avoid too continuous an assertion of personal viewpoint. This first of the *Exxon International Exhibitions,* which occurs after an extended pause necessitated by economic stringency, has been chosen and mounted by Diane Waldman, the Guggenheim's Curator of Exhibitions, who, after repeated and conscientious investigations of the state of *British Art Now,* asserts her American perspective. As is usual in ventures of this kind, Mrs. Waldman has benefited from advice from many quarters and acknowledges the extensive assistance she has

* The three *Theodoron Awards* of 1969, 1971 and 1977. as well as the very early *Younger American Painters* survey of 1954, may be cited as precursors of this recent event.

received in the course of this many-leveled enterprise. She has, however, made all final judgements herself and accepts full and undivided responsibility for them.

The participation of many organizations as sponsors, circulators and exhibitors, remains to be acknowledged. Among these, Exxon Corporation deserves the first and most prominent mention. As we had occasion to point out in the inauguration of the *1978 Exxon National Exhibition,* the Corporation has, through its support of exhibitions of current art, assumed a position of leadership among corporate sponsors that is enhanced with every new commitment of its kind and becomes increasingly visible and admirable with the passage of time. It is particularly gratifying to observe that Esso Petroleum Co., Ltd., has joined the sponsorship of the exhibition's British tour, which is also made possible by the aid and support received from The British Council as well as through the commitment of The Royal Academy to present the final showing of *British Art Now* on its premises. Finally, I would like to express our appreciation to The American Federation of Arts in New York for assuming responsibility for the circulation of the exhibition in the United States, which precedes the aforementioned showing in Britain under the auspices of the Arts Council in London.

Before completing this extensive list of acknowledgements, I should like to return once more to the central role of Exxon Corporation, this time in the context of the acquisitions which are such an important feature of these undertakings. The corporation provides acquisition funds that enable the Guggenheim Museum to purchase one work of its choice by each of the artists represented in both the *Exxon Nationals* and *Internationals.* Thus, fourteen paintings and sculptures by younger American artists were acquired in 1978, and eight more works, these by Britains, will become part of the Guggenheim Museum's collection when the present exhibition opens in New York. In a time of financial stress, acquisition funds are notoriously vulnerable and often become the first casualty of enforced economies. The opportunity to enrich our collection with works by younger artists and thereby keep pace with the developing art scene in this country and abroad may well be the most important aspect of the Exxon series.

Thomas M. Messer, *Director*
The Solomon R. Guggenheim Museum

This exhibition would not have been possible without the advice and assistance of numerous individuals, both here and in Britain. I would like to take this opportunity to thank, in particular, Ian Barker, Exhibition Officer of The British Council, who has worked closely with me on every phase of the project, and my assistant Lisa Tabak, who has seen both the exhibition and catalogue through all stages of preparation. Thanks are also due to Carol Fuerstein, Editor at the Museum, who edited the catalogue; Susan Hirschfeld, Curatorial Assistant, for her help with the catalogue; Ellen Goldhaar, for her work on the publication; Diana Eccles, Exhibition Assistant of The British Council, who compiled much of the documentation; Moira Kelly, who introduced me to the work of a number of very talented young artists; the dealers Alex Gregory-Hood, Annely and David Juda and Anthony Stokes for their most gracious cooperation; and the public and private collectors who were kind enough to lend to this exhibition. Finally, I would like to thank the artists themselves for making the experience of this exhibition a very pleasant one indeed.

D.W.

British Art Now

by Diane Waldman

At a time when the visual arts are the subject of much controversy and seem less authoritative than they have been in the last few decades, it is refreshing indeed to witness a new vitality in British art today. The reasons for this resurgence are unclear— it is impelled perhaps by a handful of artists who feel the need for change. If there is a revolution in Britain, however, it is a quiet one, without the fanfare of the fifties, or the notoriety and novelty of the sixties. There are no labels, schools, polemics, there is no consensus, no common cause. There is stylistic change on an individualized, highly personal basis.

Like American art of the sixties, British art of the same period was large in scale, affirmative in feeling, pragmatic in its approach. The heroic gesture, the intimate touch strangely in keeping with the vast space of the canvases, the painterliness, texture, tactility and intense color, the anguish of the Abstract Expressionism of the fifties had given way to an optimistic, even materialistic view of the world and wholehearted acceptance of the very mixed blessing of pop culture and advanced technology. Painting and sculpture became monuments to the commonplace object; size for the sake of size, the industrial, the synthetic, the manufactured were embraced not only by many Pop artists but by color-field painters and Minimalists as well.

By the early seventies much sixties rhetoric began to sound hollow, the issues of the decade no longer seemed as clear as they had once been, the art appeared unfocused and lacking in vitality. There ensued a kind of stalemate in art which still exists and calls to mind the lull that occurred in New York in the late 1950s. That uninventive period of second-generation Abstract Expressionists came to a close with the advent of Pop Art. The Pop artists brought with them a refreshing sense of change, a dynamism that sparked a whole series of new developments.

Whether the 1980s will usher in a similarly dazzling succession of new movements is open to question. An explosion of this sort does not seem about to occur in the States, despite the benefits of a rich source of private and public support (collectors, galleries, museums). It remains to be seen if a surge of activity will take place in Britain. The support structure there is far from encouraging, very much a skeletal one in comparison to ours or, for that matter, that of Western Europe.

Though the British must rely upon teaching and limited government funding, they are not throttled by commercialism. Financial advantages are not available to the British; they are, however, free from the pressure to create for a particular audience, to create art that is fashionable. In a climate that is not especially sympathetic to the visual arts, they have managed to go about the serious business of making serious art.

The British possess absolute determination, a fierce will to invent in the face of adversity, lack of recognition and inadequate public and private support. They are skeptical of the throwaway, trashy, technological aspects of Pop culture and much of the art of the sixties; they admire the metaphysical values and the nobility of American painting of the fifties. And they are looking back, not only to the generation that preceded them but also to icons, Oriental art, East Indian miniatures. The result is not retarditaire but refreshing and new.

New York remains the primary point of reference for British artists. Nevertheless, younger Britains are no longer as defensive or apologetic about their position in the world of art as they have been in the past. They no longer look to New York as their model. Their sense of confidence is reflected both in their attitude and in their work.

Each of the eight artists in this exhibition has achieved a clarity of expression, each is determined to reinvestigate the premises of art, each is unwilling to compromise. Their resolve speaks well not only of themselves as individuals but of the state of British art today. Although they do not represent a single direction and each was selected exclusively on the basis of his own merits, they do share certain qualities in common. Generally, they eschew monumental size for its own sake, they reject the heroic posture. If their work is small it lacks preciosity; if large, it remains related to the human dimension. The sense of intimacy despite large scale, characteristic of American painting of the 1950s, absent in much of 1960s art, is present once again in the British art of the 1970s.

The cool and rational art of Alan Green shares with Keith Milow's a rigorous sense of form and construction. Yet Green also shares with Nicholas Pope the delicate nuance of the edge which gives life and light to their work. And Milow and Pope have in common a chiseled elegance, an awareness of place and the ability to control large spaces with a minimum number of forms. John Edwards and Milow use signs, although Milow's partake of a greater symbolic residue; Green, too, is experimenting with abstract form but, unlike Edwards and Milow, he purges his vocabulary of all extra-pictorial references. While Hugh O'Donnell, unlike Green, uses extra-pictorial if abstract references, he shares with him a concern for the painting as object and with Edwards an interest in the dialogue between volumetric form and the two-dimensional field. Simon Read and Tim Head have forced us to question our concepts of perception. Read and David Nash have peopled our universe with a new and fantastic set of characters. Together they testify to the vigorous, affirmative climate of British art now.

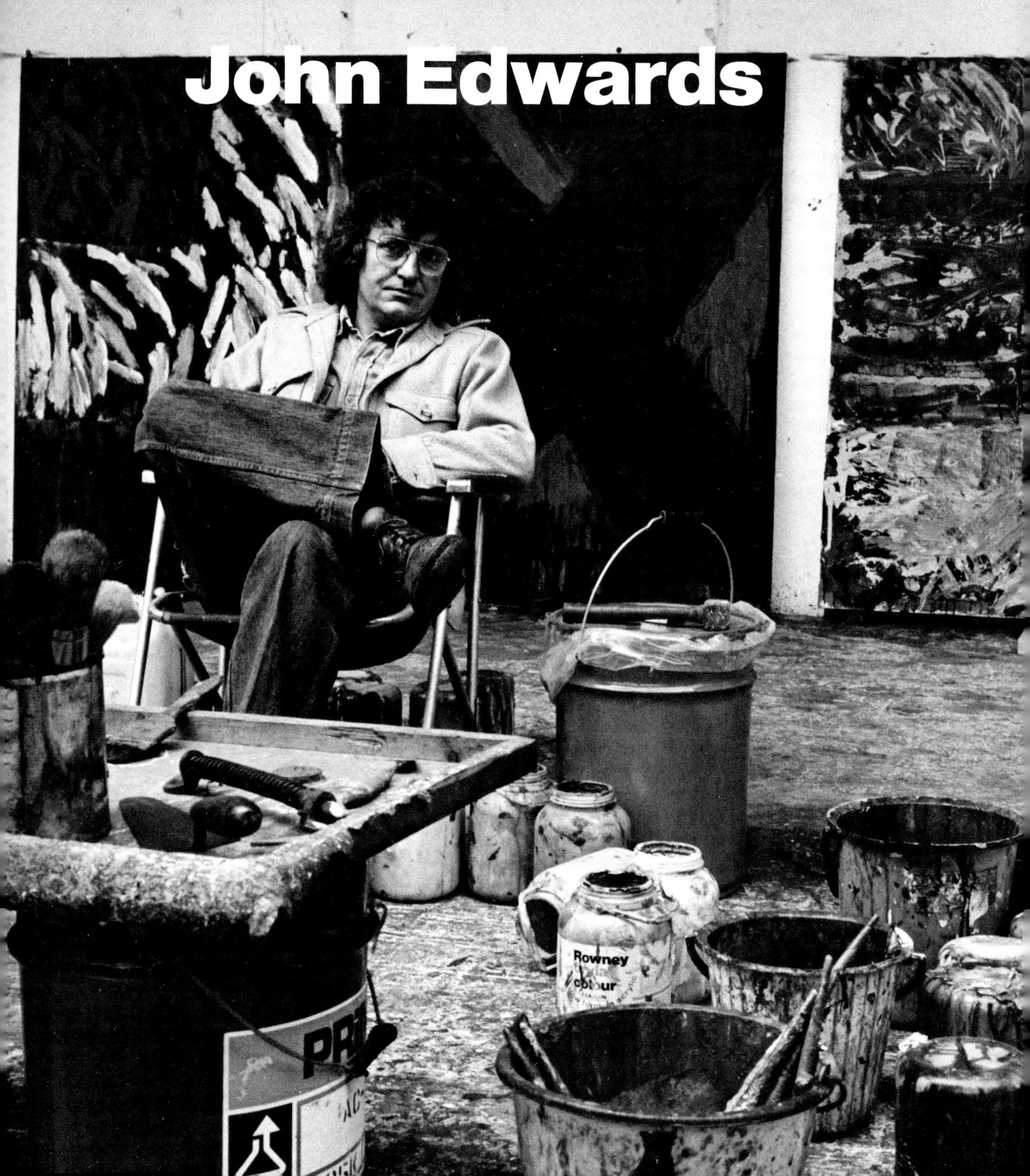
John Edwards
Rowney
colour
PRO

John Edwards' paintings of the last few years represent a significant departure from his earlier work. In his canvases prior to 1974, the figure or series of figures was securely integrated within the underlying grid of the field, and the overall or composite image was one of resolute flatness. The hard-edge works gradually gave way both formally and coloristically to a new freedom of expression: such paintings as *Green Drift,* 1977-78 (cat. no. 3) and *Red Veil,* 1978 (cat. no. 7) are dramatic examples of his recent breakthrough.

The configurations in the recent paintings are generally confined to a few very basic signs—X's, T's, crosses and arcs; these are active and often appear to be on a collision course with one another, agitating or creating an unusual friction within the field. The field no longer functions merely as ground but acts as a series of positive shapes that must be maneuvered into position with the signs so that the space of the composition does not break up. The once quiescent figure and ground have been replaced by a series of totally energized images. A sense of torsion or tension created by the figures and the figure-ground relationship threatens to tear the canvas apart. Edwards encourages this effect of warping or buckling by means of heavily scumbled surfaces, discordant textures, strident often garish colors and irregular or jagged contours. It is only by continuing to emphasize the importance of the field and the part that shape, contour and dimension play in the formulation of the painting's fictive space that he is able to bring all of the disparate elements into a unified totality.

Edwards' early interest in American color painting of the fifties and sixties, especially the work of Rothko and Noland, and his appreciation of Monet, has lately been conjoined with an awareness of the sculpture of David Smith and Anthony Caro. This new influence, more than the spatial interplay of Hofmann's "push-pull" or the expressionist virtuosity of de Kooning's paint handling (which he admires) appears to have provided the impetus for his recent innovations. Edwards' shapes, in fact, partake to some extent of the cut out, collaged, relief-like effects both sculptors have employed to great advantage. It is ironic that Smith and Caro's use of pictorial means in their sculpture has inspired Edwards to reverse that process and incorporate forms of sculptural origin into his painting.

Most recently he became interested in the scribbled paint handling of Stella's new reliefs. Edwards had, as early as 1975-76, anticipated Stella by breaking up his surfaces with similar marks, but the American's work encouraged him to be even bolder in his own experiments. Edwards' objectives, however, are vastly different from those of Stella. He does not wish to enter the area of relief but to hold to a pictorial space. Nor does he want to embellish his surfaces with the kind of random, allover graffiti that Stella employs. Popular sources, such as the spray can "art" of New York's subways or the graffiti of billboards and tenement walls, to which Stella alludes are of little interest to Edwards. Without denying the reality of the world around him, he is exclusively committed to the language of form and color of abstract painting.

Although Edwards had begun to activate his surfaces with brushstrokes and irregular shapes as early as 1974, he did not dramatically alter his vocabulary until 1977. At this time he enlarged his shapes and overlapped them so that they cut drastically into what had formerly been the most important space of the painting, the field, undermining the flatness of the picture plane, opening out the space of his painting. Despite the vitality of the monolithic images, however, the paintings seemed confined, primarily because the active brushwork remained subservient to the shapes themselves, and the field, as it had for Stella, began to appear expendable. Edwards must have recognized this because he repainted an entire series, retaining only the initial configurations. Since he continued to use acrylics rather than oils, he was able to execute new works over the old ones, keeping what he wanted, discarding the rest, in a remarkably short period. Very soon thereafter he produced another, this time entirely new, body of paintings, in which color, shape and texture function dynamically within the field.

The highly charged surfaces of Edwards' most recent canvases, the luminosity of his color—unusual in acrylics—the speed of his brushwork, the very real sense of conflict, impasse and resolution conveyed by forms that can be read as both two and three-dimensional all contribute to a sense of excitement. To the extent that Edwards works in series, his paintings are discursive; the viewer refers to a passage in one and finds pleasure in comparing or contrasting it to a related passage in another. Despite the paintings' serial nature, each is remarkably individual and complete. The impact of much serial work depends upon context for its cumulative effect. Edwards' art is invigorating and original because each painting is at once a part of a serial experience and a self-sufficient entity.

John Edwards

Born in London, 1938

Hornsey College of Art, London, 1953-56, 1958-60

National Service, Royal Air Force, 1956-58

Teaches at Brighton College of Art, 1961

Leeds University Institute, 1962-63

British Council Scholarship to Belgium, 1963-64

Teaches at St. Martin's School of Art, London; Chelsea School of Art, London; Brighton School of Art, 1964-present

Senior Lecturer in Painting at St. Martin's School of Art, 1973

Lectures at Tyler School of Art, Temple University, Philadelphia; Skidmore College of Art, Saratoga Springs, New York; Summer School, Syracuse University, New York, 1975

Artist in Residence, Syracuse University, New York, Autumn 1976

Advisor, Visual Arts Advisory Panel, Greater London Arts Association, 1977-78

Principal Lecturer at St. Martin's School of Art, 1979

Lives in London

Selected Group Exhibitions

MUBEF, Brussels, 1964

Kunstverein, Hamburg, *Britische Kunst Heute,* March-May 1968

Museum of Modern Art, Oxford, *Contemporary British Painting and Sculpture,* July 1968

Rowan Gallery, London, August-September 1968; December 1968-January 1969 (graphics); January-February 1973 (graphics); August 1974; December 1974-January 1975 (graphics); March-April 1976 (drawings); March 1977; December 1978

Leeds City Art Gallery, *Some Recent Art in Britain,* April-May 1969

Ulster Museum, Belfast, *Contemporary Prints,* July-September 1972

Walker Art Gallery, Liverpool, *John Moores Liverpool Exhibition 8,* April-July 1972; *Exhibition 9,* June-September 1974

Grosvenor House Hotel, London, *Industrial Sponsors,* July 1974

Mall Galleries, London, *CAS Art Fair,* January 1975

Cleveland Institute of Art, Ohio, *Contemporary British Art,* January 1976

Sunderland Arts Centre, *7 Artists from the Rowan Gallery,* January-February 1976

Middlesborough Art Gallery, Cleveland, United Kingdom, *Third International Drawing Biennale,* from May 1977. Traveled in United States and United Kingdom

Royal Academy of Arts, London, *British Painting 1952-1977,* September-November 1977

Newcastle upon Tyne Polytechnic Art Gallery, *Small Works,* December 1977; December 1978

Selected One-Man Exhibitions

Rowan Gallery, London, February-March 1967

Rowan Gallery, London, September-October 1968

Rowan Gallery, London, March-April 1970

Rowan Gallery, London, June-July 1971

Rowan Gallery, London, September 1972

Park Square Gallery, Leeds, April 1973

Rowan Gallery, London, August-September 1973

Rowan Gallery, London, June 1975

Lubin House, Syracuse University, New York, April 1976. Catalogue with text by Ludwig Stein

Rowan Gallery, London, May 1977

Newcastle upon Tyne Polytechnic Art Gallery, from March 1979. Traveled to Kettle's Yard, Cambridge; Mappin Art Gallery, Sheffield; Gardner Centre Gallery, University of Sussex; Morley Gallery, London. Catalogue with text by Terence Maloon

Rowan Gallery, London, May 1979

Selected Bibliography

Edwin Mullins, "Movies into 'Stills,'" *Sunday Telegraph,* February 12, 1967

John Russell, "Spectacular Re-hang," *Sunday Times,* February 19, 1967, p. 27

Norbert Lynton, "Jack Bush and John Edwards' Exhibition," *The Guardian,* February 24, 1967, p. 9

Edward Lucie-Smith, "The London Shows," *Studio International,* vol. 173, March 1967, p. 148

Charles Harrison, "UK Commentary," *Studio International,* vol. 179, March 1970, p. 117

Nigel Gosling, "From Durer to Moore," *The Observer,* June 13, 1971, p. 26

William Packer, "London Exhibitions and World Gallery Guide," *Art and Artists,* vol. 6, June 1971, p. 30

Marina Vaizey, "Sugar me sweet," *Financial Times,* September 23, 1972, p. 10

Eddie Wolfram, "London," *Art and Artists,* vol. 7, September 1972, p. 48

John Jones, "John Edwards," *Arts Review,* vol. XXV, April 21, 1973, p. 258

Tim Hilton, "Painter in a tall strait-jacket," *The Observer,* September 16, 1973, p. 34

R. J. Rees, "John Edwards," *Studio International,* vol. 186, October 1973, p. 158

Fenella Crichton, "London," *Art International,* vol. XVII, November 1973, p. 47

Barry Martin, "Interview with John Edwards," *One,* no. 5, November 1974, pp. 8-13

Rosemary Brady, "Colourful Prof visits S.U.," *Syracuse Herald Journal,* July 28, 1975, p. 13

Fenella Crichton, "London," *Art International,* vol. XIX, September 1975, p. 57

James Faure Walker, "John Edwards," *Studio International,* vol. 190, September/October 1975, p. 163

Terence Maloon, "John Edwards' Painting," *Artscribe,* no. 6, April 1977, pp. 28-30

John McEwen, "Star Struck," *The Spectator,* May 14, 1977, p. 27

T. Rendle, "Marginalia," *Architectural Review,* vol. CLXIII, April 1978, p. 192

William Feaver, "Young Professionals," *The Observer,* April 22, 1979, p. 16

Bruce Killeen, "John Edwards," *Arts Review,* vol. XXXI, April 27, 1979, p. 215

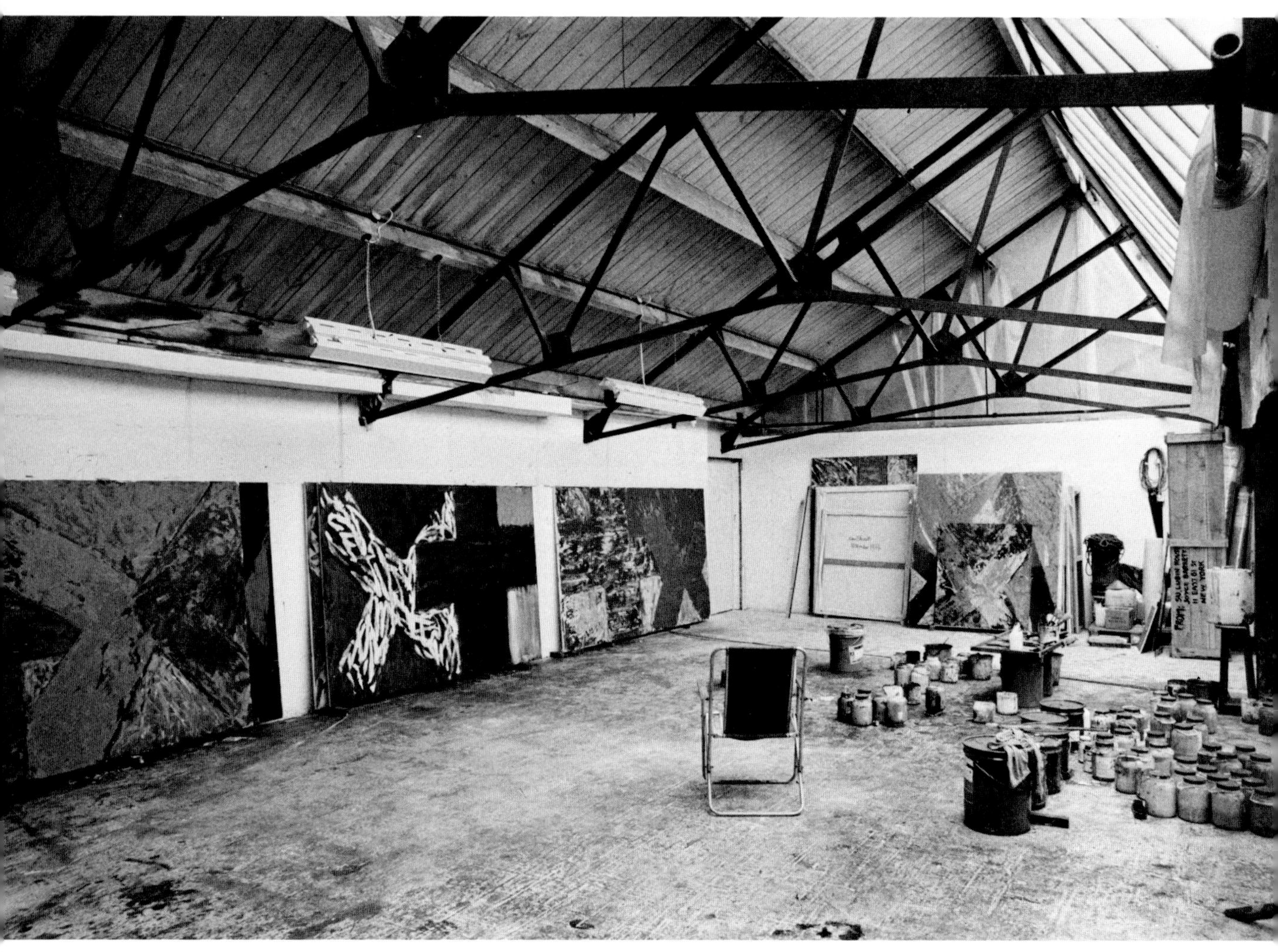

John Edwards' studio

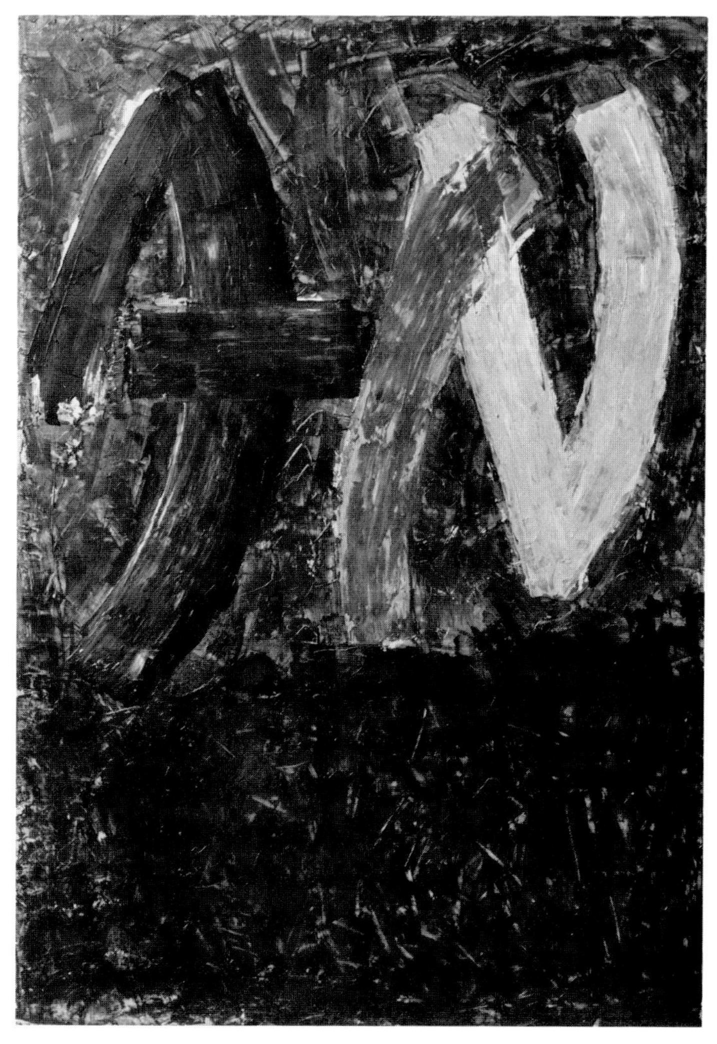

1.
Midnight Blue. 1975
Acrylic on canvas, 72 x 48″
Courtesy Rowan Gallery Ltd., London

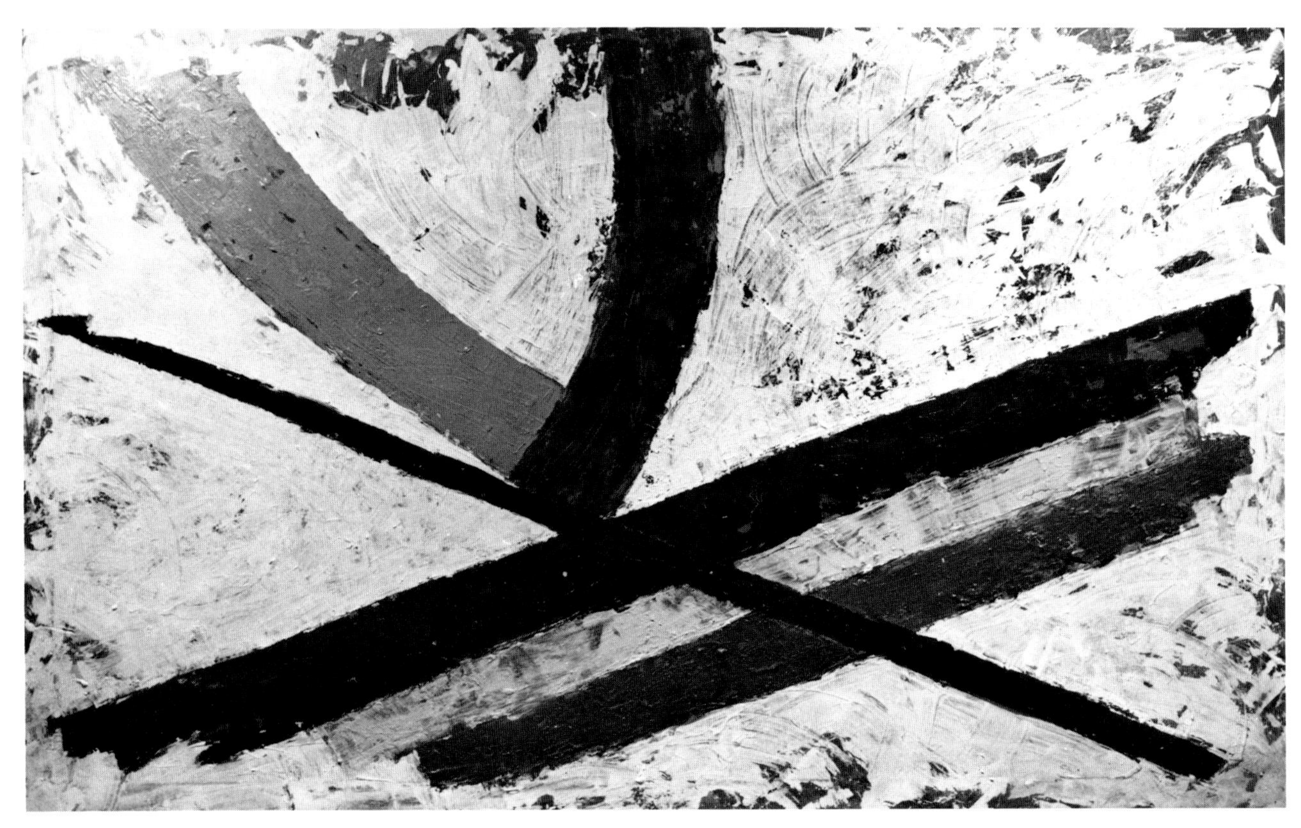

2.
Green Shimmer. 1976
Acrylic on canvas, 60 x 90″
Courtesy Rowan Gallery Ltd., London

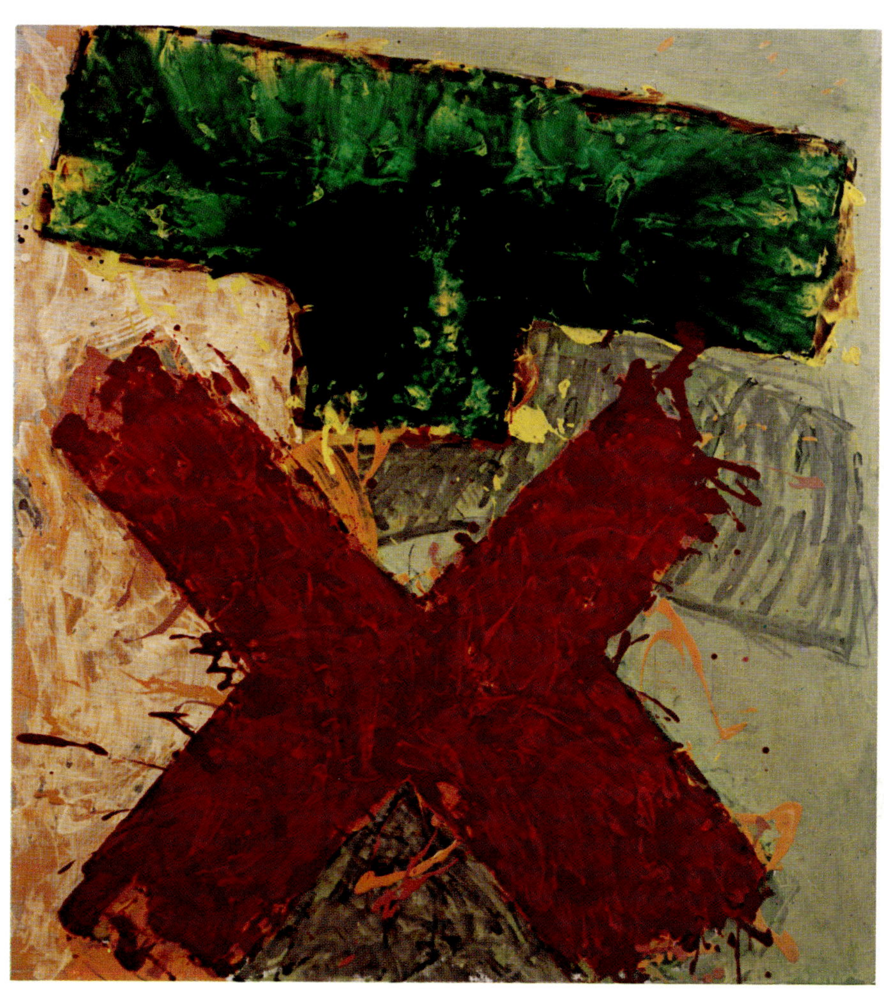

3.
Green Drift. 1977-78
Acrylic on canvas, 66 x 70"
Courtesy Rowan Gallery Ltd., London

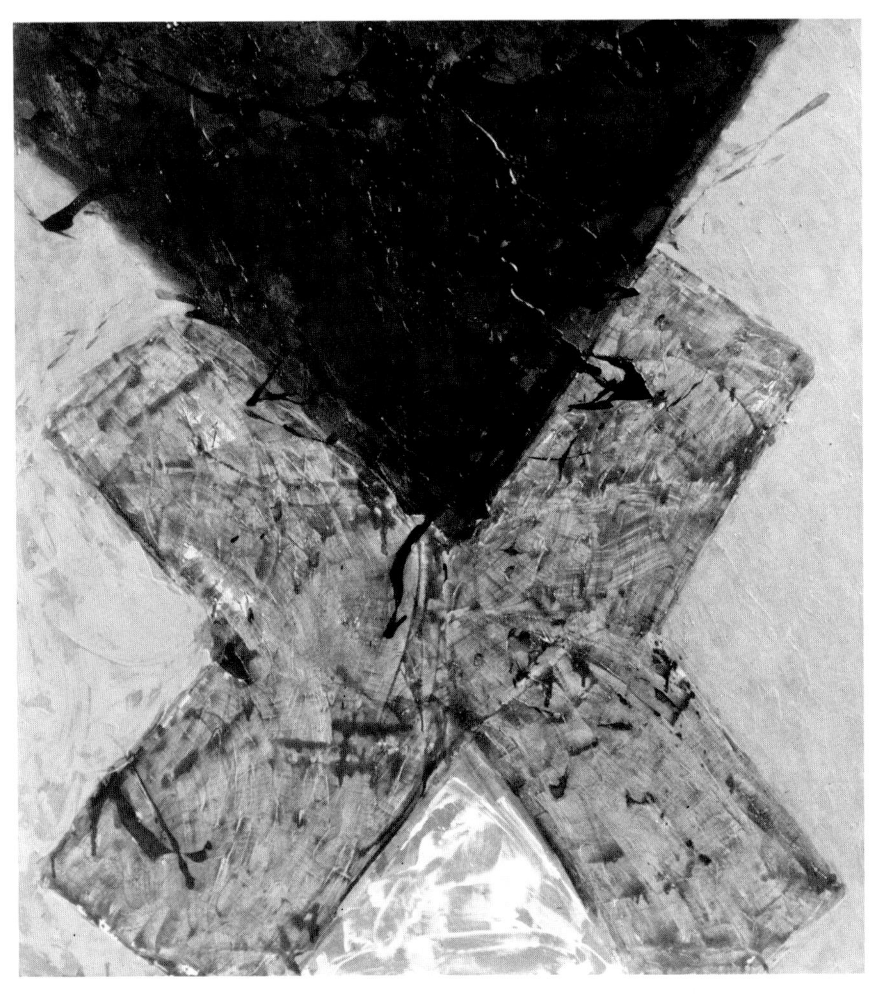

4.
Black Meadow. 1977-78
Acrylic on canvas, 66 x 60″
Collection The British Council, London

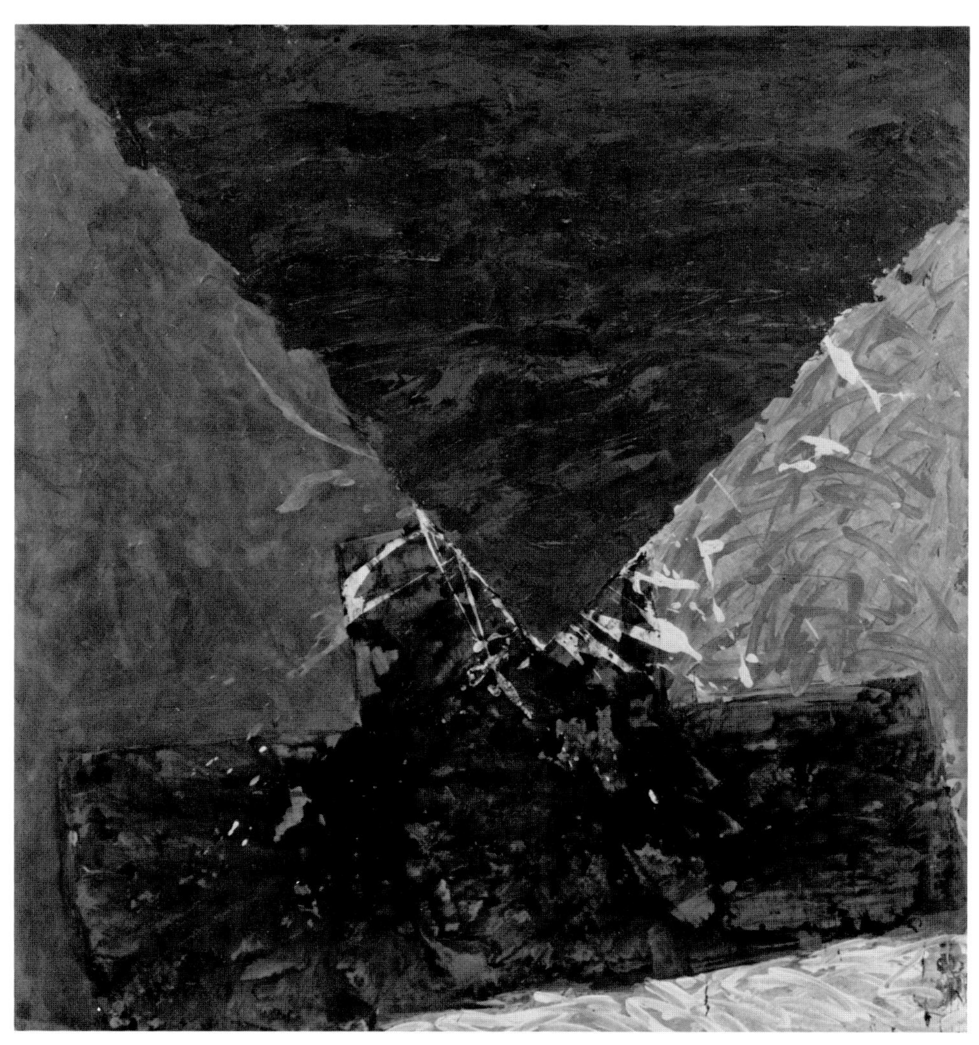

5.
Caesura. 1977-78
Acrylic on canvas, 72 x 66″
Courtesy Rowan Gallery Ltd., London

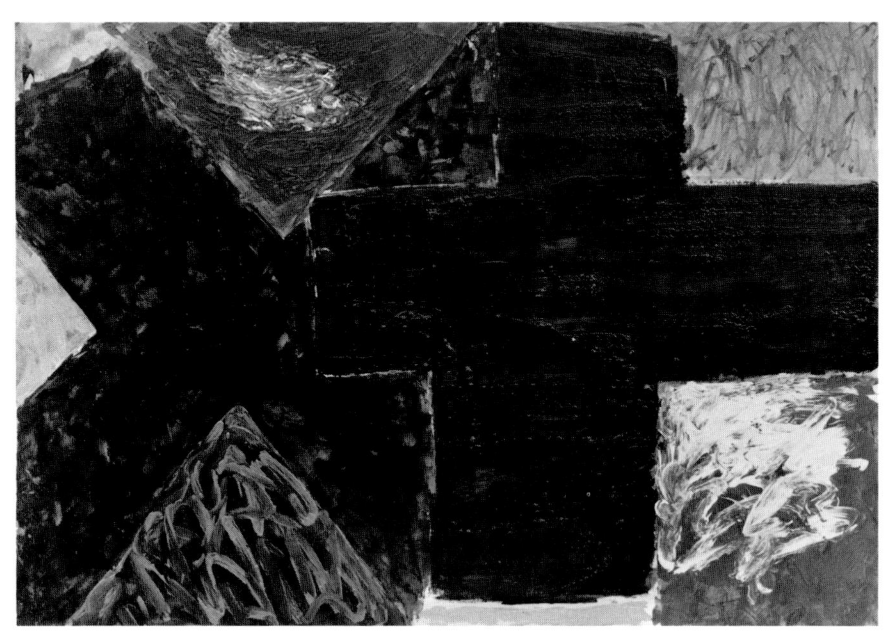

6.
Northern Lights. 1978
Acrylic on canvas, 46 x 66″
Courtesy Rowan Gallery Ltd., London

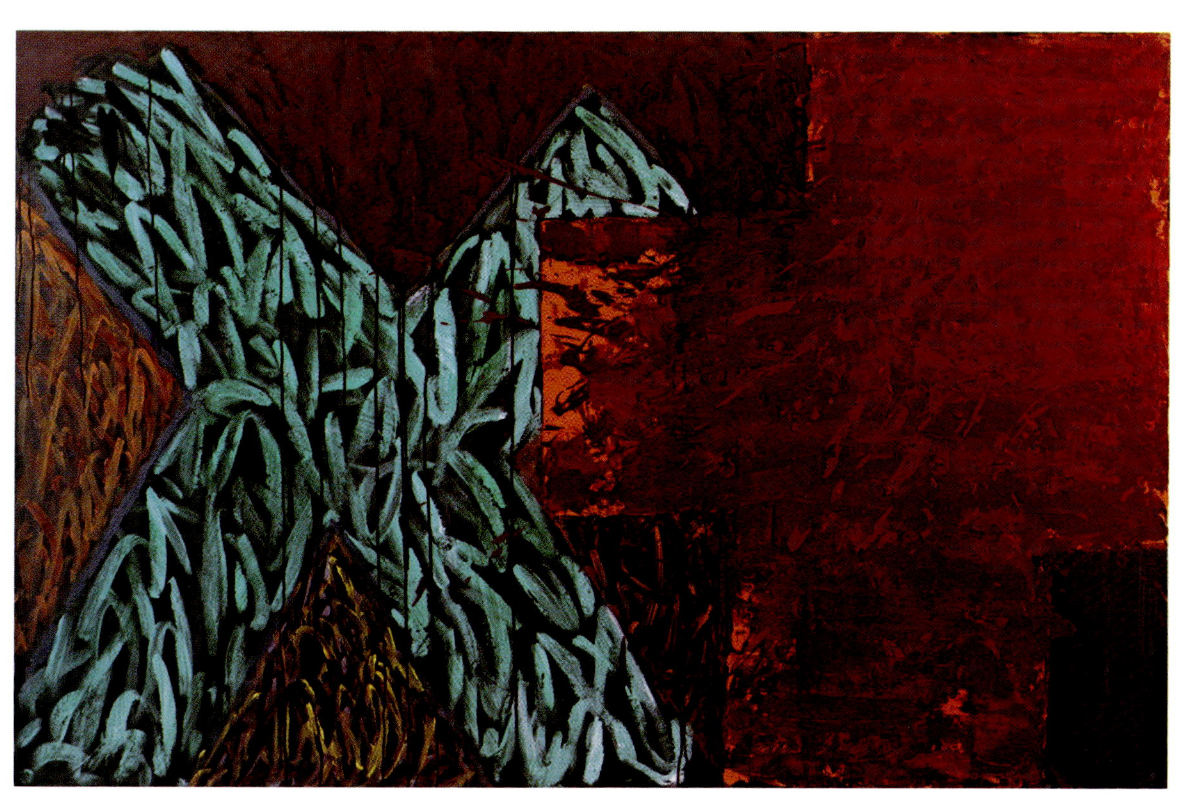

7.
Red Veil. 1978
Acrylic on canvas, 66 x 100″
Courtesy Rowan Gallery Ltd., London

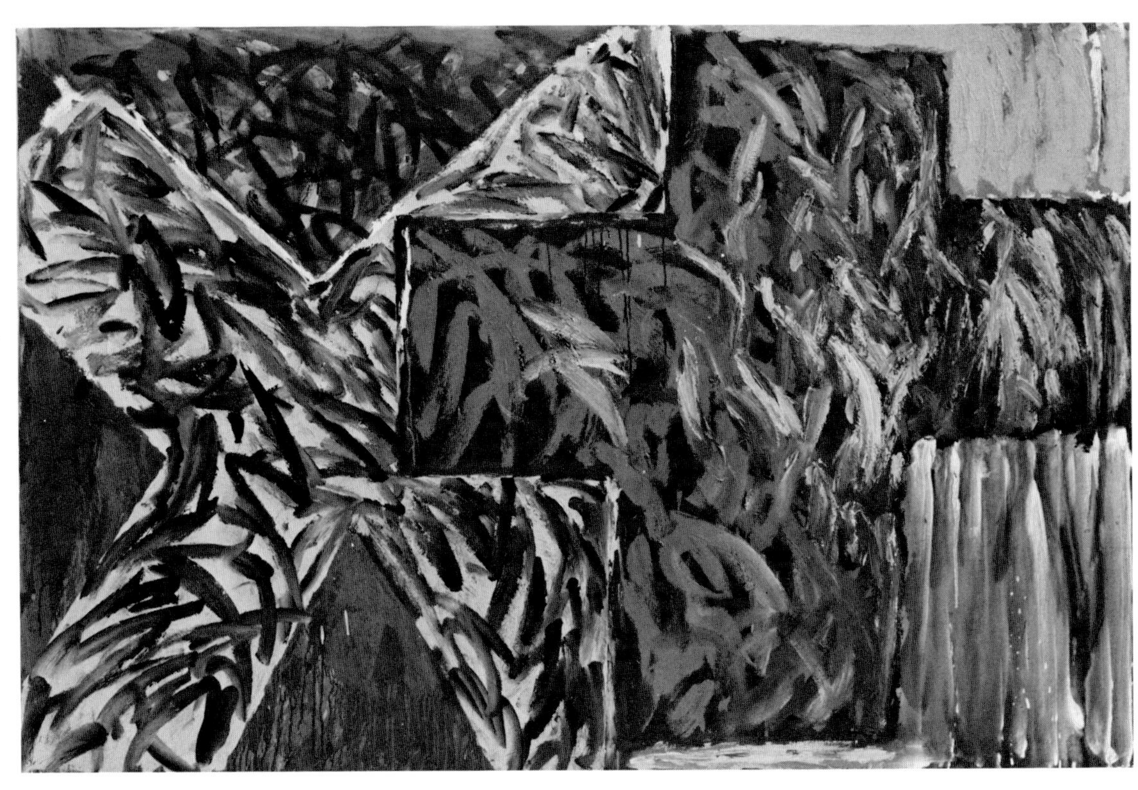

8.
Grey Echo. 1978
Acrylic on canvas, 66 x 96″
Courtesy Rowan Gallery Ltd., London

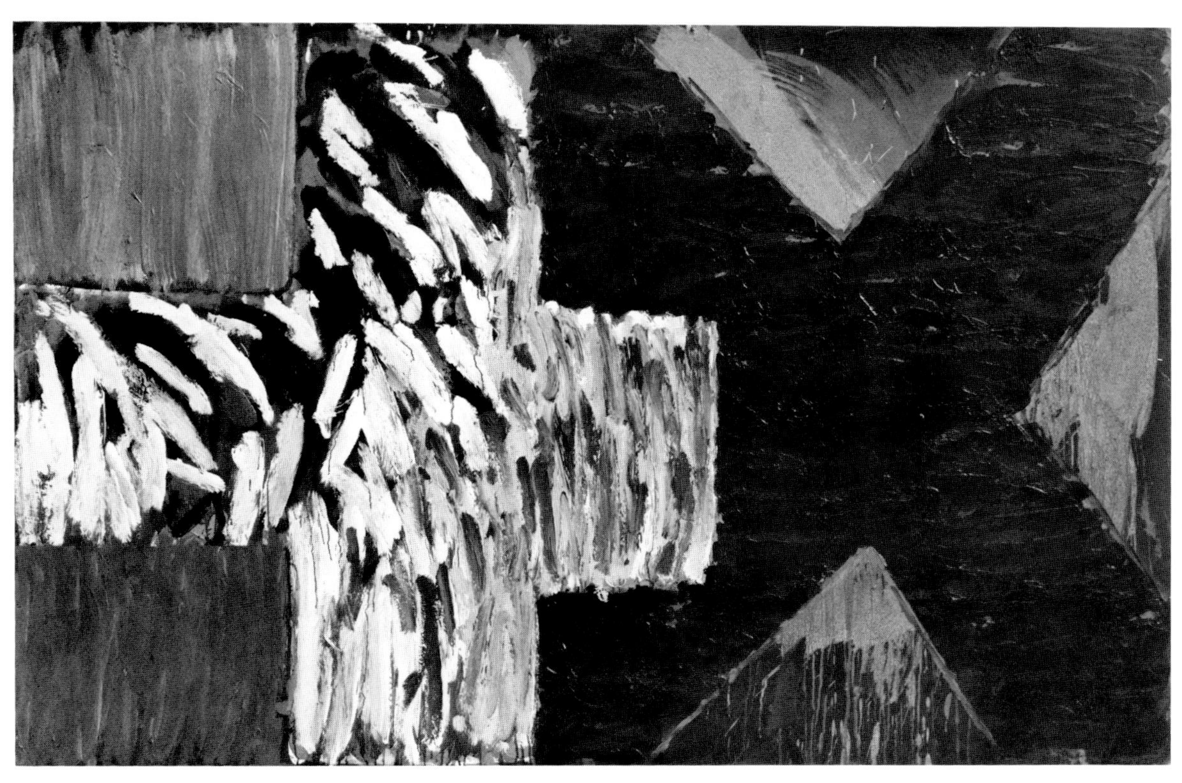

9.
Eclipse. 1978
Acrylic on canvas, 66 x 100″
Courtesy Rowan Gallery Ltd., London

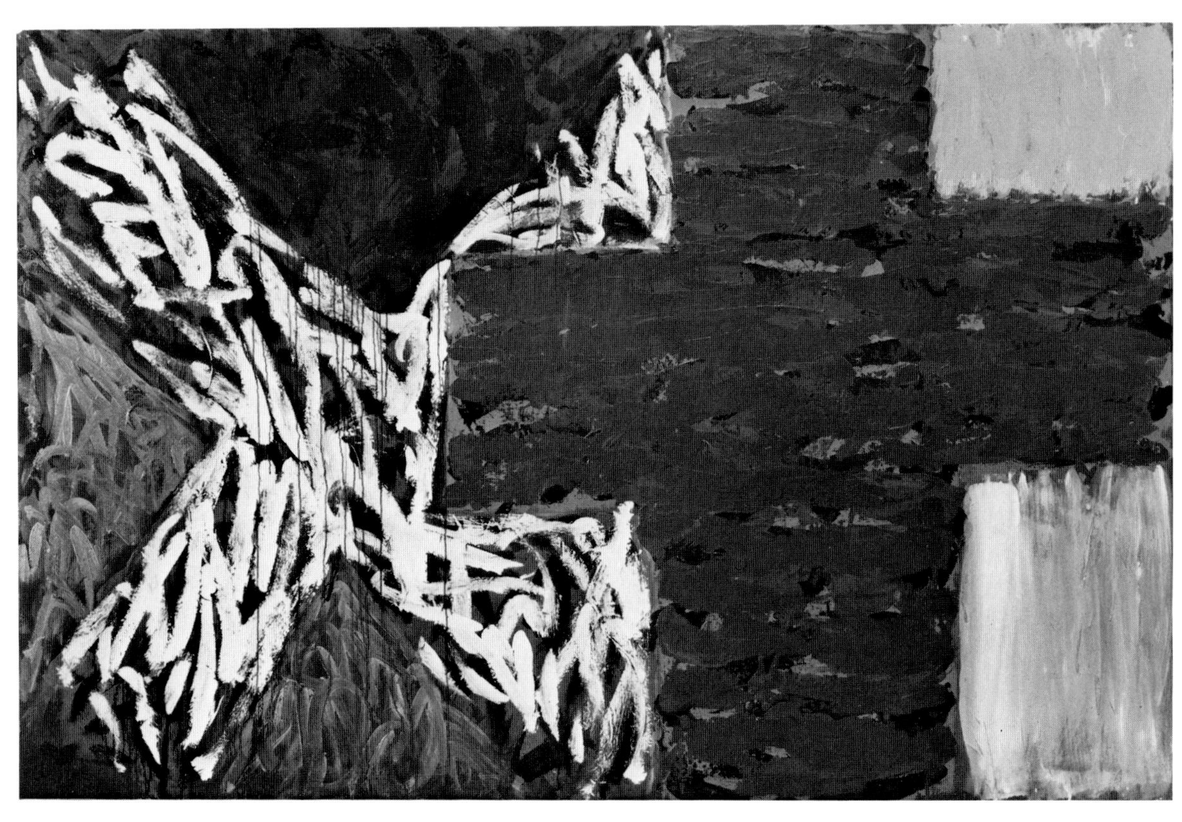

10.
Cochineal. 1978
Acrylic on canvas, 66 x 100″
Courtesy Rowan Gallery Ltd., London

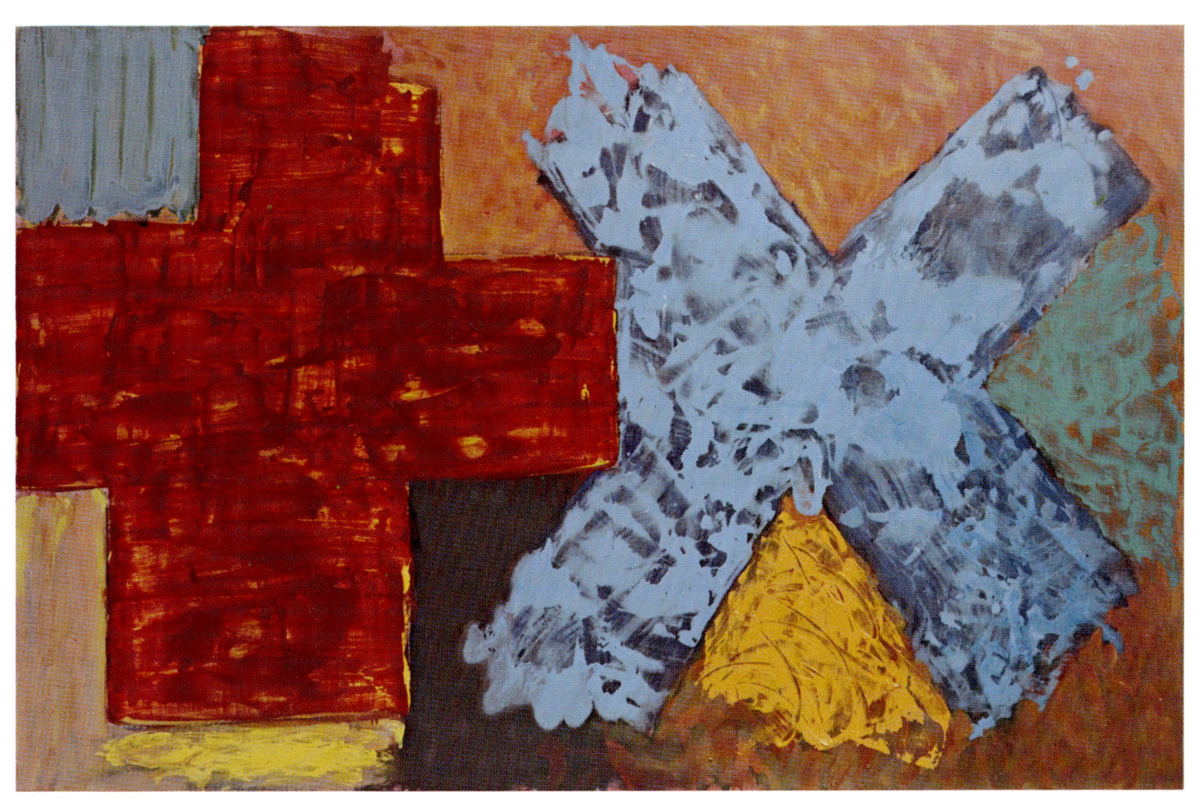

11.
della Robbia Blue. 1979
Acrylic on canvas, 66 x 96″
Courtesy Rowan Gallery Ltd., London

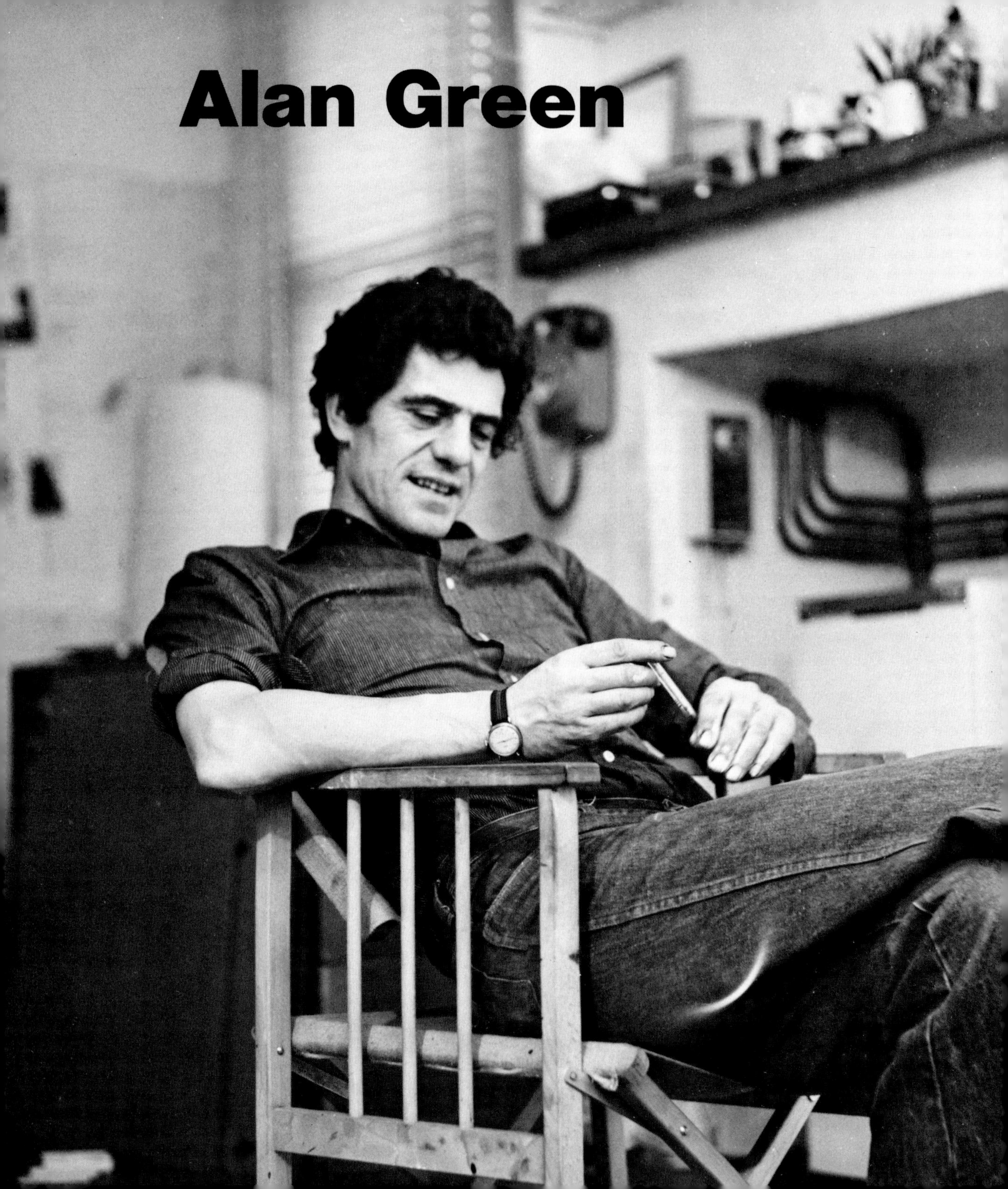
Alan Green

For Alan Green abstract painting is the ultimate reality. The authenticity of the subjective experience as conveyed through abstract form as opposed to the objective portrayal of the real world, is now commonly accepted. Whether this new tradition, now that it has been clearly defined, can continue to nourish artists, to offer them the potential for discovery, experimentation and change is currently being challenged. Green maintains that, despite the limitations inherent in the nature of abstraction, it continues to offer him far more than any form of representation.

An admirer of American painting, Green is by no means uncritical of the color abstraction produced in New York in the fifties and sixties. While he respects Ad Reinhardt's black paintings, especially for the totality of their concept, he questions the tendency of American painters to make their abstract work into icons. Nor is he a polemicist like many Americans—for Green, the actuality of paint and canvas and the creative act are sufficient reasons for the existence of his painting.

In the last few years Green has worked extensively with acrylics. He has also produced a separate, beautifully crafted body of drawings and etchings (cat. nos. 14, 15). For a time he had attempted to incorporate the activity of drawing into his painting (cat. no. 17). While his emphatic line served as a convenient structural device, it tended to suppress the vitality of his paint surface. Green's paintings began to take on a new dimension when he started to experiment wih alternatives to acrylics and to replace line and the precise divisions it created with the more random but equally articulate network of brushstrokes.

Four Vertical Reds, of 1978 (cat. no. 19), was one of the first and most ambitious of these new works. By Green's standards, it is very large: each panel is eight feet high by three feet wide, painted in oil, tempera and arcylic, each possesses its own singular identity. Because each panel is so individual in character, the work initially appears to be about internal relationships, to be self-contained rather than open-ended like much color-field painting of the past. Each uniquely subtle and vital section is augmented rather than diminished by juxtaposition with its neighbors. Ultimately, the variety of surface, texture and qualities of light not only enhances the separate frames but adds to the cumulative experience. The painting is unified by the resolute geometry, the absolute harmony of the fixed proportions of the panels and the use of a single value of red. Together the panels form a majestic sequence, imbued with a grandeur that emanates from the breadth and resonance of the whole.

Although Green has confined himself to a rather limited formal spectrum, the most recent paintings are not the product of a reductive or deductive aesthetic, nor are they dictated by predetermined modules or color choices. He approaches every painting as a singular experience, as an opportunity to experiment with a new format and range of colors. Among his recent, enormously varied works are another four panel painting, this one with sections of uniform height and medium but four different widths, and four different greys (cat. no. 22); a stunning brown canvas, its edges lit by a soft but palpable, very narrow band of pink which comes alive only with prolonged observation (cat. no. 20); and an equally striking canvas whose white lead field is illuminated by a red lead ground revealed at the edges and intermittently flickering through the entire surface (cat. no. 23).

Green's experimentation with materials other than acrylic has altered not only his process but his imagery as well. Acrylic is a fast-drying medium and lends itself to rapid execution. The result of such a swift painting technique is often work which invites immediate response rather than prolonged viewing. As Green has slowed down the process of painting, he has also slowed down the viewing experience. While he is not involved with the contemplative process of an artist like Rothko or the metaphysical discourse of many fifties painters, Green is nevertheless concerned with the act of painting and the evidence of that act. In this he is turning away from the speed of much sixties art and moving towards a more thoughtful form of abstract painting. By introducing duration into his work, he is able to create a vastly more rewarding series of images.

Although color is the basis of Green's art, his paintings are not statements about color per se. Their subject is not the interaction of color, the naming of colors, the alignment of color; rather they are about pushing color to its limits. Green's titles indicate his concern with the varieties of experience generated by color. As he recently noted, "One is called 'Last Red' because it's the darkest possible red I could make before it was no longer a red.... At the moment I've got a painting called 'Blue Space,' and it's exactly that; it has a 1½″ space at the top with Prussian Blue beneath, and it's all about that space."[1]

For Green the act of painting involves not only color and process but the nature of painting as object. In this respect his work is closer to that of Jasper Johns than to much recent color painting. However, unlike Johns, Green does not create emblematic equivalents of real objects or introduce irony to question the language of painting. As Stella did in his early black and metallic series, he acknowledges the objectness of the canvas through its surface, the thickness of the support, edge and pigment. He wishes to retain both the feeling of the objective reality of the painting itself and the sense of the magic inherent in the act of painting. To this end, he cultivates a certain spontaneity, a randomness of paint application, an asymmetry of proportion. It is this quixotic mix of calculation and intuition that endows his color painting with its elusive individuality.

Abstract painters have related their personal visions to the larger human experience in various ways. Often they have resorted to polemics to justify their work or have couched their dialogue in philosophical terms. Or they have made of abstraction a system of logical constructs, a form of geometry that has often reduced rather than enhanced the experience of pure painting. Green, however, celebrates the beauty of painting in his attempt to convey his belief that abstract painting is self-sufficient and that the more personal the experience, the greater and more universal is its ultimate meaning.

1. Rippon, Peter, "Painting Now: Alan Green," *Artscribe,* no. 5, February 1977, p. 7

Alan Green

Born in London, 1932

Beckenham School of Art, Kent, 1949-53

National Service, Korea and Japan, 1953-55

Royal College of Art, London, 1955-58

R.C.A. Major Travelling Scholarship, France and Italy, 1958-59

Teaches at Hornsey College of Art, London, 1959-61; Leeds College of Art, 1961-66; Ravensbourne College of Art and Design, Kent, 1966-74

Intaglio Print Prize, *4th British International Print Biennale,* Bradford City Art Gallery, 1974

Giles Bequest Prize for a British Printmaker, *5th British International Print Biennale,* Bradford City Art Gallery, 1976

Third Prize, *6 Miedzy narodowe Biennale Grafiki/ VIe Internationale Biennale de la Gravure,* Krakow, 1976

Purchase Prize, *XII Mednarodni Bienale Grafike,* Ljubljana, Yugoslavia, 1977

RTE Grapics Award, Limerick, Ireland, 1977

Writers Award, *Listowel Graphic Art Open Exhibition,* Ireland, 1978

Grand Prize, *4 Norske Internasjonale Grafikk Biennale,* Fredrikstad, Norway, 1978

Prize of the Museum of Modern Art, Rijeka, *XIII Mednarodni Bienale Grafike,* Ljubljana, Yugoslavia, 1979

Prize of the National Museum of Art, Osaka, *11th International Biennale Exhibition of Prints,* Tokyo, 1979

National Westminster Bank Prize, *6th British International Print Biennale,* Bradford City Art Gallery, 1979

Lives in London

Selected Group Exhibitions

R.B.A. Galleries, London, *Young Contemporaries,* May 1957; 1958

Walker Art Gallery, Liverpool, *John Moores Liverpool Exhibition 5,* November 1965; *Exhibition 6,* November 1967; *Exhibition 8,* April-June 1972; *Exhibition 9,* June-September 1974; *Exhibition 11,* November 1978-February 1979

Welsh Arts Council, Cardiff, *Structure 66,* June 1966

Camden Arts Council, London, *"Survey 67" Abstract Painting,* June 1967. Catalogue with text by Paul Overy

Fredrikstad Bibliotek, Norway, *1 Norske Internasjonale Grafikk Biennale,* October 1967; *4 Norske Internasjonale Grafikk Biennale,* August 1978

Galerie Heide Hildebrand, Klagenfurt, Austria, *Junge Engländer,* September 1967

Galerie Onnasch, Berlin, *British Movements,* October 1969

Bradford City Art Gallery, *2nd British International Print Biennale,* September-December 1970; *4th British International Print Biennale,* July 1974; *5th British International Print Biennale,* June 1976; *6th British International Print Biennale,* May-July 1979

Alexandra Palace, London, *Art Spectrum London,* August 1971

Musée d'Art Moderne de la Ville de Paris, *La Peinture anglaise aujourd'hui,* February 1973

Kunsthalle Düsseldorf, *Prospekt '73,* September 1973

XII Bienal de São Paulo, Brazil, October 1973

Palais de l'Europe, Menton, France, *Xe Biennale d'Art: The Process of Painting,* July 1974. Catalogue with text by Melanie Sandiford

Hayward Gallery, London, *British Painting 74,* September 1974

Galerie Rencontres, Paris, *Critique théorie art no. 3,* April 1975. Catalogue with text by Catherine Millet

Comune Rimini and Museo Castelvecchio, Verona, *Empirica,* June 1975

Schweizer Mustermesse, Basel, *British Exhibition Art 6 '75,* June 1975

Nordjylands Kunst Museum, Oslo, *Tendencies in Modern Painting,* 1975

6 Miedzy narodowe Biennale Grafiki / VIe Internationale Biennale de la Gravure, Krakow, 1976

Galleria Civica Comune di Modena, Italy, *Cronica,* March 1976

Galleria d'Arte Moderna, Bologna, *Europa America l'Astrazione Determinata 60-76,* May 1976

Istituto Italo Latino Americano, Rome, *I Colori della Pittura una situazione europa,* July 1976

Moderna galerija, Ljubljana, Yugoslavia, *XII Mednarodni Biennale Grafike,* May 1977; *XIII Mednarodni Biennale Grafike,* May 1979

Young Hoffman, Gallery, Chicago, *Five British Painters,* April 1977

Kassel, Germany, *Documenta VI,* June 1977

Royal Academy of Arts, London, *British Painting 1952-77,* September-November 1977

Rheinisches Landesmuseum, Bonn, *Bilder Ohne Bilder,* December 1977

The Mechanized Image (An Historical Perspective of 20th Century Prints), from February 1978. Organized by The Arts Council of Great Britain, traveled to Abbotsholme School, Uttoxeter; Portsmouth City Museum and Art Gallery; Graves Art Gallery, Sheffield; Ferens Art Gallery, Kingston upon Hull; Camden Arts Centre, London; Hatton Gallery, Newcastle upon Tyne; Aberdeen Art Gallery and Museum

Listowel Graphic Art Open Exhibition, Ireland, 1978

Lunds Konsthal, Sweden, *Brittiskt 60-70-tal,* April 1979

Peterloo Gallery, Manchester, *Alan Green-Nigel Hall,* May 1979

Tokyo, *11th Internationale Biennale Exhibition of Prints,* June 1979

Waddington Graphics, London, *Understanding Prints,* September 1979

Selected One-Man Exhibitions

A.I.A. Gallery, London, May 1963

Annely Juda Fine Art, London, October 1970

Annely Juda Fine Art, London, March 1973

Galerie Liatowitsch, Basel, July 1973

Galerie Hervé Alexandre, Brussels, March-April 1974

Galerie Art in Progress, Munich, April-May 1974

Studio La Città, Verona, February 1975. Catalogue with text by Charles Spencer

Annely Juda Fine Art, London, April 1975

Galerie Hervé Alexandre, Brussels, June 1975 (drawings)

Galerie de Gestlo, Hamburg, September-October 1975

Galleria Vinciana, Milan, October 1975

Oliver Dowling Gallery, Dublin, January 1976 (prints)

Annely Juda Fine Art and Tate Gallery, London, *Alan Green Etchings 73-76,* from September 1976. Traveled to Mappin Art Gallery, Sheffield; University of Newcastle upon Tyne; Galerie Klaus Lupke, Frankfurt

Painting Box Gallery, Zürich, November 1976-January 1977

Galerie Arnesen, Copenhagen, December 1976

Galerie Art in Progress, Munich, January 1977

Galerie Art in Progress, Düsseldorf, September 1977

Nina Freudenheim Gallery, Buffalo, and Susan Caldwell Inc., New York, April-May 1978. Catalogue with text by John McEwen

Oliver Dowling Gallery, Dublin, May 1978

The Roundhouse Gallery, London, September-October 1978

Annely Juda Fine Art, London, October 1978

Galerie Palluel, Paris, October-November 1978. Catalogue with text by Gerhard Weber

Kunsthalle Bielefeld, *Alan Green—Paintings 1969-79,* September-October 1979. Catalogue with texts by Dr. Erich Franz, Martine Lignon and Dr. Bernd Growe

Artline, The Hague, December 1979

Galerie Loyse Oppenheim, Nyon, Switzerland, November-December 1979

Selected Bibliography

Andrew Forge, "A Note on some Recent Pictures by Alan Green," *Studio International,* vol. 185, February 1973, pp. 76-77

John Russell, "Durable Lines," *Sunday Times,* March 18, 1973, p. 28

Nigel Gosling, "Simply Singing," *The Observer,* March 25, 1973, p. 35

Marina Vaizey, "Alan Green," *Financial Times,* April 3, 1973, p. 3

Andrew Forge, "Alan Green on his paintings," *Studio International,* vol. 186, October 1973, pp. 144-145

Laslo Glozer, "Bilder die von Malerei handeln," *Suddeutsche Zeitung,* no. 102, May 3, 1974

Bernard Denvir, "Alan Green; A Dialogue," *Art International,* vol. XVIII, November 1974, pp. 47-48

Judy Marle, "Judy Marle on Alan Green's new exhibition," *The Guardian,* April 25, 1975, p. 14

William Packer, "Alan Green," *Financial Times,* April 25, 1975, p. 3

Peter Rippon, "Alan Green," *Artscribe,* no. 5, February 1977, p. 7

Colin Naylor and Genesis P. Orridge, eds., *Contemporary Artists,* London, 1977

John McEwen, "Monochrome," *The Spectator,* October 7, 1978, p. 24

Martine Lignon, "Paintings about Colour," *Art Monthly,* no. 21, November 1978, pp. 18-19

Michael Billam, "Alan Green at Annely Juda," *Artscribe,* no. 15, December 1978, pp. 56-57

Gerhard Weber, "Alan Green, La peinture ne s'explique pas," *Art Press International,* no. 23, December 1978, p. 14

Pat Gilmour, *Understanding Prints: A Contemporary Guide,* London, 1979

Colin Naylor and Genesis P. Orridge, eds., *Contemporary Artists,* London, 1979

Alan Green in his studio

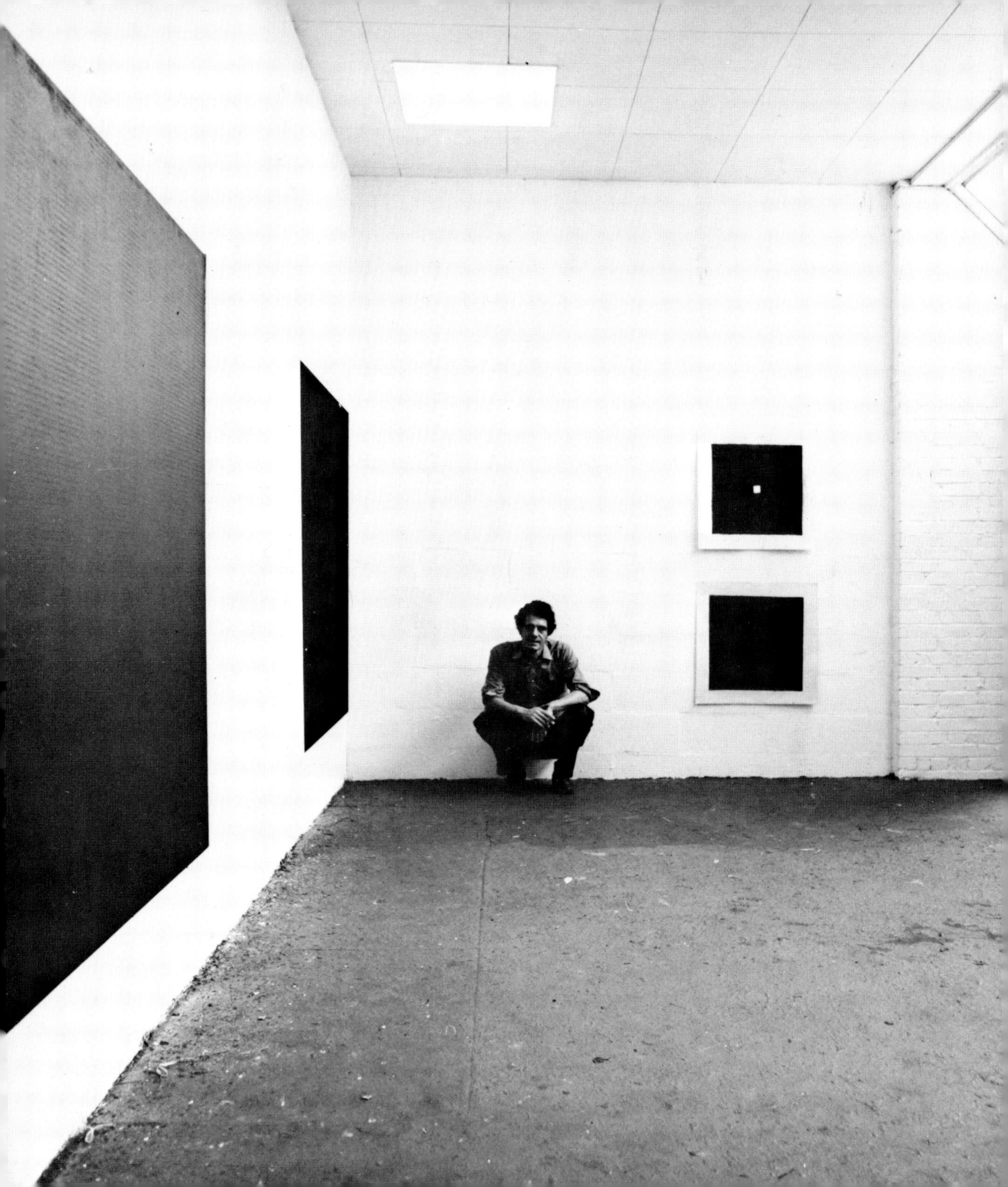

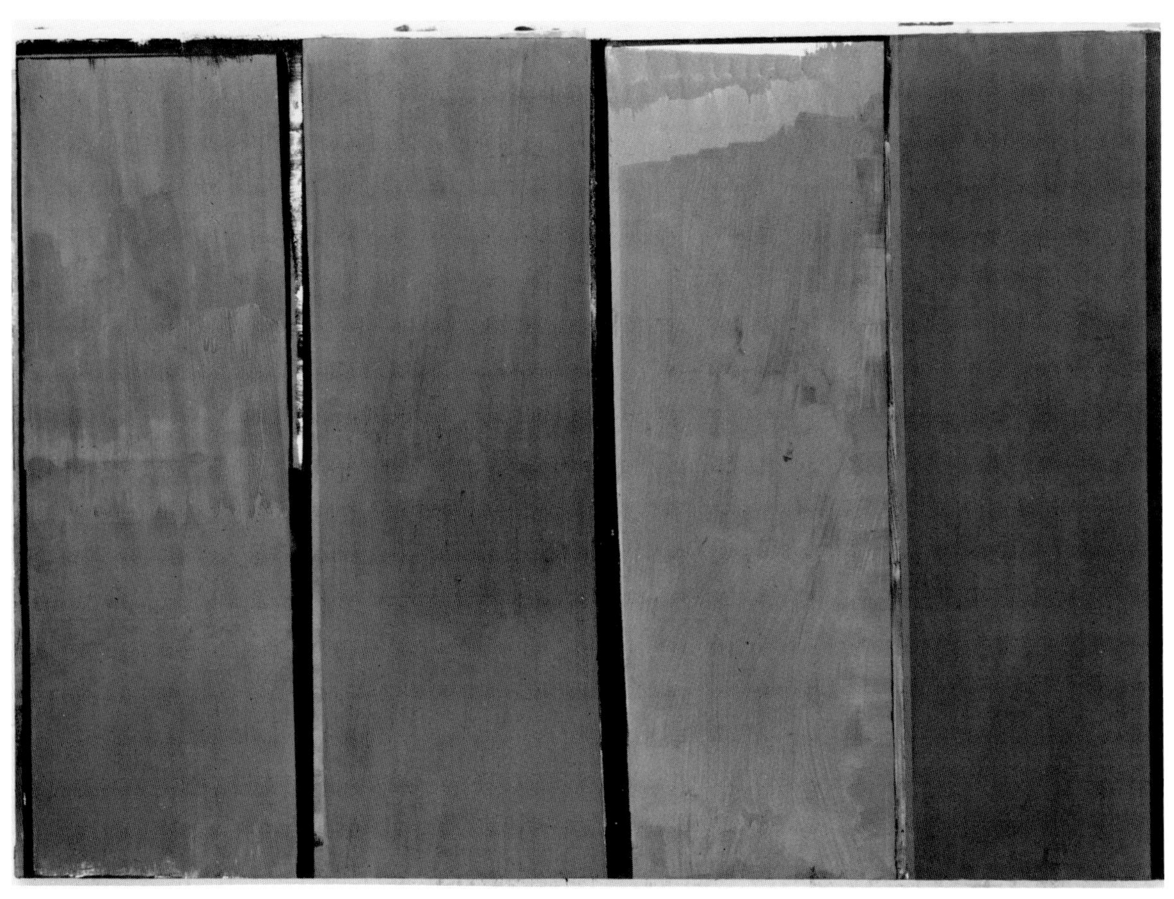

12.
Towards Grey. 1973
Acrylic on canvas, 72 x 98″
Galerie Art and Progress, Düsseldorf

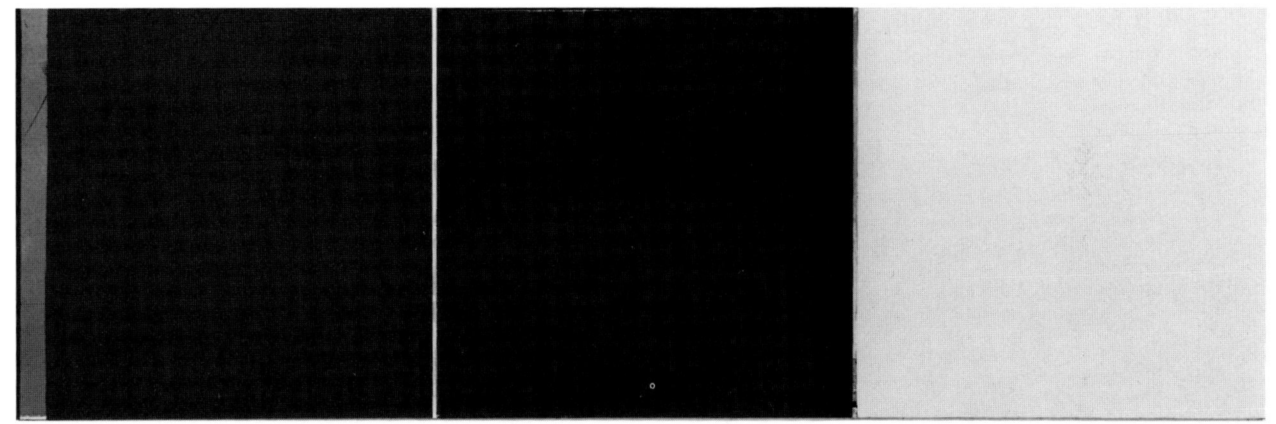

13.
Three Squared (3 Parts). 1975
Acrylic on canvas, 48 x 144"
Courtesy Annely Juda Fine Art, London

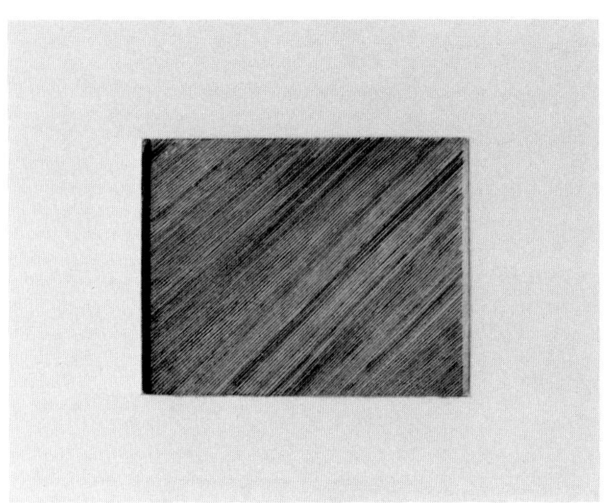

14.
Four to One: ¼ Black Diagonal. 1976
Etching, 28 x 33¼ ″
Collection The British Council, London

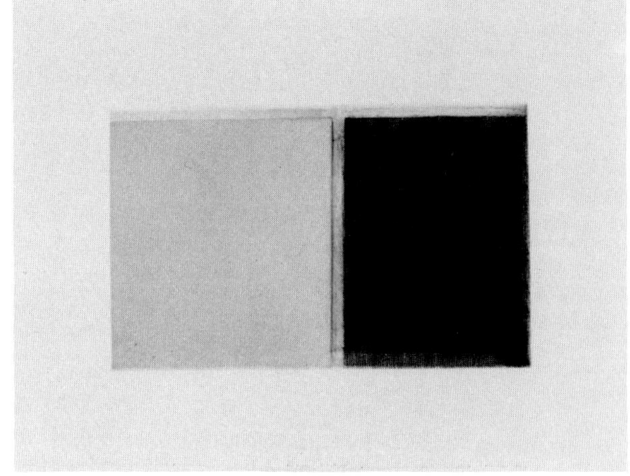

15.
Four to One: ½ to the Right. 1976
Etching, 28 x 33¼ ″
Collection The British Council, London

16.
Extended Blue. 1976
Oil on canvas, 65 x 65″
Collection The Solomon R. Guggenheim Museum,
New York 79.2524

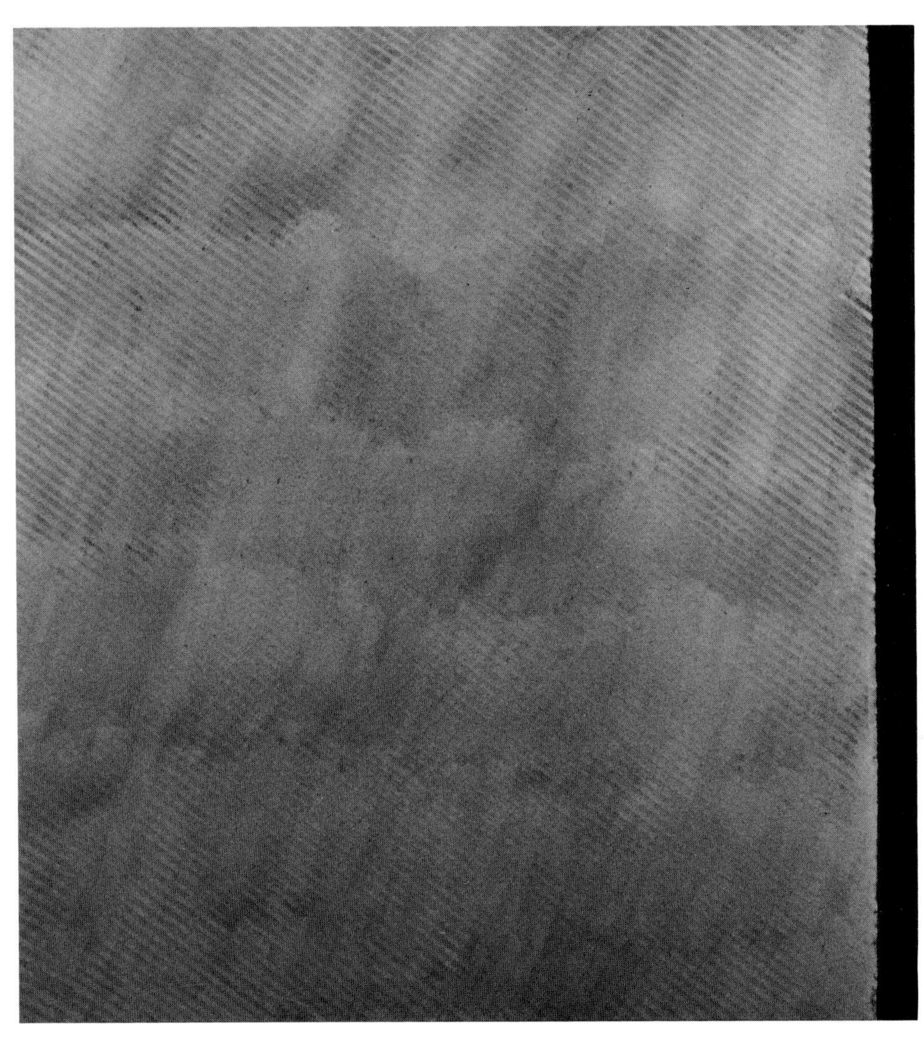

17.
Silver and Black. 1977
Acrylic on canvas, 76 x 69″
Courtesy Susan Caldwell, Inc., New York

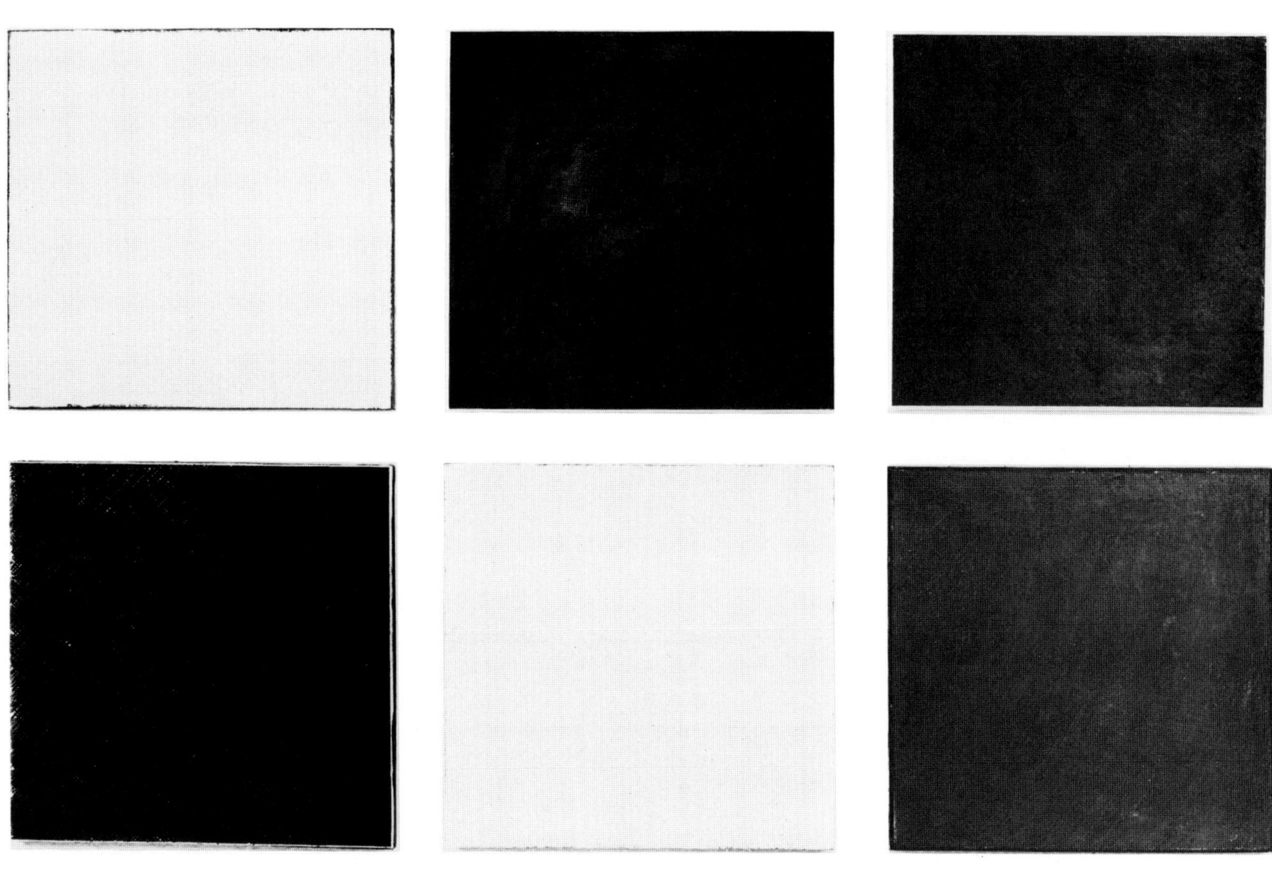

18.
Six Separate Panels. 1978
Each 23¾ x 23¾ "
Courtesy Annely Juda Fine Art, London

White on Brown Panel
Acrylic on paper on canvas

White Lead-Black Panel
Oil on canvas

Black Jap Panel
Oil on paper on canvas

Line Black Panel
Tempera on paper on canvas

White Lead Panel
Oil on canvas

Dark Red Panel
Oil on canvas

19.
Four Vertical Reds. 1978
Oil, tempera and acrylic on canvas, 96 x 144¼″
Collection of the artist

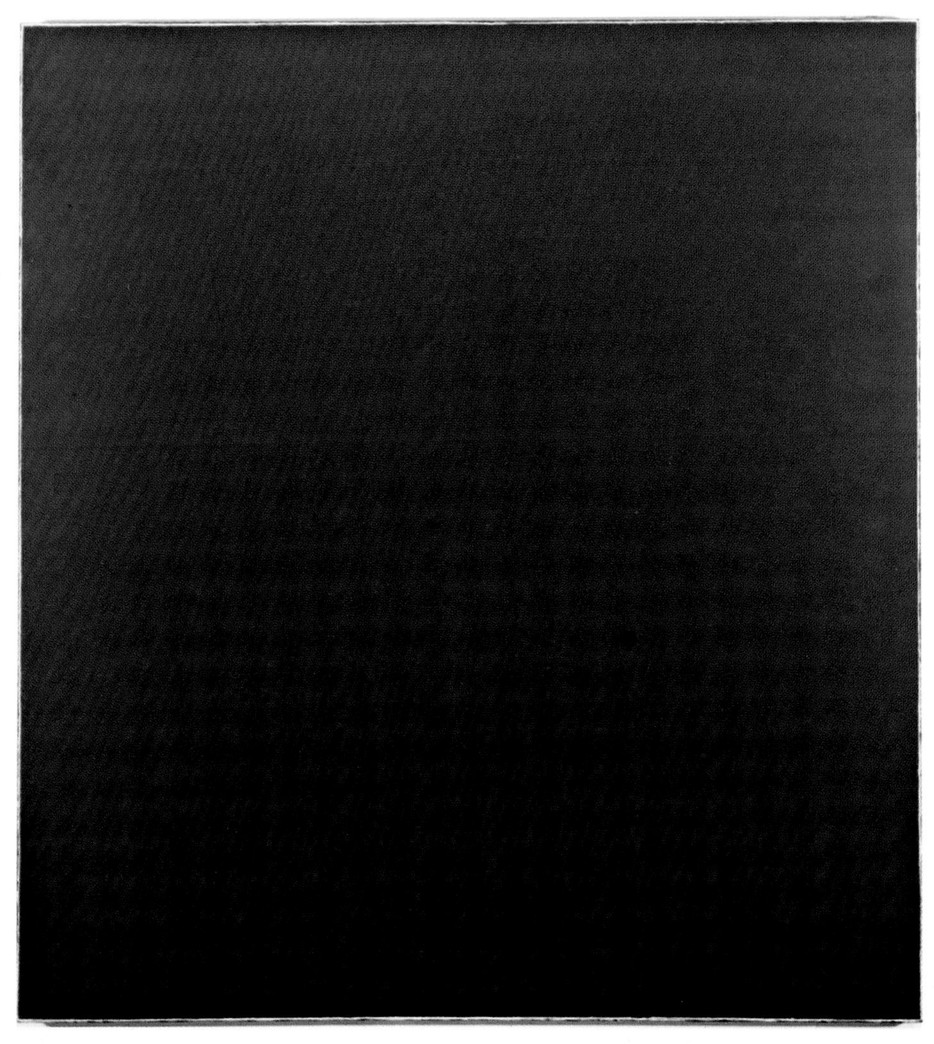

20.
Umber. 1978
Oil on canvas, 74½ x 66⅞ ″
Courtesy Annely Juda Fine Art, London

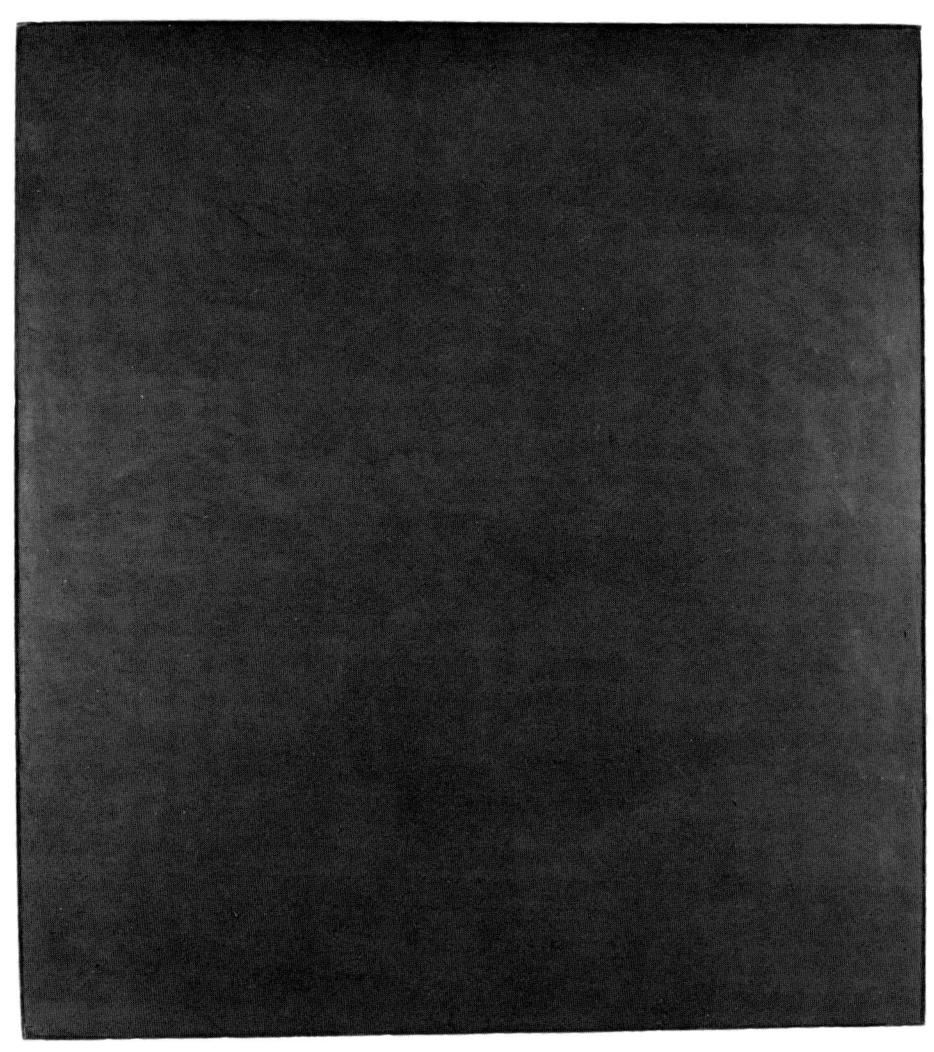

21.
Reduced Blue. 1979
Oil on canvas, 74½ x 67″
Courtesy Annely Juda Fine Art, London

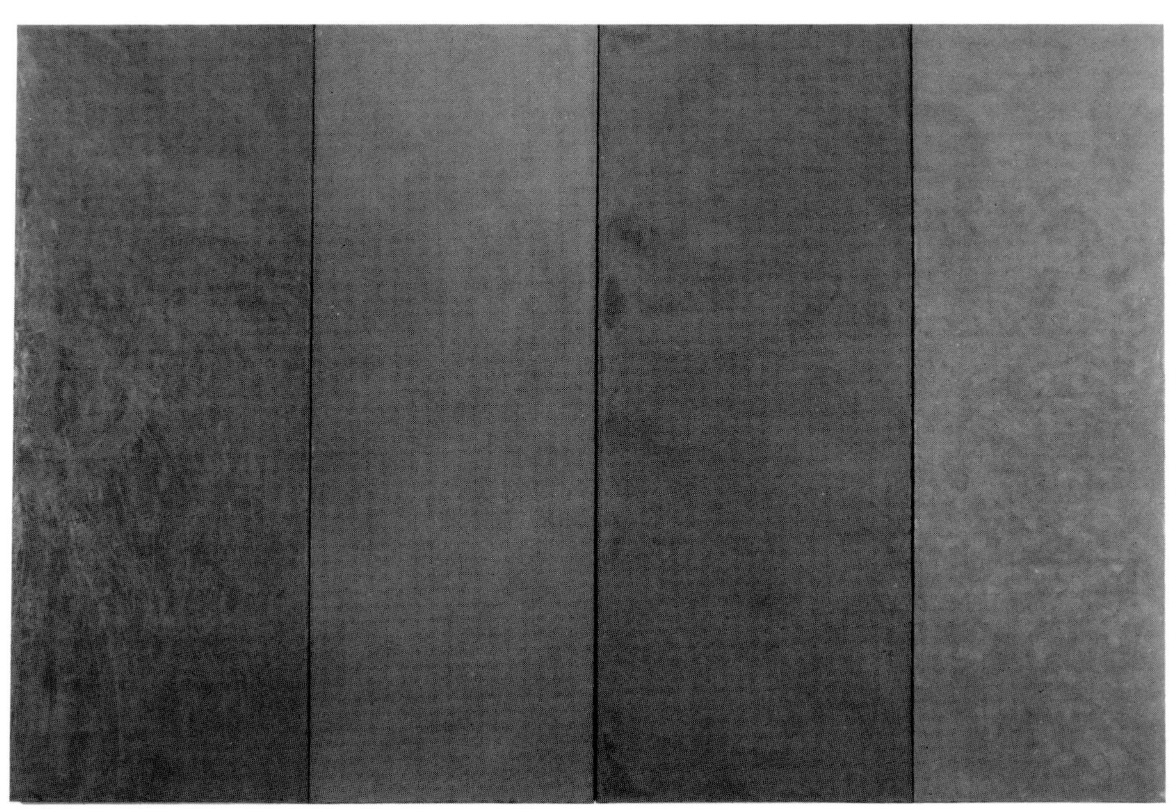

22.
Four Grey Panels. 1979
Oil on canvas, 81⅛ x 118½ "
Collection The British Council, London

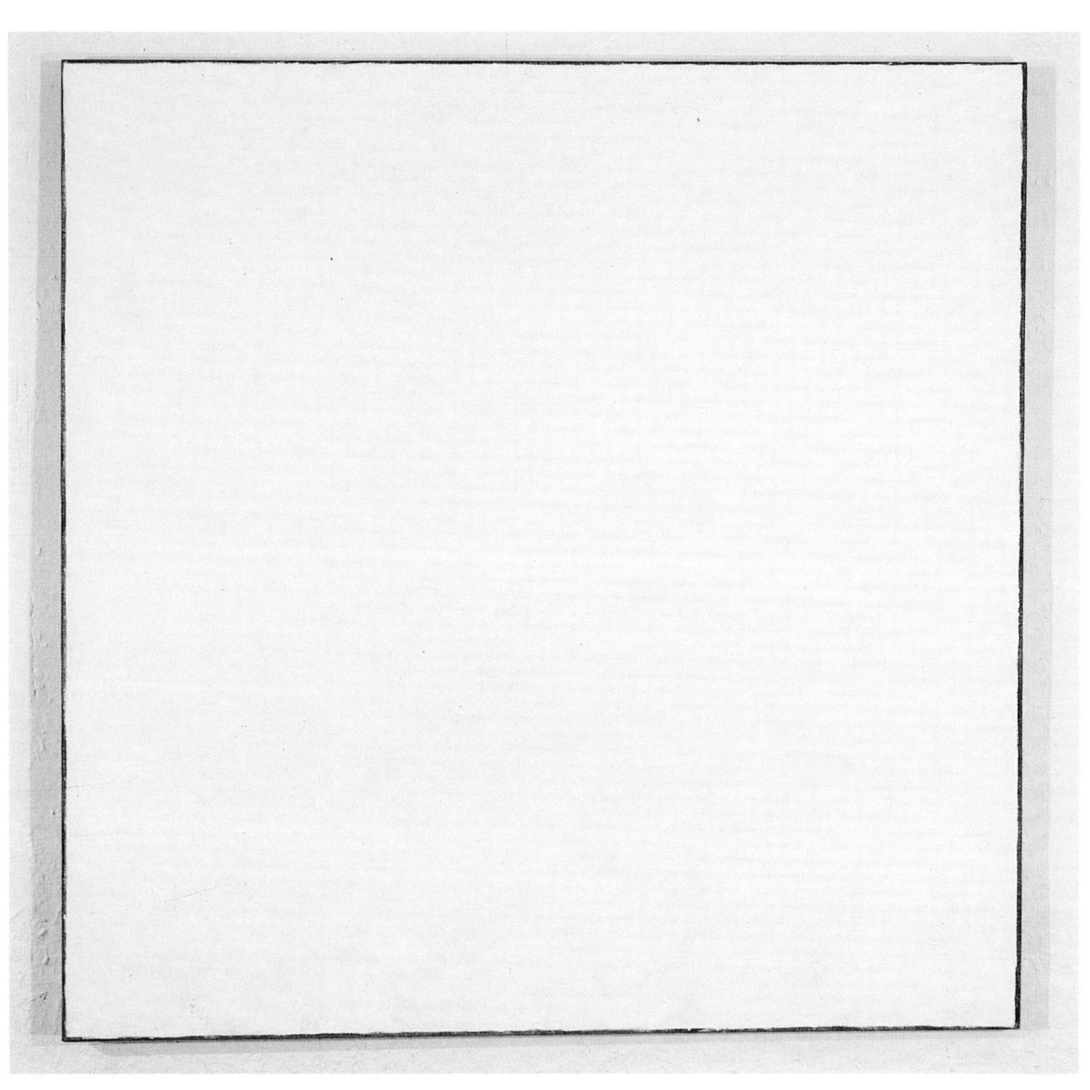

23.
White Lead over Red Lead. 1979
Oil on canvas, 65½ x 64½ ″
Courtesy Annely Juda Fine Art, London

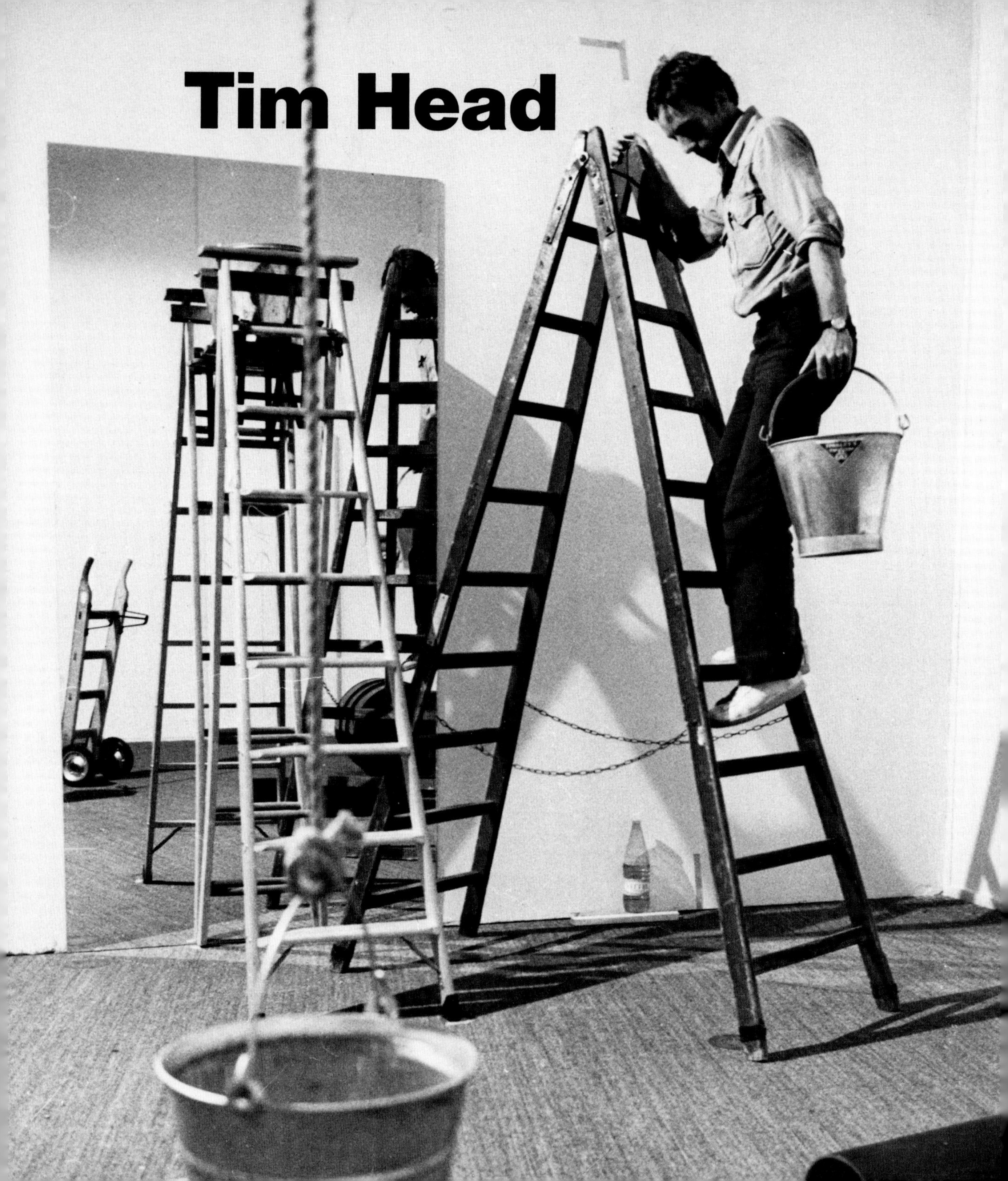
Tim Head

The enduring questions about the nature of reality and illusion are central to Tim Head's work. The artist organizes his tableaux of commonplace, everyday subjects into events of uncommon reality. He achieves this sense of ambiguity through the simplest of devices, using slide projections and occasionally introducing a few mundane objects into his pieces. By means of projections he creates a very palpable space which he then rearranges so that the viewer experiences not only a sense of displacement but a confusion as to what is real and what is illusion.

Head's work to date consists of environmental pieces made expressly for specific sites. One of his most memorable settings (cat. no. 27), at the now defunct Garage in Covent Garden, was composed of infra-red shots of the gallery interior, with many pillars functioning as markers or signs. Eerie and unreal in that light, "reality" seemed to assert itself only at the juncture where an actual column and its photographic duplicate were perfectly aligned. Yet, because of the peculiar nature of the light, one remained uncertain as to which, the actual column or the photographic image, was the truest reality.

More recently, at the Anthony Stokes Gallery, Head installed a work entitled *Appearance/Apparition,* 1977 (cat. no. 30), in which a negative rather than positive slide of a male nude was projected into a niche-like space. The peculiarly insistent presence of what one knew to be a figure without substance violated not only the spectator's space but touched upon his perceptions and ultimately upon his physical being as well. There could not have been a greater feeling of reality had the actual model been in the room. In fact, in a peculiar reversal of normal perception, the illusion seemed more compelling than the tangible figure. The larger-than-life size projected image enhanced rather than diminished this effect. Head is not involved with the metaphysical dimensions of Surrealism, the transformation of the commonplace object that is central to Pop Art or the prosaic imagery and slick advertising techniques of Photo Realism. On the contrary, he is searching for the margin of existence in that narrow space between the real and the imagined.

His work is most haunting when he uses few tangible objects, as in *Present* (cat. no. 33), installed in 1978 at the Rowan Gallery. Here the projection was of the image of a horse which stood gazing calmly back at the spectator. So convincing was the illusion of the horse and the space in which it was positioned that only with great difficulty could one come to terms with it as fiction and grasp the physical reality of the surroundings.

Head uses a real context, like the Garage, and real subjects, as his point of departure. For the Rowan installation, he actually brought a horse onto the premises and photographed it there. But the animal and the space have been presented to us so that we see them, not as they appear in reality, but projected in reverse, as mirror images. The idiosyncratic nature of objects and space that double back upon themselves does not undermine the sense that the apparitions do exist in fact. By entering the magical world that Head has created, much as one enters Lewis Carroll's *Alice in Wonderland,* one begins to perceive that an alternative reality can exist.

The disorientation or dislocation that Tim Head's work engenders is based upon the very real participation of the spectator. It is only by our interrupting an image, by crossing and crisscrossing the space in which the installations exist, that we can begin to measure our own reality and compare it with the image surrounding us. Although it seemed at first fairly straightforward, even unremarkable, Head's installation at the Museum of Modern Art in Oxford in 1972, his first show, was profoundly disturbing. Head had simply photographed three of the four walls of the gallery and then projected the images back on the original walls. The photographic images, however, were out of sync with the walls upon which they were superimposed. The artist also altered the site very effectively, repositioning five mirrors after he photographed the room. Since neither the real nor projected reflections corresponded with one another, the viewer was no longer able to separate one from the other, to distinguish fact from fiction. The same sense of disorientation occurred at Head's Whitechapel Gallery exhibition in 1974. The pro-

Tim Head installing piece for *10ᵉ Biennale de Paris,* 1977

jected image of an open door invited the visitor to enter the gallery; the actual entrance, however, remained firmly shut.

Head uses props from the world of reality in order to question both the way we perceive external reality and the conventions we have come to accept as signals for that reality. Renaissance perspectival treatment—the window frame onto the real world—had long been the accepted pictorial formula. In his work, Head acknowledges the dramatic breaks with this tradition and alludes both to earlier alternatives and to more recent examples. One thinks, for example, of Van Eyck's *Giovanni Arnolfini and his Bride* or Piranesi's staircases as well as Oldenburg's oversized props and the theater of Robert Morris' sculpture. In installations like those at the Whitechapel, the Garage, the Rowan, the artist does not simply substitute the irrational for the rational but attempts to present a new visual construct.

By subtly inverting illusion and reality, Head has altered the rules by which we measure existence; as a consequence, he has altered the rules by which we perceive art. It would be difficult to imagine a more successful means of achieving this result than through projection: the projected image and the ambient light of projection are already a distortion of space and human scale. What we know, or at least what we can measure, has lost its effectiveness as a tool with which we can grasp actuality. Head offers us the suggestion of another dimension, another equally plausible reality, the theater of the imagination.

Tim Head

Born in London, 1946

University of Newcastle upon Tyne, Department of Fine Art, 1965-69

Does research on British artists and assists with *Niki de Saint Phalle* exhibition at Stedilijk Museum, Amsterdam, Summer 1967

Assistant to Claes Oldenburg, New York, Summer 1968

St. Martin's School of Art, London, 1969-70

Assistant to artist for *Robert Morris* exhibition at Tate Gallery, London, Spring 1971

Teaches at Goldsmiths' College School of Art, London, 1971-present; Slade School of Fine Art, London, 1976-present

Calouste Gulbenkian Foundation Visual Arts Award, 1975

Artist in Residence, Clare Hall and Kettle's Yard, Cambridge, 1977-78

Lives in London

Selected Group Exhibitions

Alexandra Palace, London, *Art Spectrum London,* August 1971

South London Art Gallery, March 1972

Grabowski Gallery, London, April 1972

Holland Park, London, *Open Air Sculpture Exhibition,* June 1972

Gallery House, London, March 1973

Musée d'Art Moderne de la Ville de Paris, *8e Biennale de Paris: Internationale des jeunes artistes,* September 1973

Rowan Gallery, London, December 1974 (graphics); December 1975; December 1977

Garage Gallery, London, October 1975

Palazzo Reale, Milan, *Arte Inglese Oggi,* February 1976. Catalogue with statement by the artist and text by Richard Cork

Künstlerhaus Graz, Austria, *Zeit, Worte und die Kamera: Fotoarbeiten englischer Künstler,* October 1976

Fitzwilliam Museum, Cambridge, *Tolly Cobbold/ Eastern Arts National Art Exhibition,* from April 1977. Traveled to Ipswich Museums, High Street Art Gallery, Corn Exchange, Ipswich; Graves Art Gallery, Sheffield; Camden Arts Centre, London

Kassel, Germany, *Documenta VI,* June 1977

Musée d'Art Moderne de la Ville de Paris, *10e Biennale de Paris: Manifestation internationale des jeunes artistes,* September 1977

Arnolfini Gallery, Bristol, *On Site,* September-October 1977

Fredrikstad, Norway, *British Artists' Prints 1972-77,* from September 1977. Organized by The British Council, traveled in Scandinavia

Kettle's Yard Gallery, Cambridge, *Reflected Images,* October-November 1977. Catalogue with text by Fenella Crichton

ARC II, Musée d'Art Moderne de la Ville de Paris, *Un Certain art anglais . . .,* January-March 1979. Catalogue with text by Michael Compton

Palais des Beaux Arts, Brussels, *JP II,* March-April 1979. Catalogue with text by the artist

Arts Gallery of New South Wales, Sydney, *3rd Biennale of Sydney,* April-May 1979

Bradford City Art Gallery, *6th British International Print Biennale,* May-July 1979

Nigel Greenwood Inc. Ltd., London, *Front Gallery/ Back Gallery,* July-September 1979

One-Man Exhibitions

Museum of Modern Art, Oxford, June 1972

Artist's studio, London, *Interference,* July 1973

Whitechapel Art Gallery, London, April 1974

Garage Gallery, London, *Infra-red/3 Shots in the Dark,* June 1974

Rowan Gallery, London, *Displacements,* January 1975

Arnolfini Gallery, Bristol, *Interference,* November 1975

Rowan Gallery, London, November 1976

Anthony Stokes Gallery, London, *Appearance/ Apparition,* November 1977

Rowan Gallery, London, *Present,* April 1978

Henie-Onstad Kunstcenter, Høvikodden, Norway, June 1978

Kettle's Yard, Cambridge, *Back to Front,* June 1978

Institute of Modern Art, Brisbane, May 1979

Galerie Bama, Paris, November 1979

Paola Betti, Milan, November 1979

Selected Bibliography

By the artist

Reconstructions, Idea Books, London, 1973

"Glossary—a preliminary sketch," *Flash Art,* no. 48-49, October/November 1974, p. 39

On the artist

Michael Shepherd, "Euan Uglow and Tim Head," *Arts Review,* vol. XXVI, May 3, 1974, p. 239

Marina Vaizey, "Slogans in style," *Sunday Times,* January 12, 1975, p. 32

Paul Overy, "Artist's artist," *The Times,* January 14, 1975, p. 13

Richard Cork, "How the camera lies," *The Evening Standard,* January 16, 1975, p. 24

Caroline Tisdall, "Tim Head Exhibition in London," *The Guardian,* January 16, 1975, p. 12

Nigel Gosling, "Revelations at the supermarket," *The Observer,* January 18, 1975, p. 28

Peter Fuller, "Tim Head, Rowan Gallery," *Arts Review,* vol. XXVI, January 24, 1975, p. 36

William Feaver, "Tim Head," *Financial Times,* January 27, 1975, p. 3

Rosetta Brooks, "Tim Head," *Studio International,* vol. 189, March/April 1975, p. 150

Fenella Crichton, "London," *Art International/Art Spectrum,* vol. XIX, May 1975, p. 40

John Tagg, "In Camera. A projected interview on the work of Tim Head," *Studio International,* vol. 190, July/August 1975, pp. 55-59

Fenella Crichton, "Space as Conundrum: The work of Tim Head," *Art International/Art Spectrum,* vol. XIX, October 1975, pp. 54-55, 68

William Feaver, "Showing the Flag," *The Observer,* March 14, 1976, p. 30

Brian Wallworth, "Tim Head," *Arts Review,* vol. XXVIII, November 26, 1976, p. 647

Adrian Searle, "Tim Head at the Rowan Gallery," *Artscribe,* no. 5, February 1977, p. 16

France Huser, "Calligraphies et graffiti," *Le Nouvel Observateur,* January 29, 1979, pp. 69-70

Suzanne Page, "Un certain art anglais . . . à l'ARC," *L'Oeil,* no. 282-283, January-February 1979, pp. 64-65

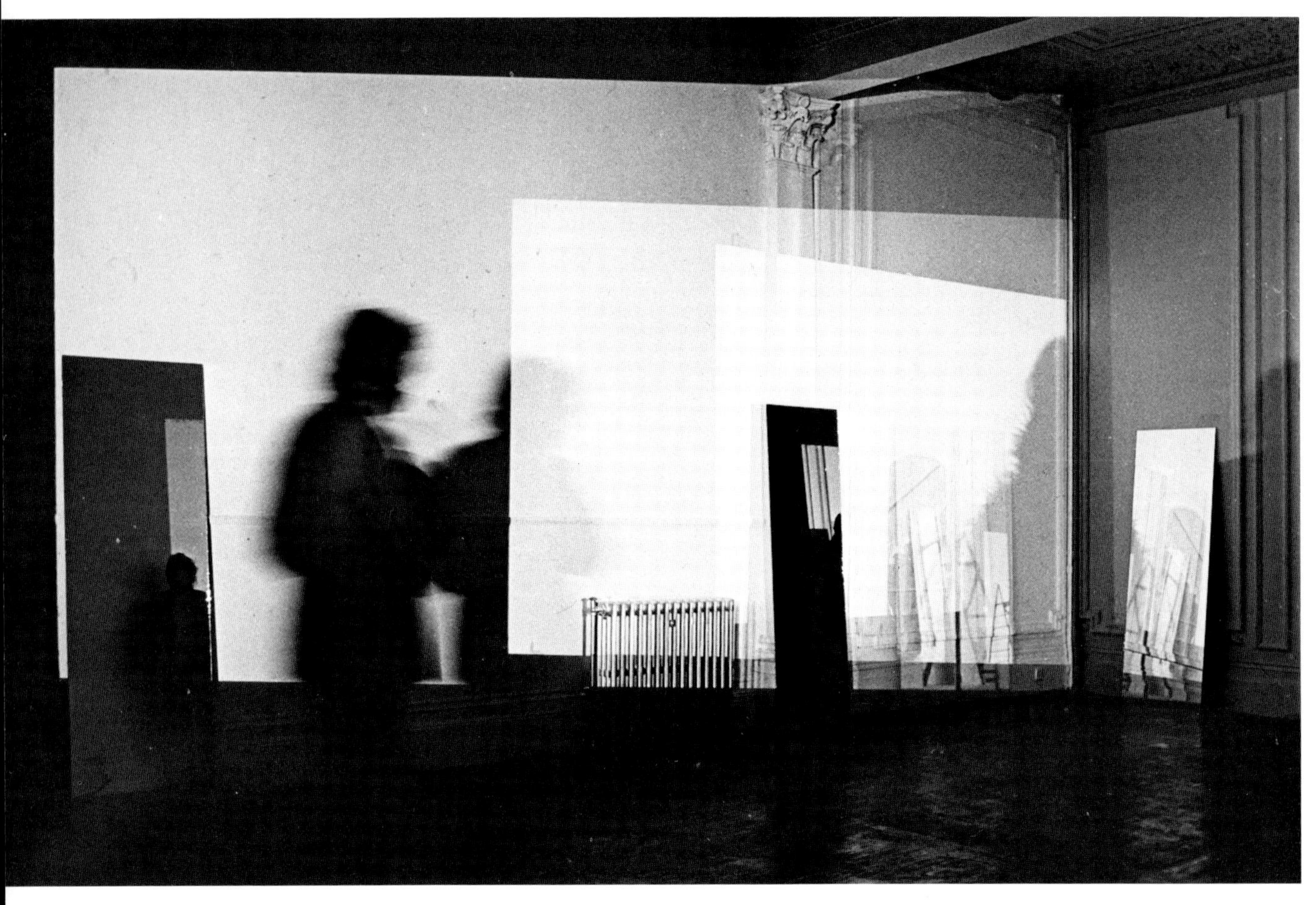

24.
Installation at Whitechapel Art Gallery, London,
1974
Slide projections and mirrors

25.
Installation at Gallery House, London, 1973
Slide projections and mirrors

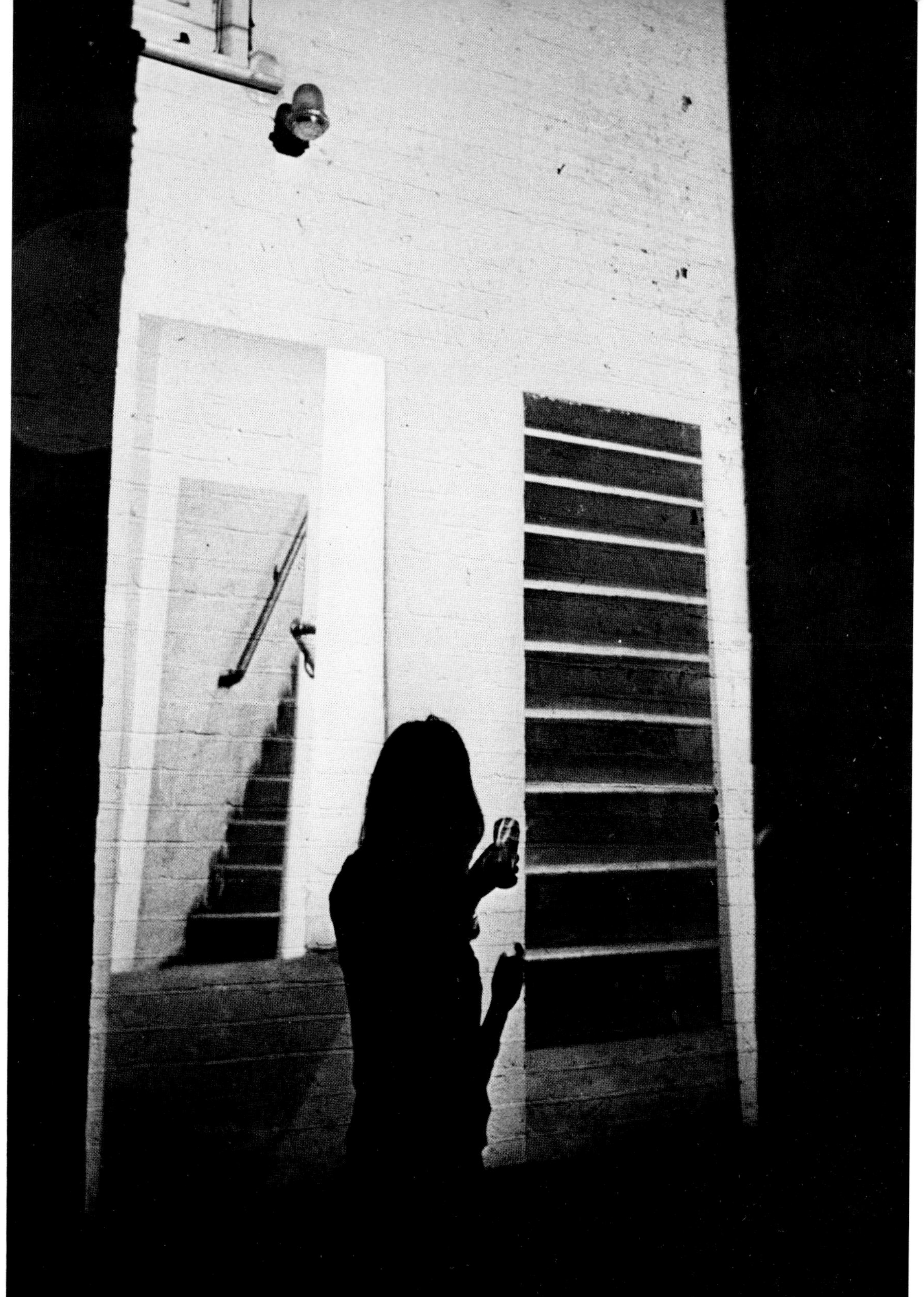

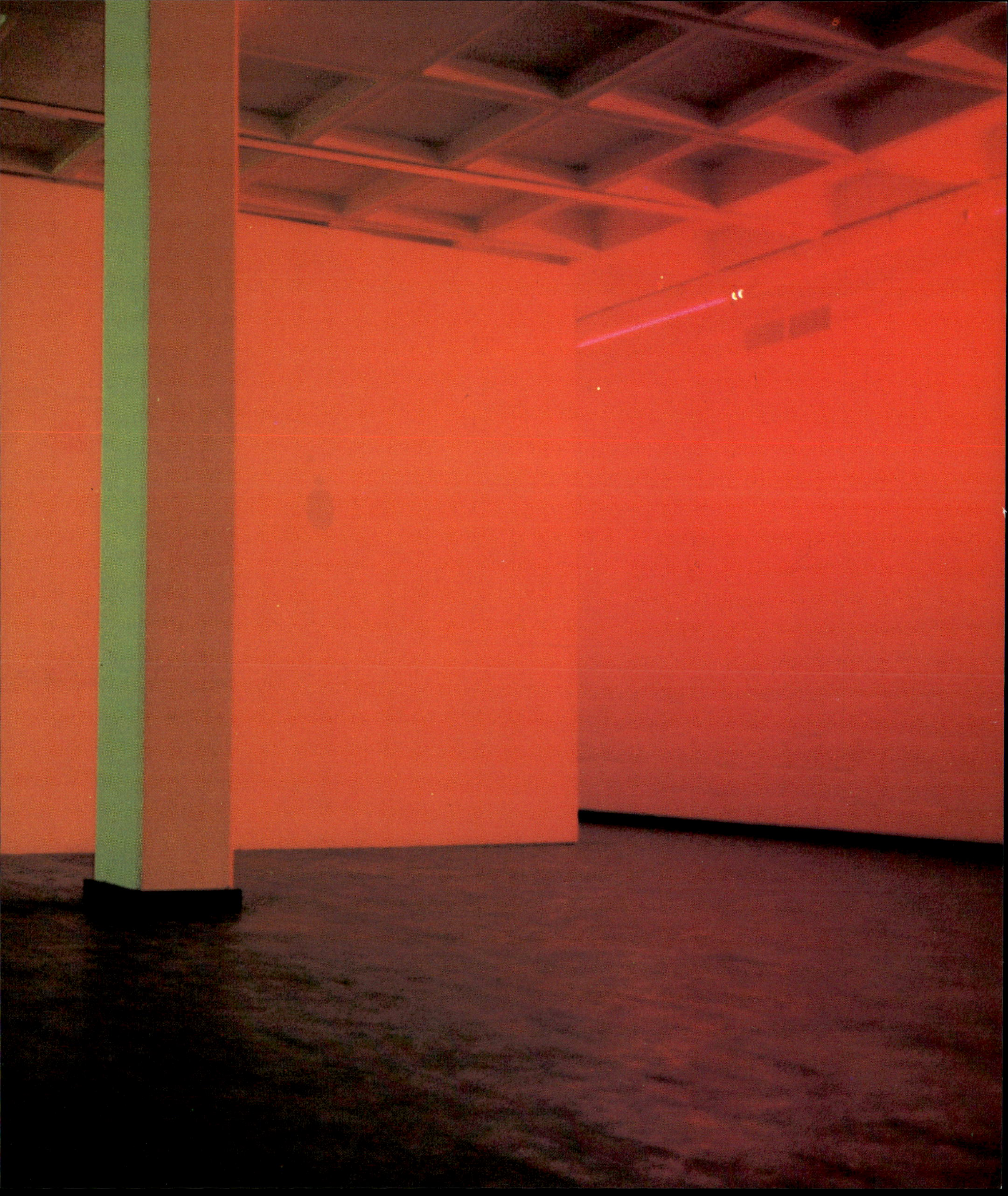

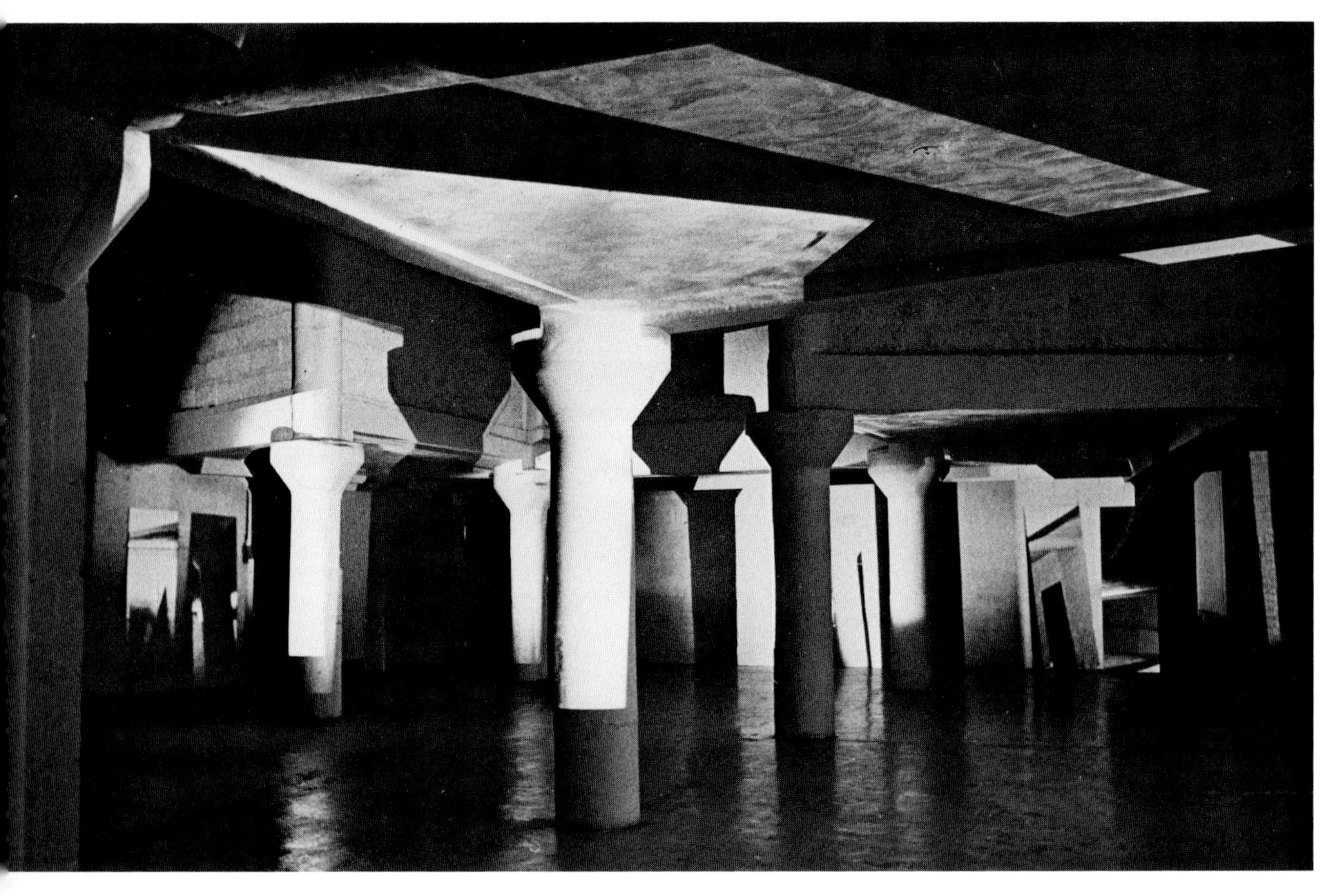

26.   p. 50
Interference, Installation at Arnolfini Gallery, Bristol, 1975
Colored lights, mirrors and wood constructions

27.
Infra-Red/3 Shots in the Dark, Installation at Garage Gallery, London, 1974
Slide projections and mirrors

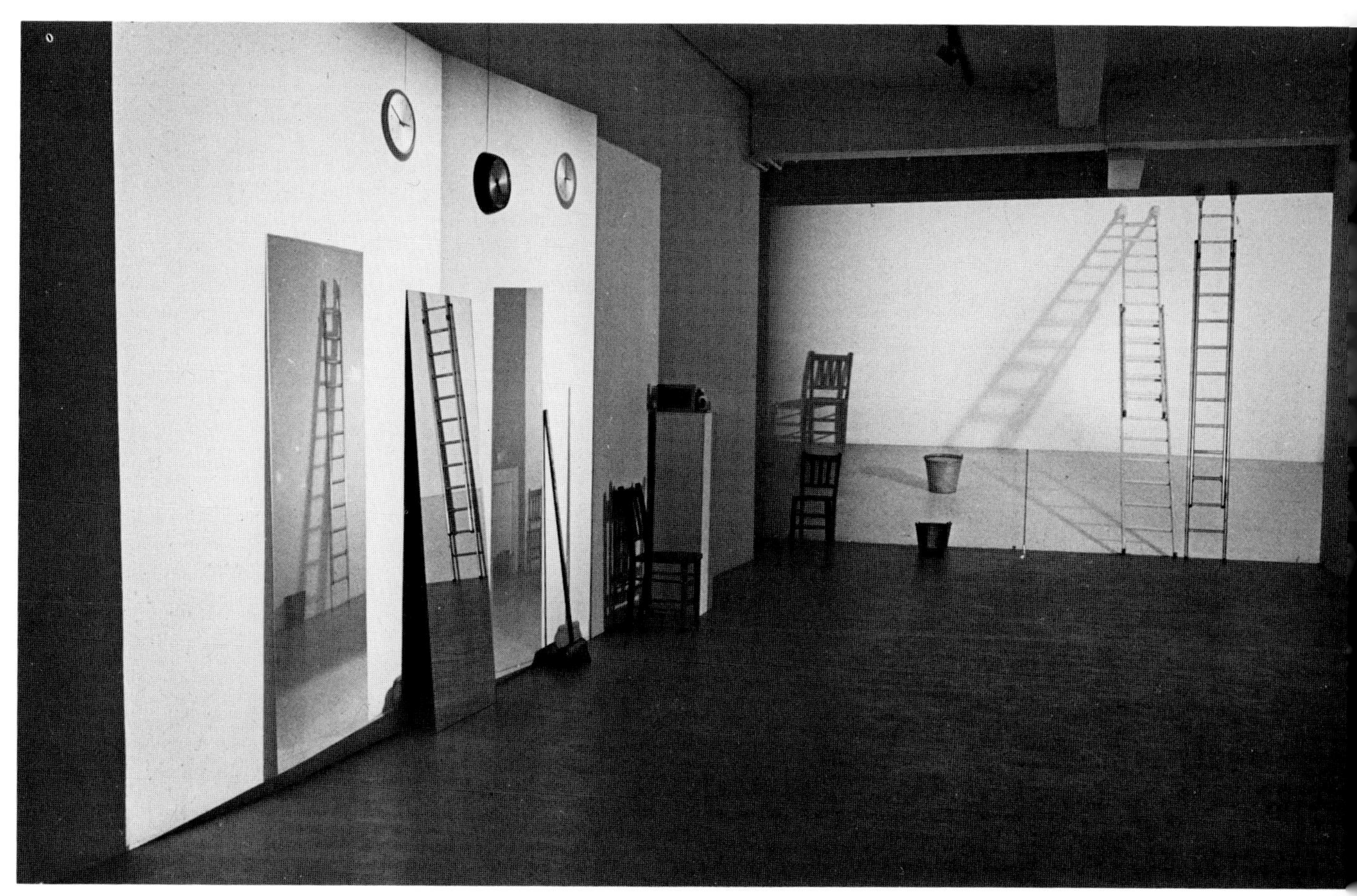

28.

Displacements, Installation at Rowan Gallery,
London, 1975
Slide projections, mirrors and objects
Collection The Trustees of the Tate Gallery,
London

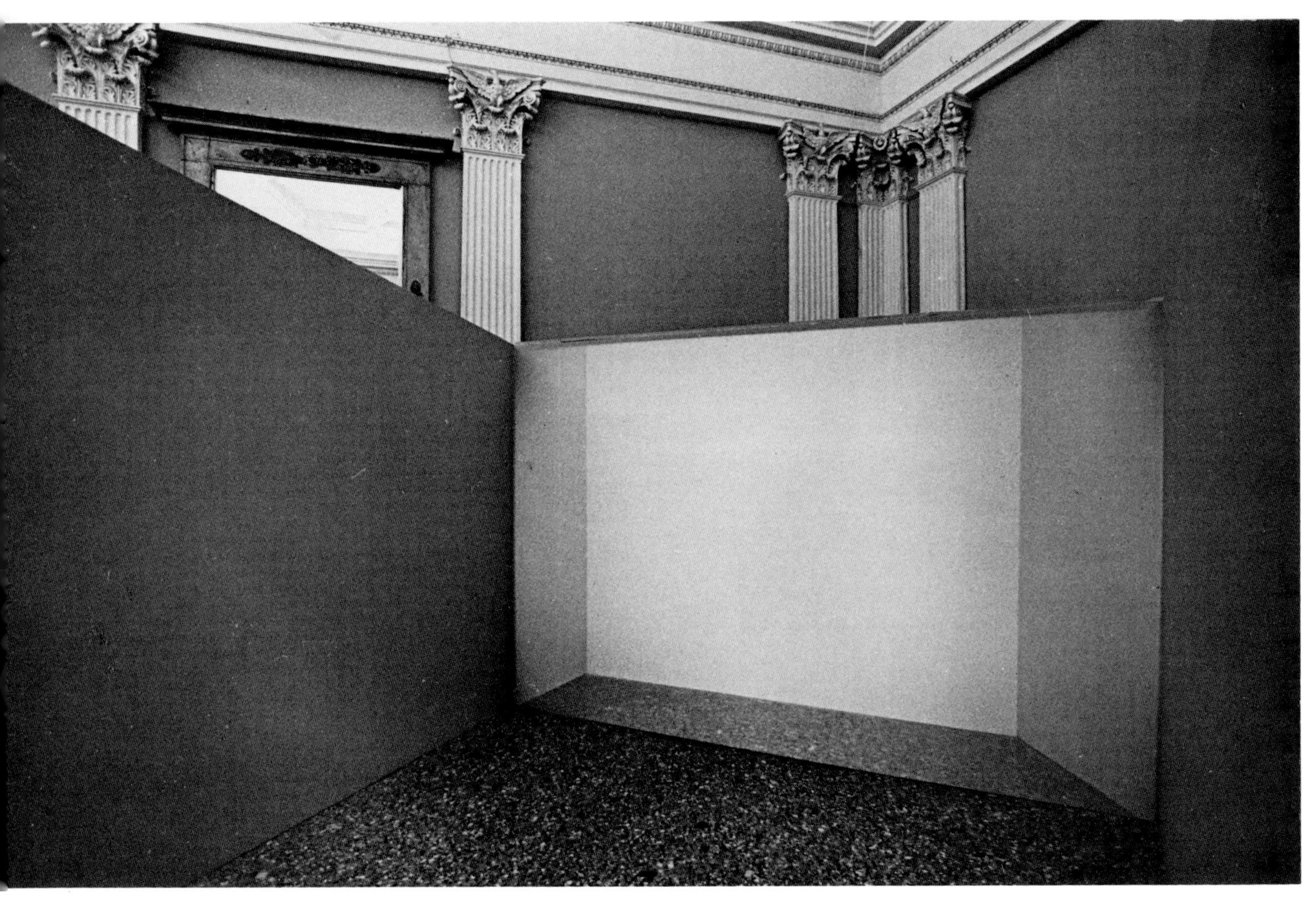

29.
Installation at Arte Inglese Oggi, Sala degli Specci, Palazzo Reale, Milan, 1976
Slide projections and wood constructions

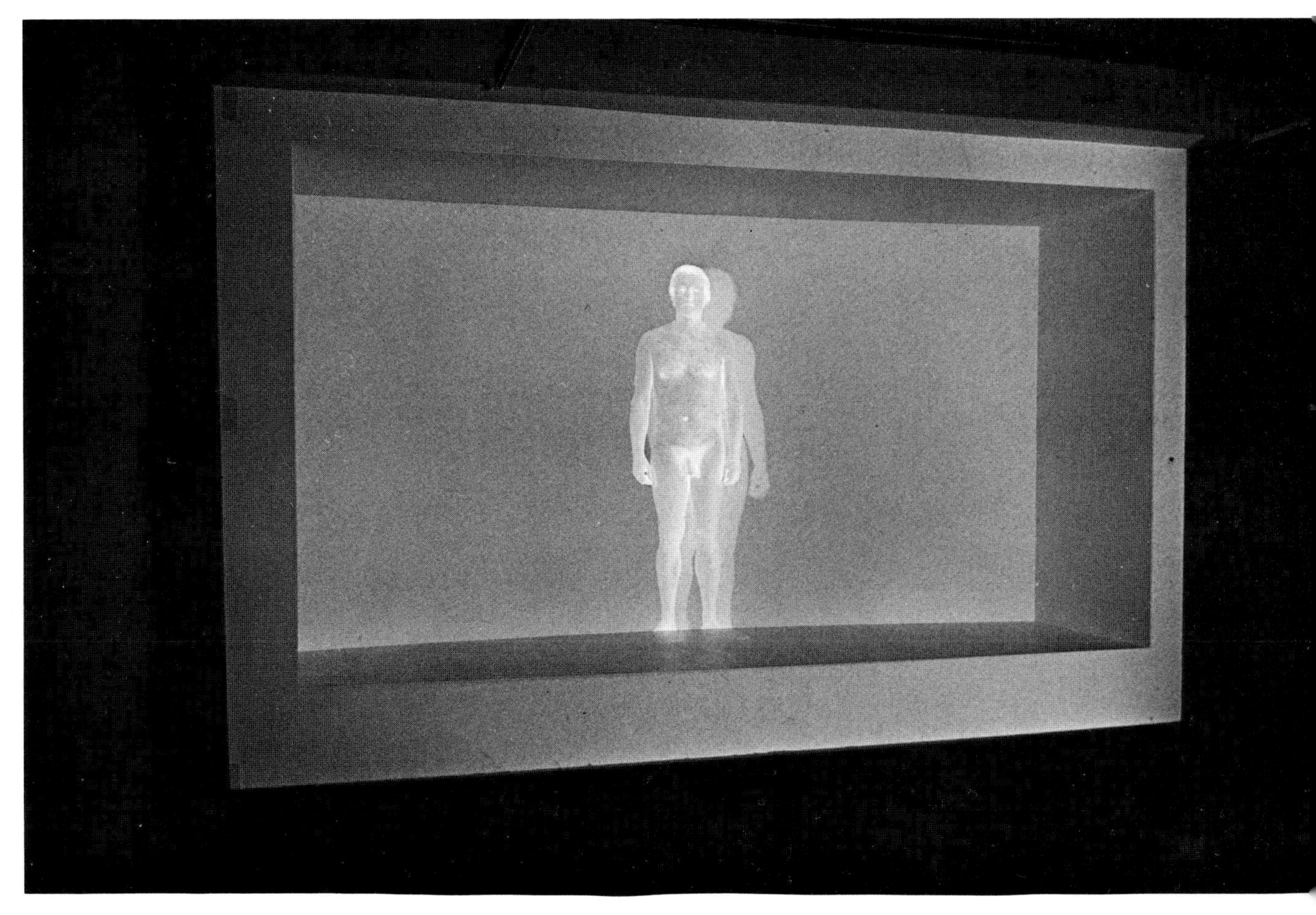# 30.

Appearance/Apparition, Installation at Anthony
Stokes Gallery, London, 1977
Slide projection

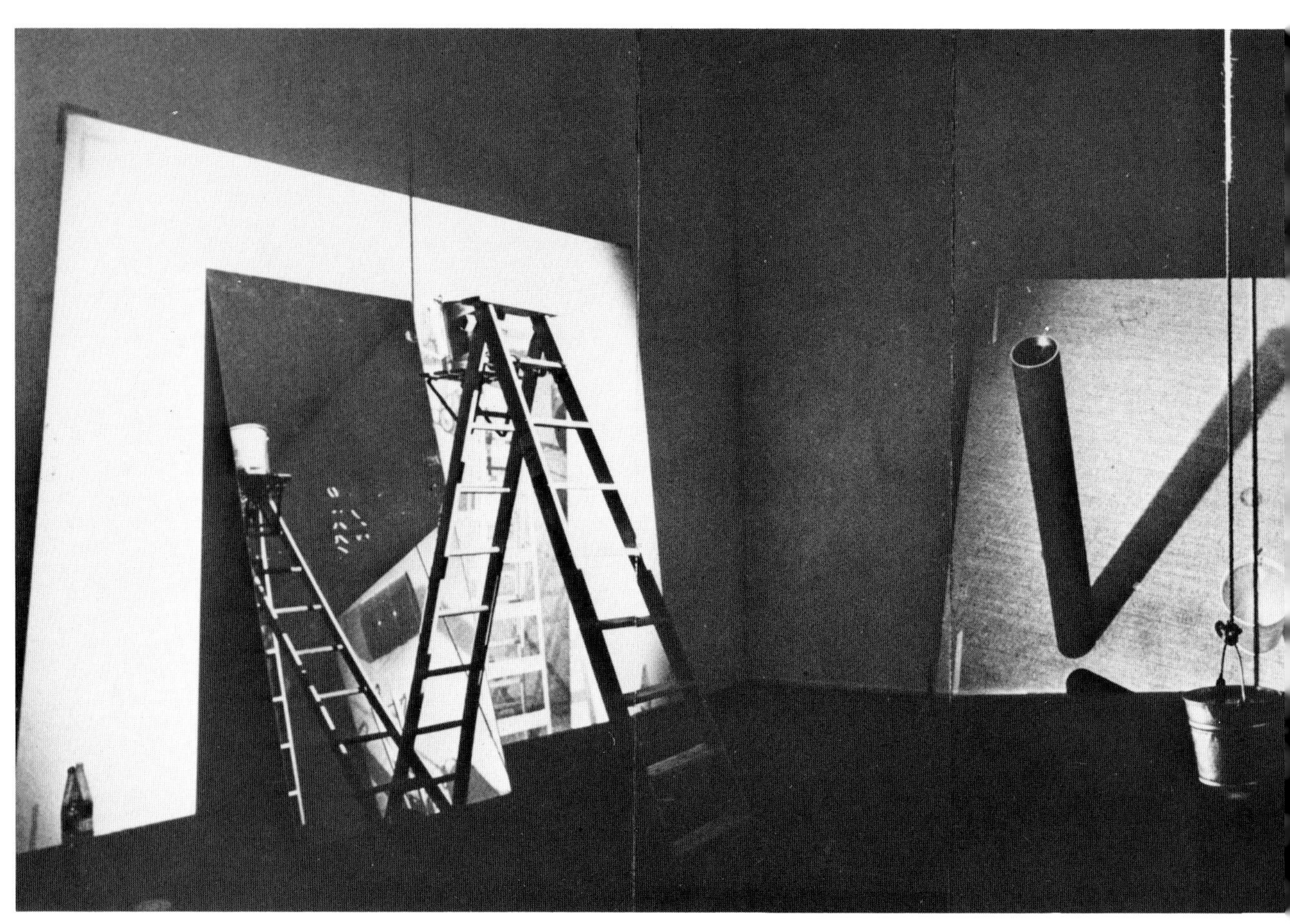

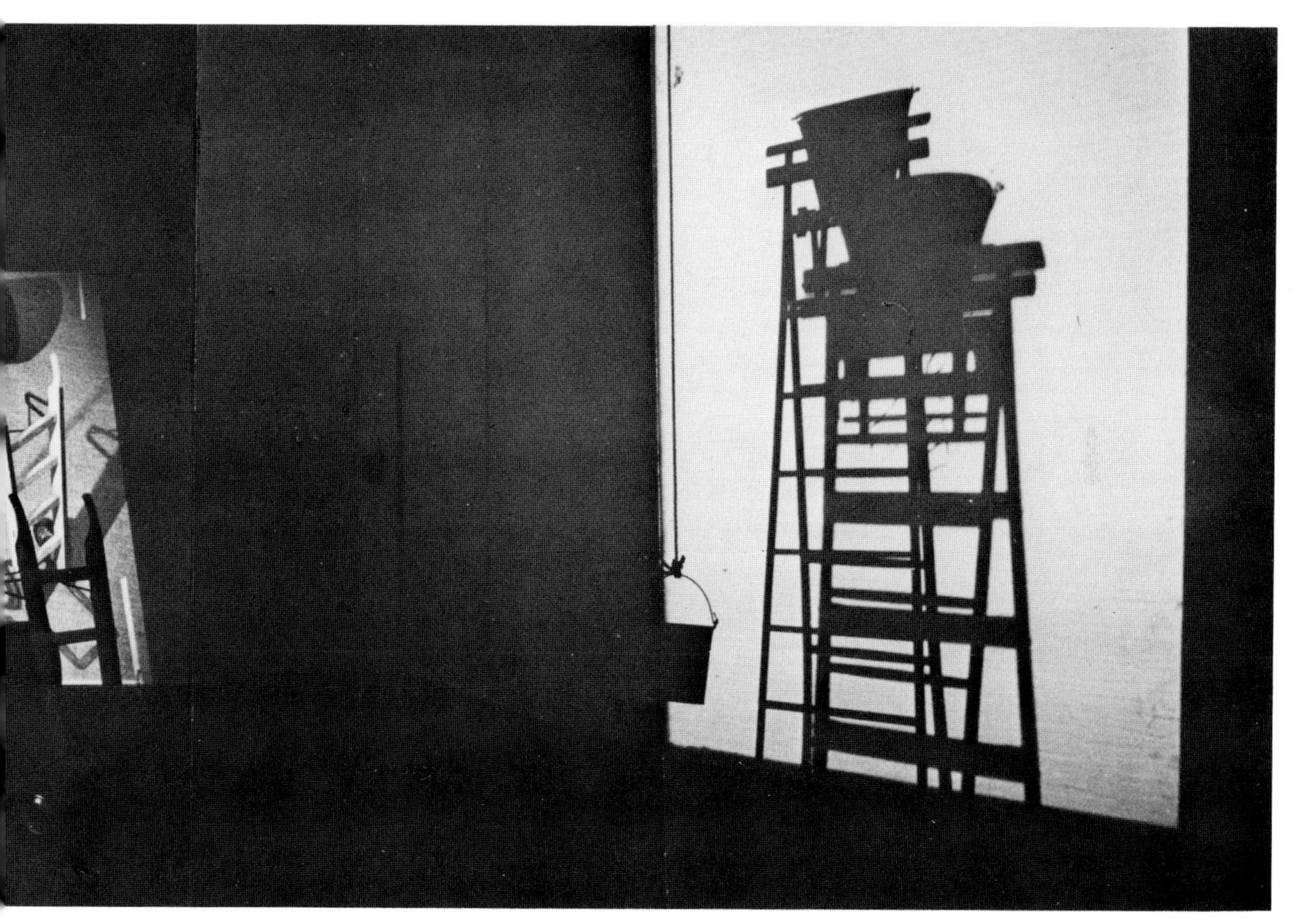

31.
Dislocations, Installation at *10ᵉ Biennale de Paris,*
1977
Slide projections, mirrors and objects

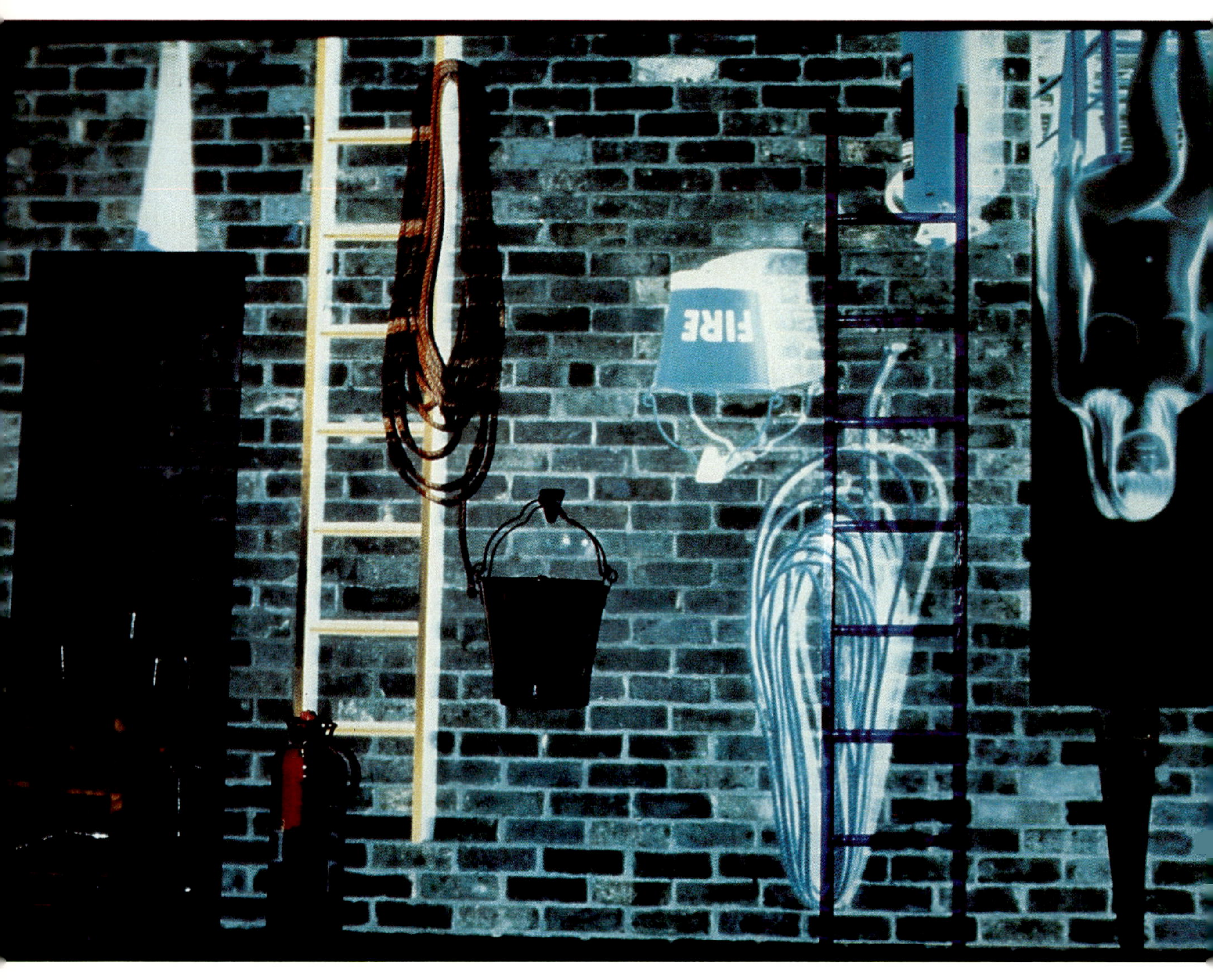

32.
Still Life. 1977-78
Slide projection, mirrors and objects
Collection The British Council, London

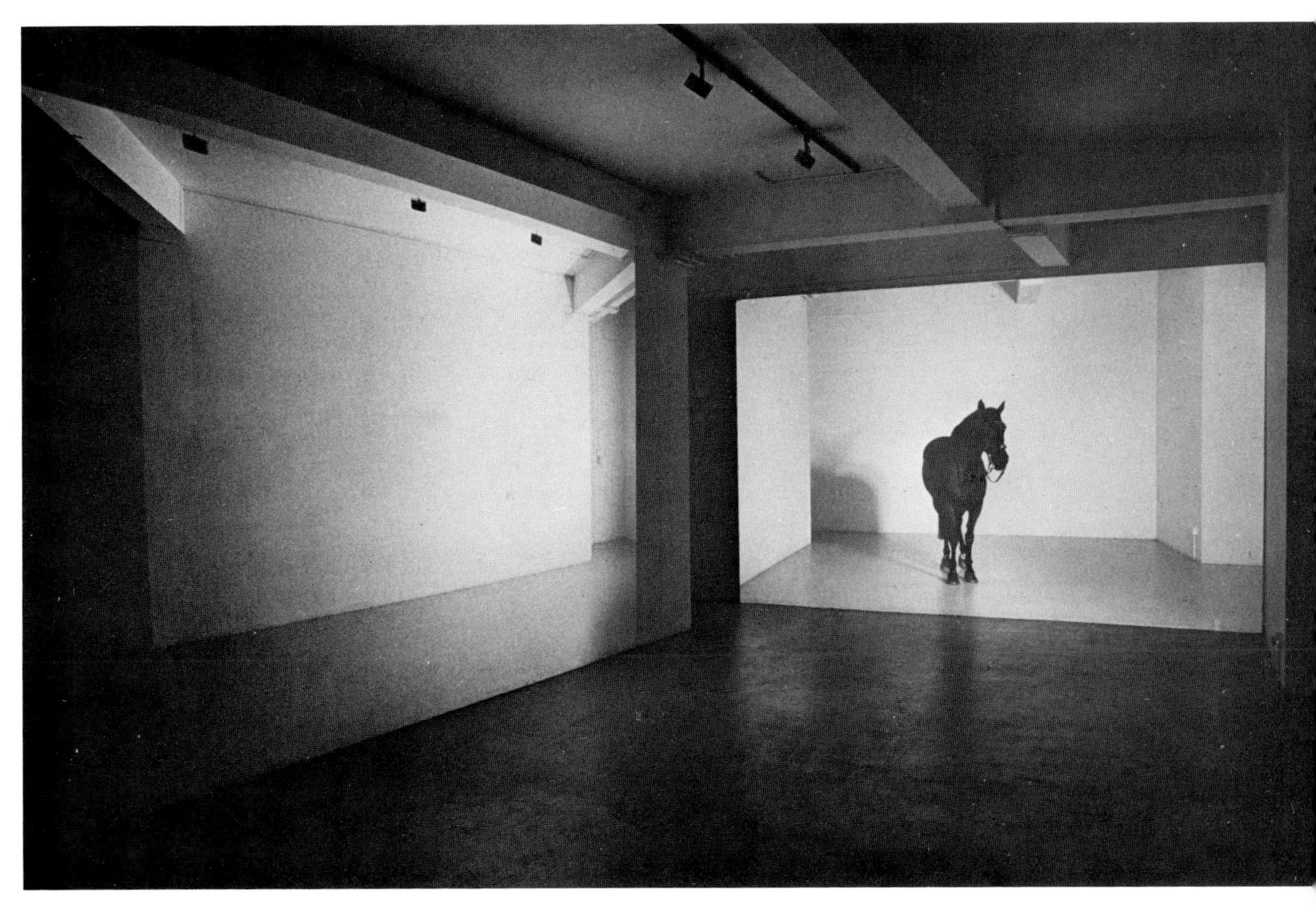

33.
Present, Installation at Rowan Gallery, London,
1978
Slide projections

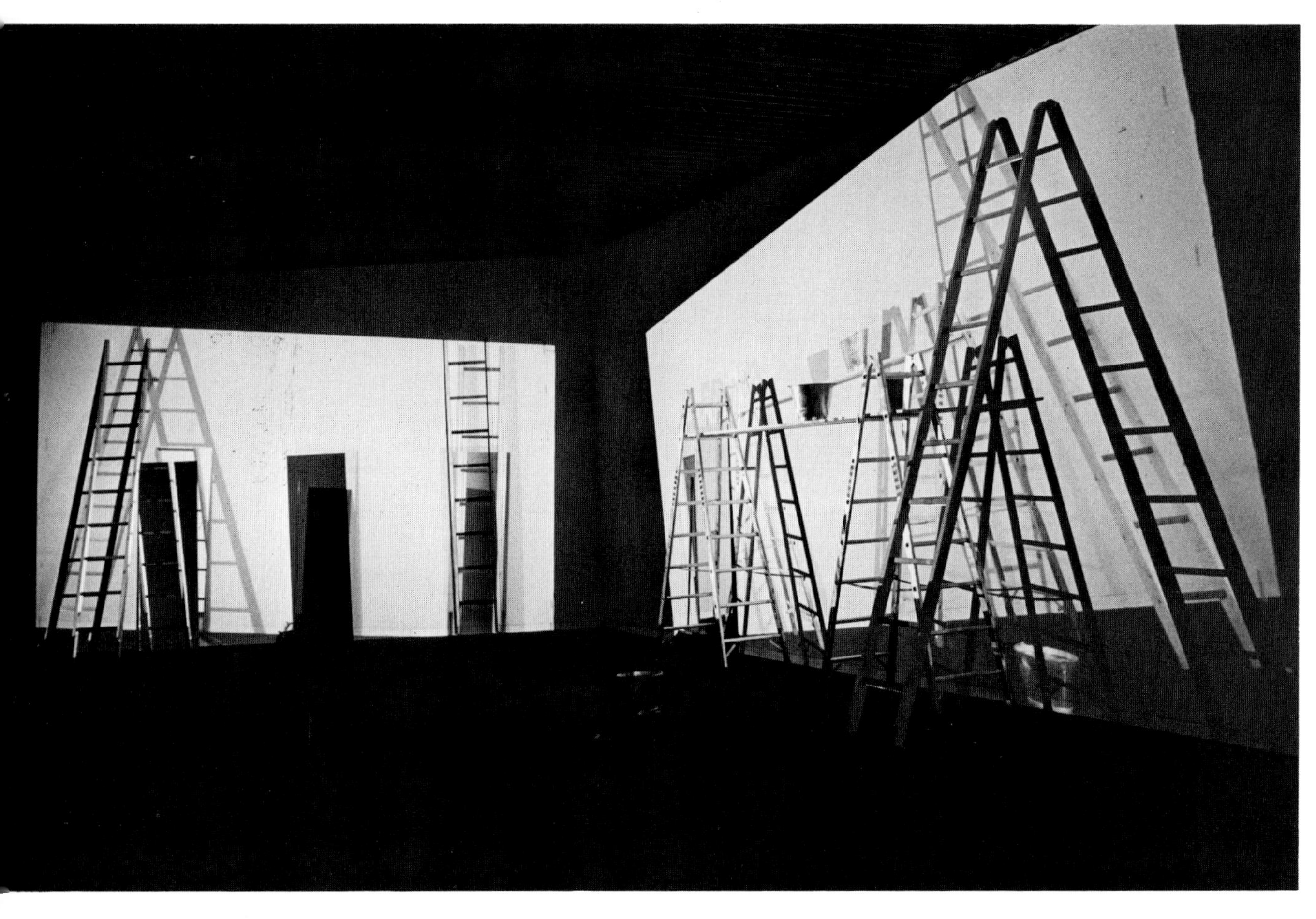

34.
Installation at Henie-Onstad Kunstcenter, Høvikod-
den, Norway, 1978
Slide projections, mirrors and objects

35.
Transparency, Installation at *3rd Biennale of Sydney,*
April-May 1979
Slide projections

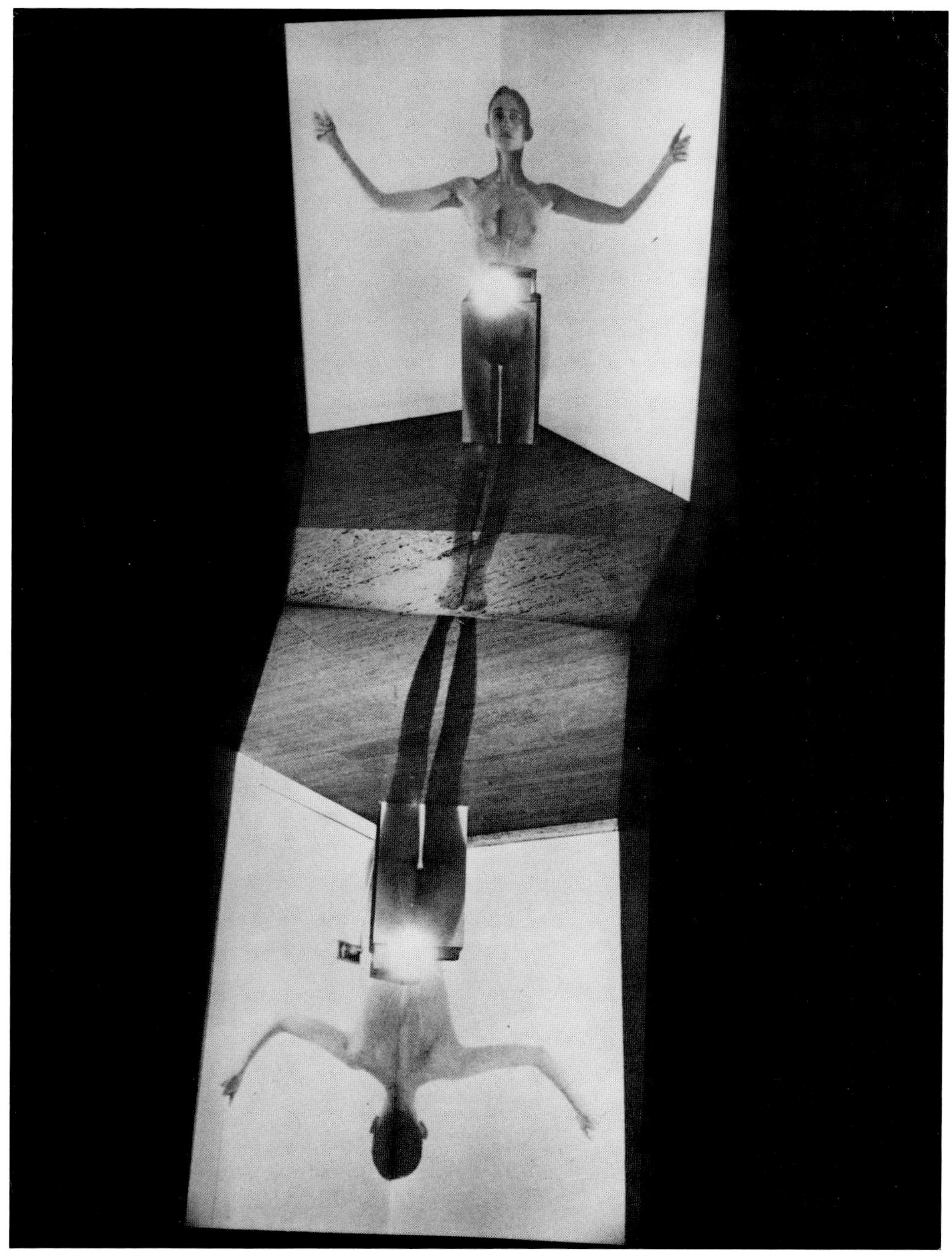

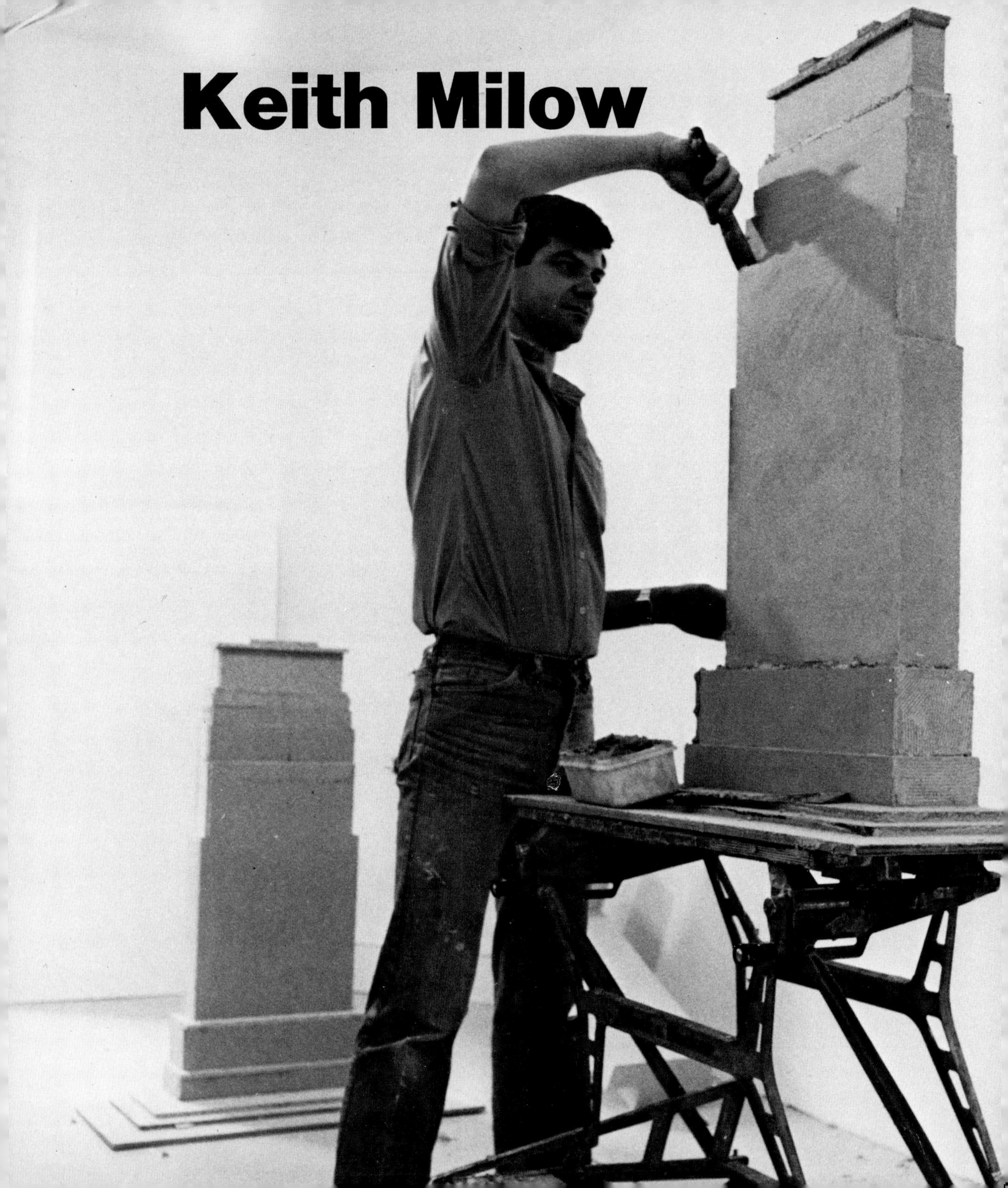

Keith Milow

Spare yet sensuous, painterly yet concerned with the nature of the object, Keith Milow's newest work expresses the quiet authority and confidence of an artist who has reached an important plateau. The culmination of a long and complex evolution, the imagery of much of his recent work derives from the configuration of the cross. In 1972, some months before he left Britain for New York on a Harkness Fellowship, Milow installed his first cross—a wall painting in Utrecht. It was not until near the end of his stay in New York, in 1974, that Milow began to make constructions in the shape of the cross.

It was not the crosses, however, but another series, *Split/Definitive* (cat. no. 39) of 1976, that he chose to show at the Nigel Greenwood Gallery in London in 1976. Each of the four panels of raw plywood in the series was hung at a right angle to the wall: thus, from the normal viewing position (facing the wall) only the panel edge was visible. The group was divided into two pairs of two panels, the upper one hung with its image facing in, the bottom painting with its image facing out. The image on each panel was divided diagonally in half, with the alternating sections painted the cool reserved green Milow typically favors. To comprehend the image as a totality, the spectator was forced to navigate the entire space of the installation.

By obliging the viewer to walk around each of the panels, Milow made a two-dimensional image operate in three-dimensional space. While the space in which these panels functioned was real, the images bordered on the implausible. For the panels were not only fragmented but cast triangular shadows which echoed the shapes of the images and thus undermined the reality of the works themselves.

In his concern with the play of reality against unreality, Milow may be compared with Tim Head. Both artists are deeply involved with the physical world and use structural, architectural and environmental references. Both have employed illusionism, mirror images, inversion, displacement and superimposition. Head, however, is primarily interested in suspending our belief in what we perceive and depends upon certain phenomena—cues from the environment, real or recognizable props, an element of theater—to force this suspension of belief upon us. Milow, on the other hand, has introduced fictive objects into real space with somewhat different intentions, namely to question the nature of art, to heighten the conflict between object and illusion. His is a Johnsian dialogue, committed to the investigation of objective reality, the illusionistic depiction of the subject and to the documentation of the process of transforming the one into the other.

In the *Split/Definitive* series, indeed in all Milow's work prior to the crosses, the Duchampian play upon the meaning of objects was so intricate and indirect that it often obscured our direct apprehension and enjoyment of the image. However, we are forced to confront the subject of Milow's crosses directly because their symbolic meaning is so powerful. The crosses are so austere, so pareddown we perceive them also as abstract shapes. Thus we comprehend them as both many-layered symbol and pure form.

He uses the cross, much as as he has used other images, as an object to build upon, transform and re-create. The cross, however, is a loaded image. Milow neither denies nor encourages its symbolic associations. Nor does he engage in the kind of play Walter de Maria encourages when he makes symbols work as games. Milow wishes to maintain a dialogue between the forms and symbols of the real world and pure abstraction. Because his crosses are neither too emphatically symbolic nor too resolutely abstract, they are among his most successful works.

Trained primarily as a painter but intensely interested in architecture, especially in the work of Frank Lloyd Wright, Milow attempts in his crosses to work with the space of the object and the space the object occupies, with the anchoring of real space with real objects. Whereas in the *Split/Definitive* series, the object completes itself only as part of the environment, the crosses are totalities which articulate the space around them. Milow does not seek to act in the "gap between art and life" like Rauschenberg and, for that matter, Head, but tries to wrest from his cruciform structures the power to control relatively large areas of space.

Keith Milow working on *Cenotaph*

To date Milow has produced over one hundred crosses. They range from a mere few inches to eight feet in height and were initially constructed of plywood coated with iron or copper powder. Surface oxidation, which occurs when the artist applies salt and vinegar to the iron or copper coating, has given them the patina of age. Although Milow followed roughly the same procedure in each of these works, the results were often strikingly different: for he allowed an element of chance to come into play so that the random brushstroke or accidental drip activated an otherwise rigorously controlled structure.

The cross itself derived initially from the configuration and proportions of the traditional Christian symbol. Thus Milow has often used a representational image for his point of departure, as an earlier series based on a ship indicates. After painting the ship, he cut the canvas into L-shaped segments and replaced each strip with from one to eight layers of resin. Although the original image was obliterated in the process, Milow created another equally plausible reality. Other L-shaped resin pieces are not based on images of ships. *Improved Reproductions 12345* 6 *. . . B, 1970,* for example (cat. no. 36), is part of a sequence based on a chalk drawing of a Caro table sculpture *(LXIII, 1968)* shown at the Hayward Gallery.

As the series evolved, Milow substituted concrete and plaster for iron and copper. He developed a number of constructions (cat. nos. 45, 46), which he has painted a soft pinkish tone and oriented diagonally, whose configurations derive from but only remotely resemble the forms of his original crosses. While they retain an iconic quality, these pieces are more closely related to the crosses of Malevich or the constructions of Rodchenko than to the crosses of Christianity, underlining Milow's emphasis upon the significance of the object as a formal rather than symbolic entity. He is concerned primarily with the object's purity of shape, the space it anchors, and the materials, textures and colors that transform it from a literal symbol into an abstract construct. The soft and seductive pink used in the asymmetrical crosses has a similar effect to the cool and memorable green of much of his work.

Color functions on two levels, as a self-sufficient entity and also as a comment on the nature of color. This duality enriches the many-leveled complexities of his sculpture.

Like his crosses, Milow's cenotaphs (see cat. nos. 47, 48) carry with them the residue of another time and place. Despite the cenotaph's powerful implicit symbolism, Milow once again forces us to consider these objects not merely for their historical resonance but as pure form. Like the earlier *Split/ Definitive* series, the cenotaphs are part of an architectural construct, but they do not depend upon the environment for their completion: they control the space they enclose while they maintain their autonomy. The shadows cast by the cenotaphs, as in the *Split/Definitive* series and the crosses, become vital components of the images. The symbolic content of the crosses and of the cenotaphs has been reduced as Milow's renewed interest in painting painting becomes apparent. Layers of complexity, both pictorial and extra-pictorial, contribute a sense of immediacy to a subject drawn from remote times. Milow has infused very ancient signs and symbols with renewed life and a new formal dimension.

Keith Milow

Born in London, 1945

Camberwell School of Art, London, 1962-67

Royal College of Art, London, 1967-68

Experimental work at Royal Court Theatre, London, 1968

Teaches at Ealing School of Art, London, 1968-70

Gregory Fellowship as Artist in Residence, University of Leeds, 1970

Harkness Fellowship to New York, 1972-74

Teaches at Chelsea School of Art, London, 1975-present

Calouste Gulbenkian Foundation Visual Arts Award, 1976

Equal First Prize, *Tolly Cobbold/Eastern Arts 2nd National Exhibition,* 1979

Lives in London

Selected Group Exhibitions

Tate Gallery, London, *Young Contemporaries,* January-February 1967

Lisson Gallery, London, April-May 1967

Festival of the City of London, February-March 1968

Axiom Gallery, London, August-September 1968

Palazzo Strozzi, Florence, *Mostra Mercato d'Arte Contemporanea,* November 1968

Richard Feigen Gallery, New York, November-December 1969

Hayward Gallery, London, *Six at the Hayward,* November-December 1969. Catalogue with text by Michael Compton

Bradford City Art Gallery, *2nd British International Print Biennale,* September-December 1970

Tokyo, *7th International Biennale Exhibition of Prints,* November 1970-January 1971

The Museum of Modern Art, New York, *A Selection of Drawings and Watercolors from the Museum Collection,* May-October 1971

Leeds City Art Gallery, *Art Spectrum North,* from June 1971. Traveled to Laing Art Gallery, Newcastle upon Tyne; Manchester City Art Gallery

XI Bienal de São Paulo, Brazil, September-November 1971. Traveled in South America

Walker Art Gallery, Liverpool, *John Moores Liverpool Exhibition 8,* April-July 1972; *Exhibition 9,* June-September 1974; *Exhibition 11,* November 1978-February 1979

Hayward Gallery, London, *The New Art,* August 1972. Catalogue with interview by Anne Seymour

Camden Arts Centre, London, *Photography into Art,* December 1972-January 1973

The Museum of Modern Art, New York, *Homers,* May 1973

Palais des Beaux Arts, Brussels, *Henry Moore to Gilbert and George: Modern British Art from the Tate Gallery,* September-November 1973. Catalogue with text by Anne Seymour

Serpentine Gallery, London, *Art as Thought Process,* December 1973-January 1974. Catalogue with text by Michael Compton

Palais de l'Europe, Menton, France, *Xe Biennale d'Art: The Process of Painting,* July 1974. Catalogue with text by Melanie Sandiford

Hayward Gallery, London, *British Painting, 74,* July 1974

Galerie Jacomo Santiveri, Paris, *Buckley, Milow, Hall,* March-April 1975

Schweizer Mustermesse, Basel, *British Exhibition Art 6 '75,* June 1975

Palazzo Reale, Milan, *Arte Inglese Oggi,* February 1976. Catalogue with text by Norbert Lynton

Recent British Art, from May 1976. Organized by The British Council, traveled to Yugoslavia, Greece, Hungary, Austria, Poland, Norway, Finland, Sweden, Portugal. Catalogue with text by David Thompson

The Dubose Gallery, Houston, *Six English Artists,* November 1976

Palais de l'Europe, Menton, France, *XIe Biennale Internationale d'Art: Art as Thought Process,* 1976

Felicity Samuel Gallery, London, *Photographs-works,* February-March 1977

Young Hoffman Gallery, Chicago, *5 British Artists,* April-May 1977

Hayward Gallery, London, *Hayward Annual,* May-September 1977

Musée d'Art Moderne de la Ville de Paris, *10e Biennale de Paris: Manifestation Internationale des jeunes artistes,* September 1977

Royal Academy of Arts, London, *British Painting 1952-1977,* September-November 1977

Kettle's Yard Gallery, Cambridge, *Reflected Images,* October-November 1977. Catalogue with text by Fenella Crichton

Fitzwilliam Museum, Cambridge, *Tolly Cobbold/ Eastern Arts 2nd National Exhibition,* from April 1979. Traveled to The Castle Museum, Norwich; Christchurch Mansion, Ipswich; Camden Arts Centre, London; Graves Art Gallery, Sheffield

Selected One-Man Exhibitions

Institute of Contemporary Arts, London, February-March 1971

Park Square Gallery, Leeds, July 1971 (prints); April-May 1972 (drawings)

Kings College, Cambridge, January 1972

Utrecht, The Netherlands, *Utrechtkring,* February 1972. Catalogue with text by Jeroen Grosfeld

Leeds City Art Gallery, *Gregory Fellows Exhibition,* March-April 1972

J. Duffy & Sons, New York, April-May 1973

Nigel Greenwood Inc. Ltd., London, November-December 1973

Nigel Greenwood Inc. Ltd., London, November 1974

Galerie Jacomo Santiveri, Paris, May 1975

Arnolfini Gallery, Bristol, October-November 1975

Hester Van Royen Gallery, London, October-November 1975 (drawings)

Kettle's Yard Gallery, Cambridge, April-May 1976. Catalogue with text by William Feaver

Nigel Greenwood Inc. Ltd., London, June 1976

Galerie Albert Baronian, Brussels, March-April 1977

Park Square Gallery, Leeds, and Walker Art Gallery, Liverpool, November 1977

Nigel Greenwood Inc. Ltd., London, *A series of watercolours "Dedicated to . . .,"* April-May 1978

Roundhouse Gallery, London, *Just Crosses,* August-September 1978

Selected Bibliography

Richard Morphet, *Improved Reproductions, Notes in Progress on Keith Milow,* London, May 1970

Marina Vaizey, "Keith Milow and Diter Rot," *Financial Times,* March 11, 1971

William Feaver, "Keith Milow," *Art International,* vol. XVI, October 1972, pp. 34-37, 131

William Feaver, "London Letter," *Art International,* vol. XVI, November 1972, pp. 38-39

William Feaver, "Keith Milow," *Financial Times,* November 14, 1974, p. 3

William Feaver, "Keith Milow," *Art Spectrum,* vol. 1, January 1975, p. 47

Simon Wilson, "Keith Milow," *Studio International,* vol. 193, September/October 1976, pp. 213-214

Joseph Masheck, "Cruciformality," *Artforum,* vol. XV, Summer 1977, pp. 56-63

Joseph Masheck, "Hard-core painting," *Artforum,* vol. XVI, April 1978, pp. 46-55

Adrian Lewis, "Keith Milow at Nigel Greenwood," *Artscribe,* no. 12, June 1978, p. 58

Joseph Masheck, "Iconicity," *Artforum,* vol. XVII, January 1979, pp. 30-41

Joseph Masheck, "Pictures of Art," *Artforum,* vol. XVII, May 1979, pp. 26-37

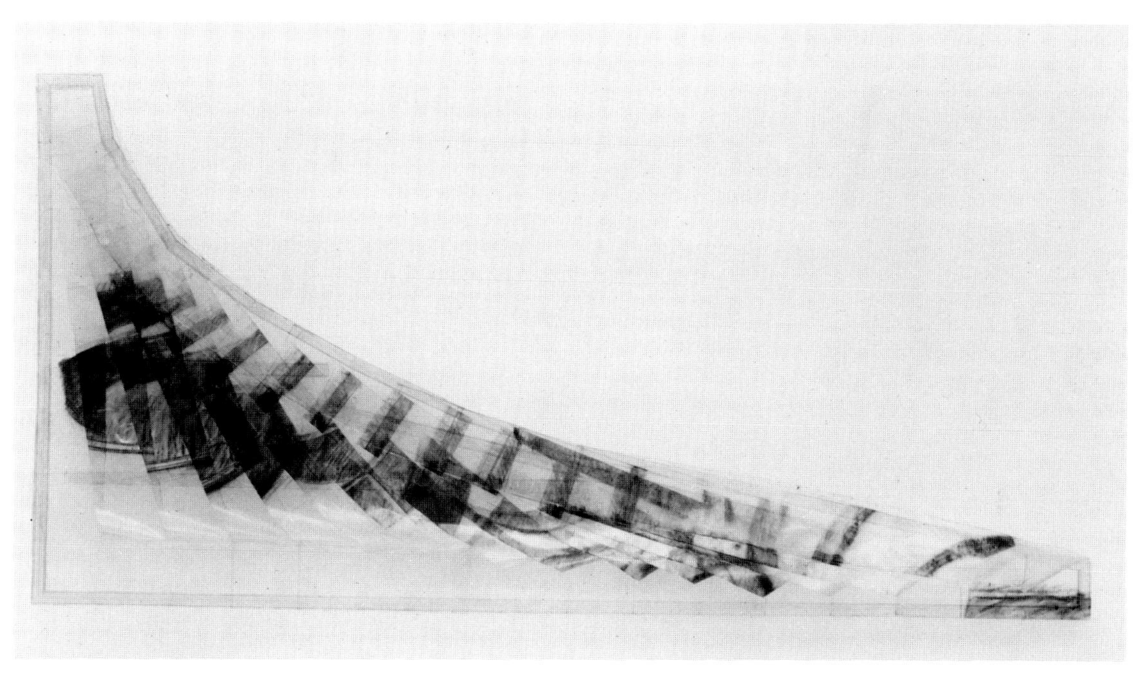

36.
Improved Reproductions, 12345 $\boxed{6}$ *. . . B,* 1970
Resin, charcoal and fiberglas, 48 x 84"
Collection The Trustees of the Tate Gallery, London

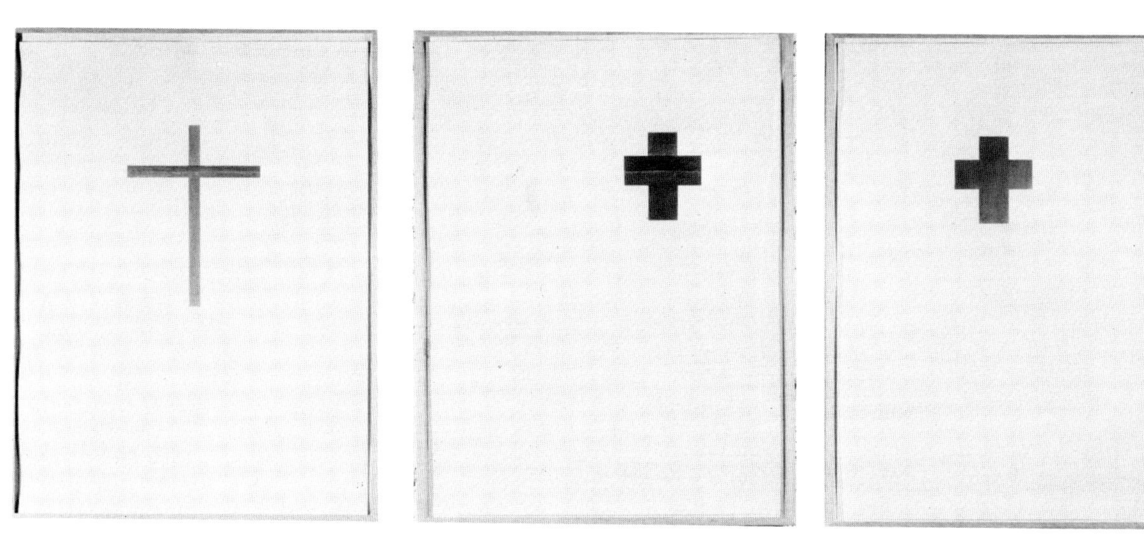

37.
Two and One Crosses, Two. 1974
Metallic crayon on paper, each 40 x 30″
Collection Michael Findlay, New York

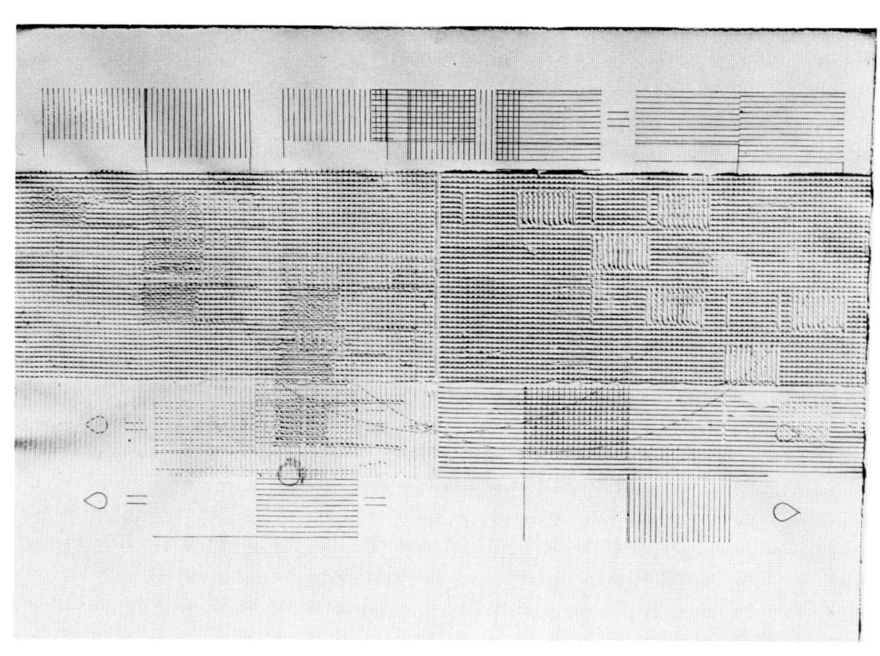

38.
Infinity Drawing 10/15B/75. 1975
Iron powder and aquatec-jel on paper, 22½ x 30⅞ ″
Collection The British Council, London

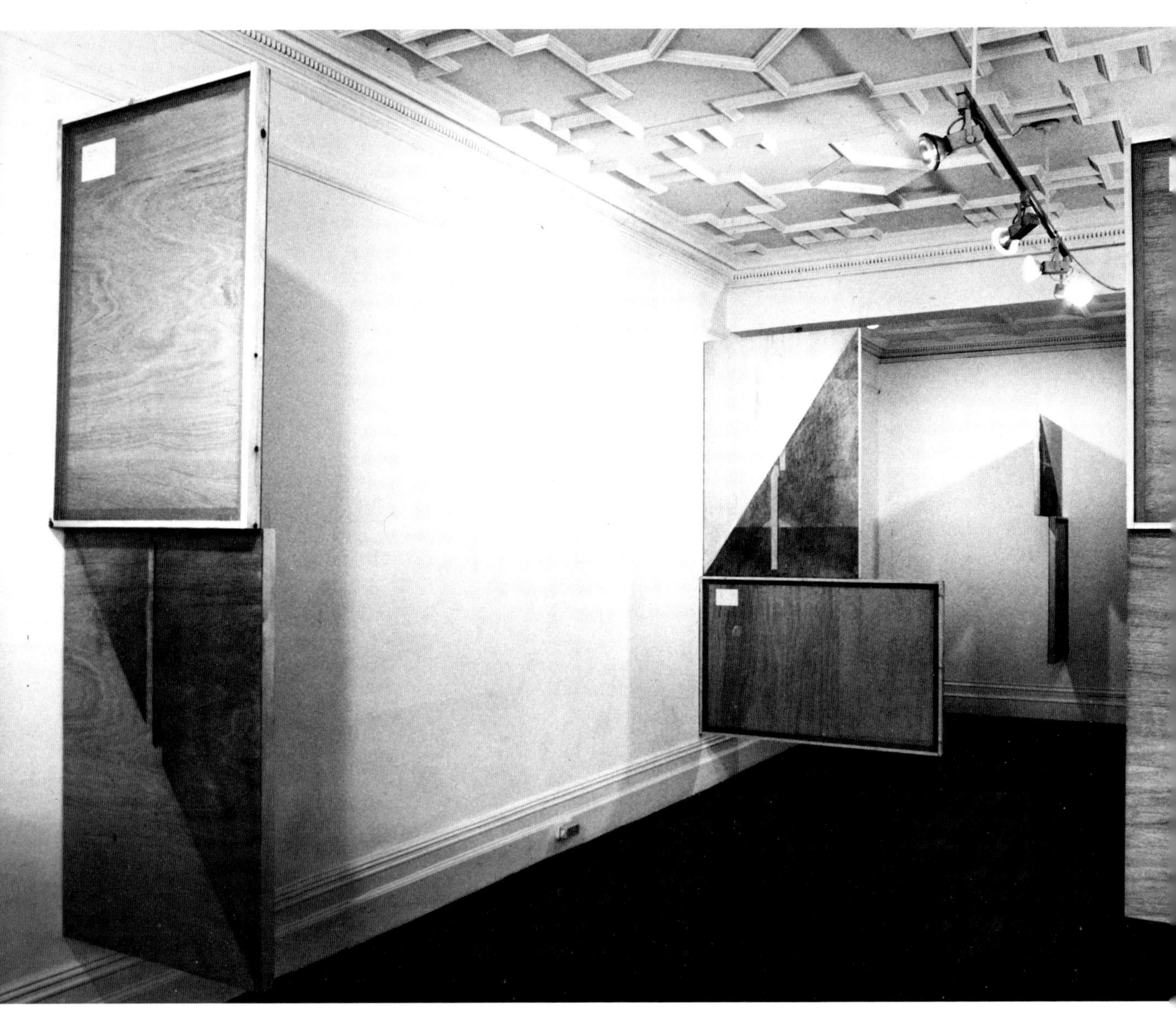

39.
1st Split Definitive series, Installation at Nigel
Greenwood Inc. Ltd., London, June 1976

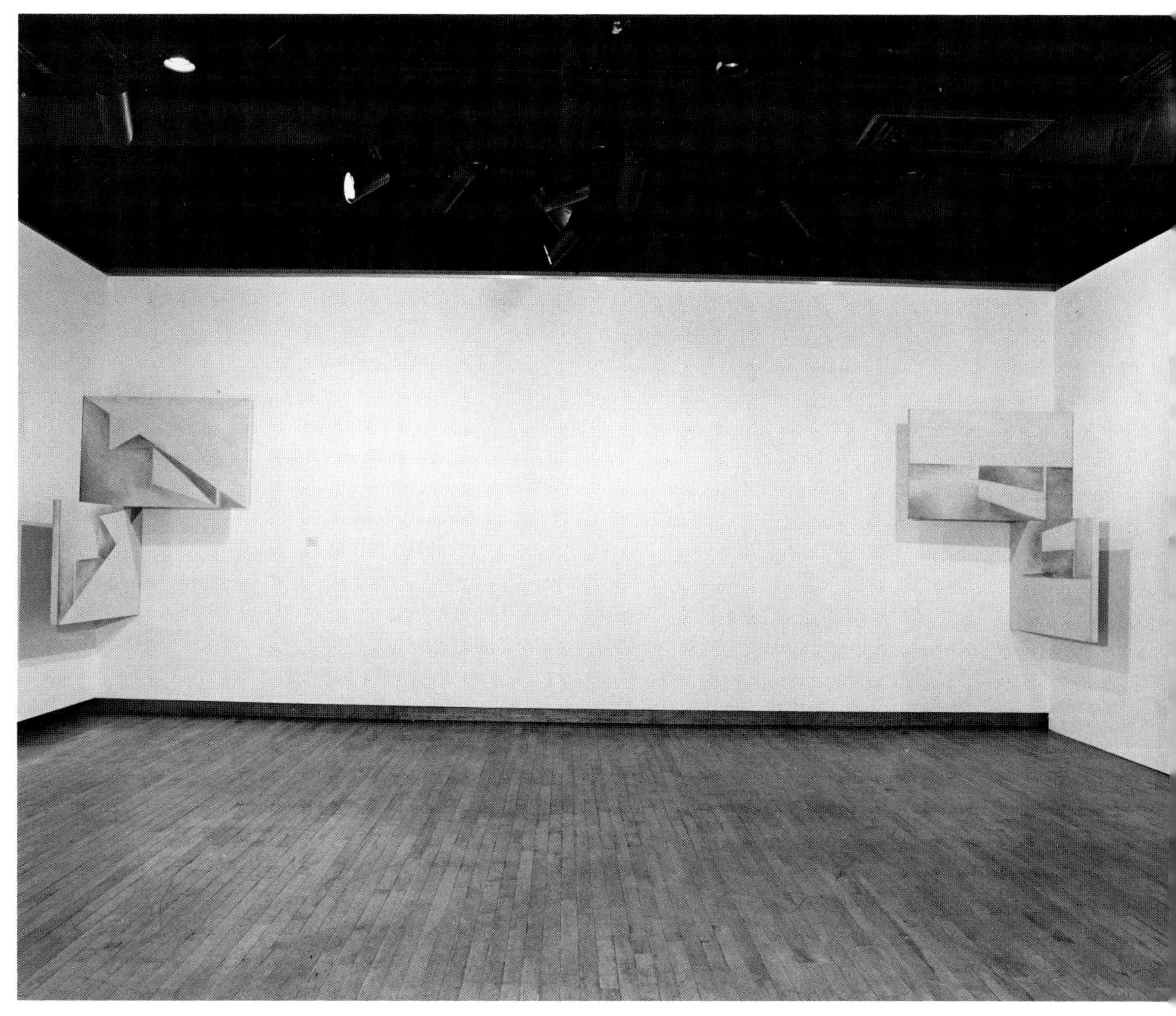

40.
2nd Split Definitive series, Installation at the Hayward Gallery, London, 1977

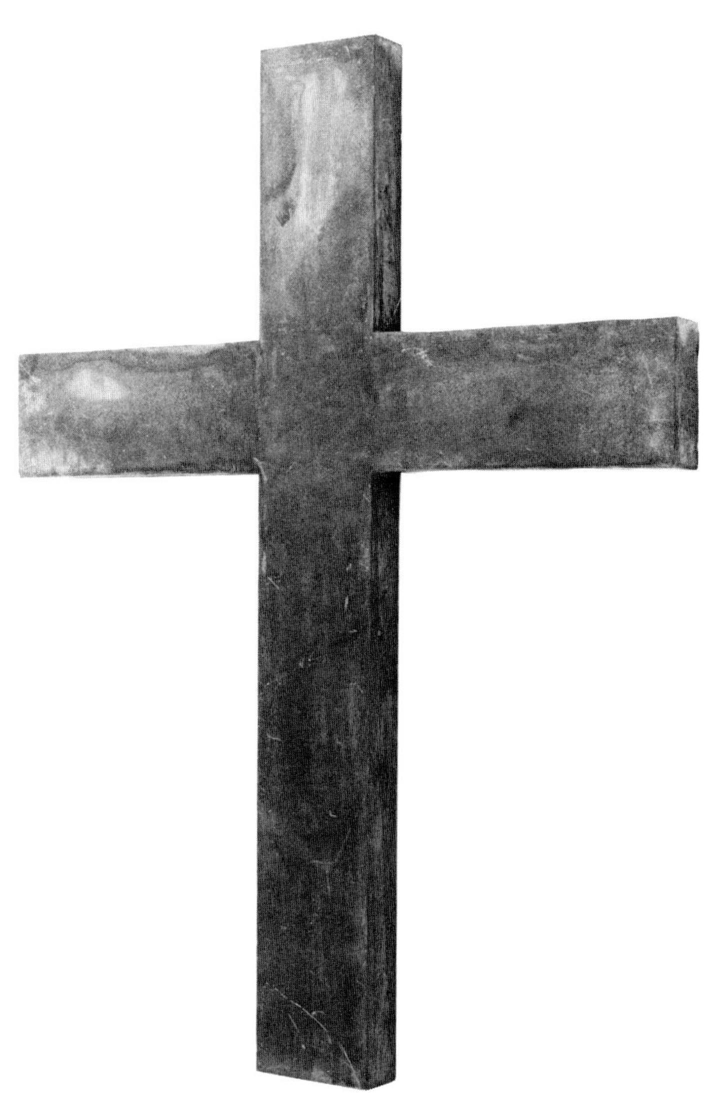

41.
Forty Sixth Cross. 1976
Iron powder and acrylic on wood, 40 x 30 x 2″
Courtesy Rowan Gallery Ltd., London

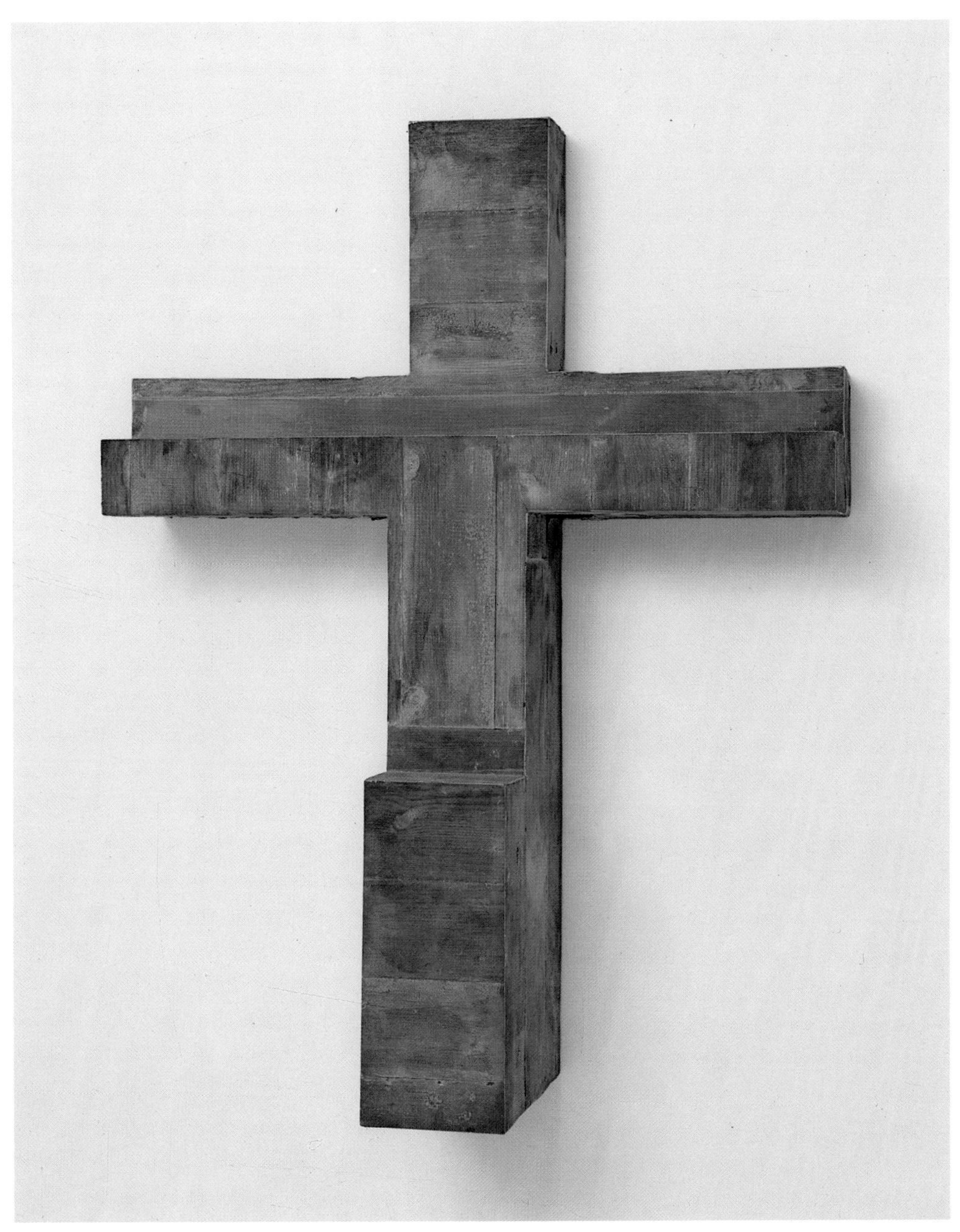

42.
Ninety Fifth Cross. 1978
Concrete, resin and fiberglas, 40 x 30 x 11¼ ″
Collection Silas Rhodes

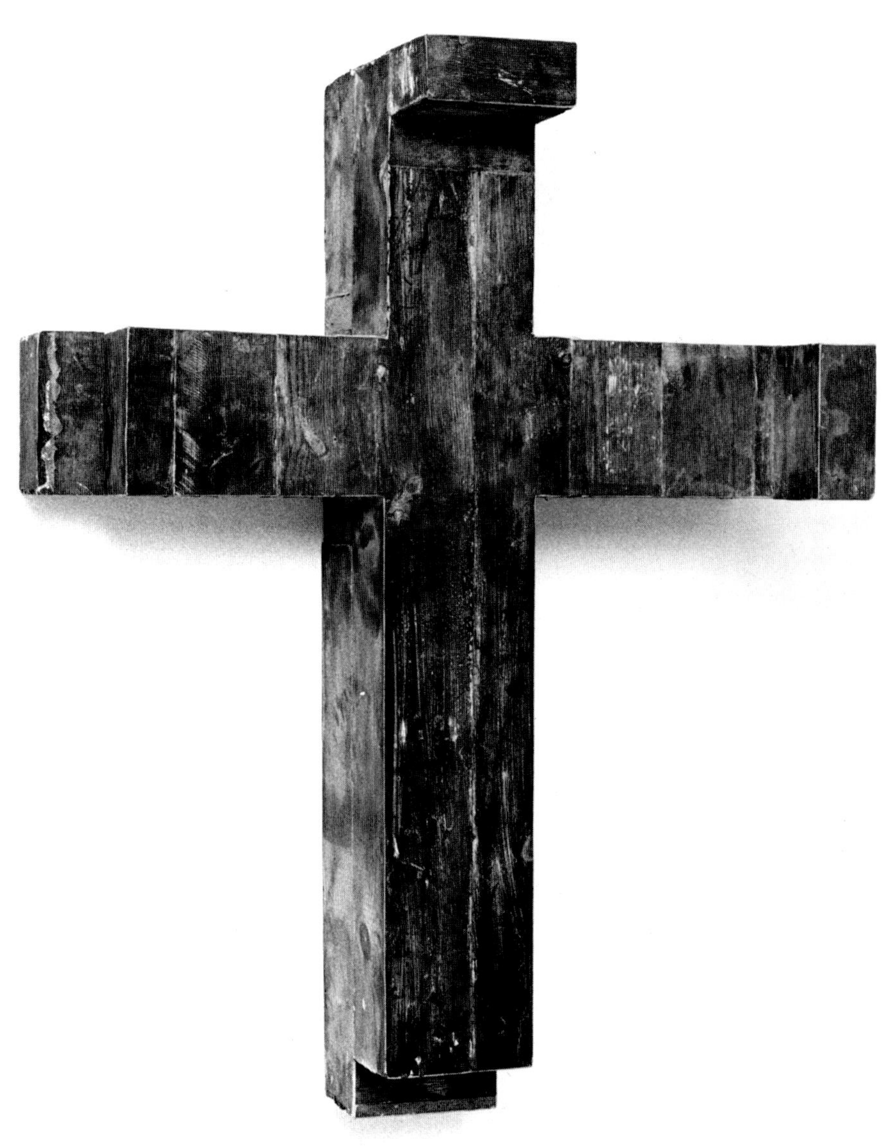

43.
Ninety Sixth Cross. 1978
Concrete, resin and fiberglas, 40 x 30 x 11¼ ″
Courtesy Rowan Gallery Ltd., London

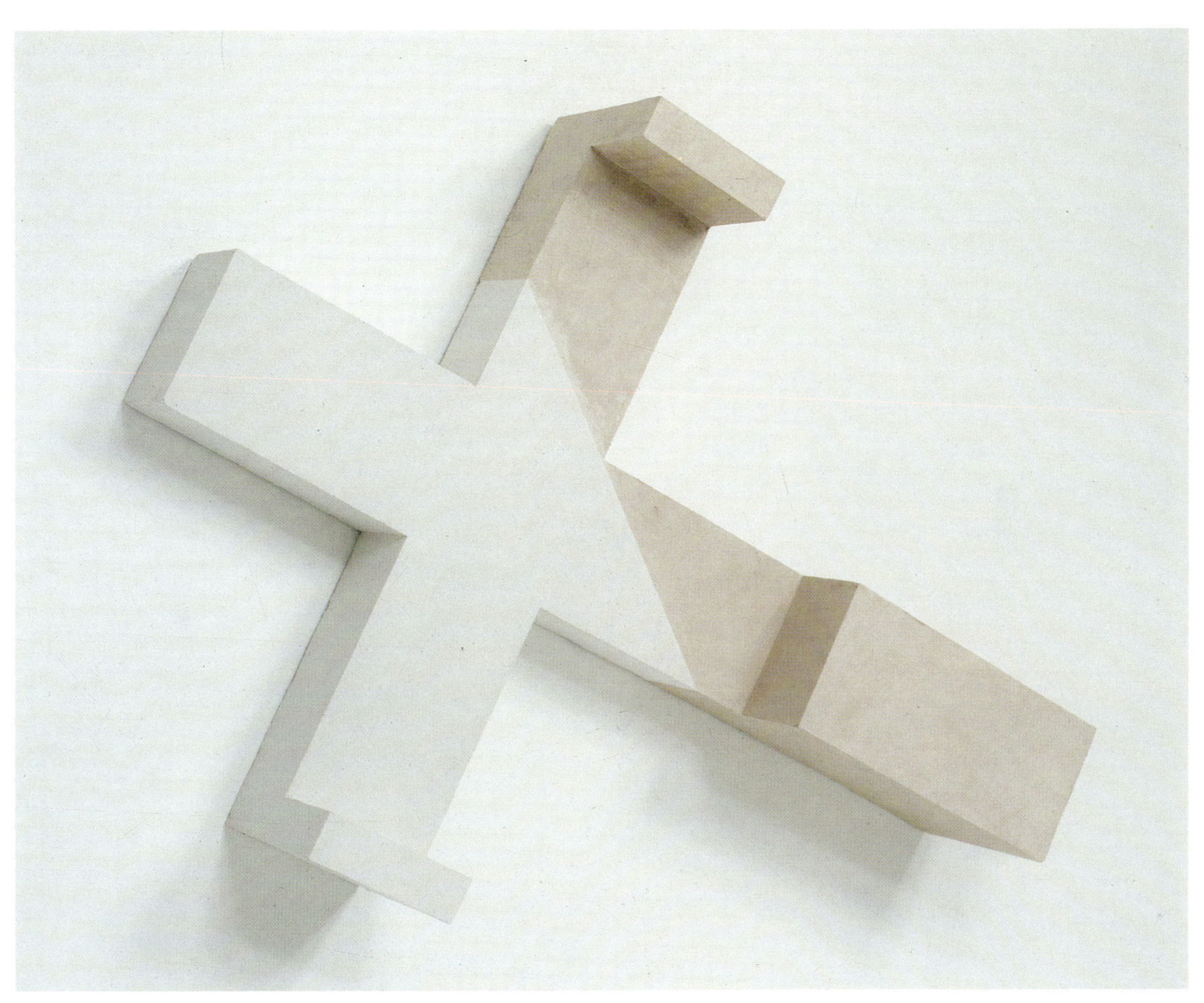

44.
One Hundredth Cross. 1978-79
Plaster, sirapite and acrylic on wood, 29½ x 38 x
7½ "
Courtesy Rowan Gallery Ltd., London

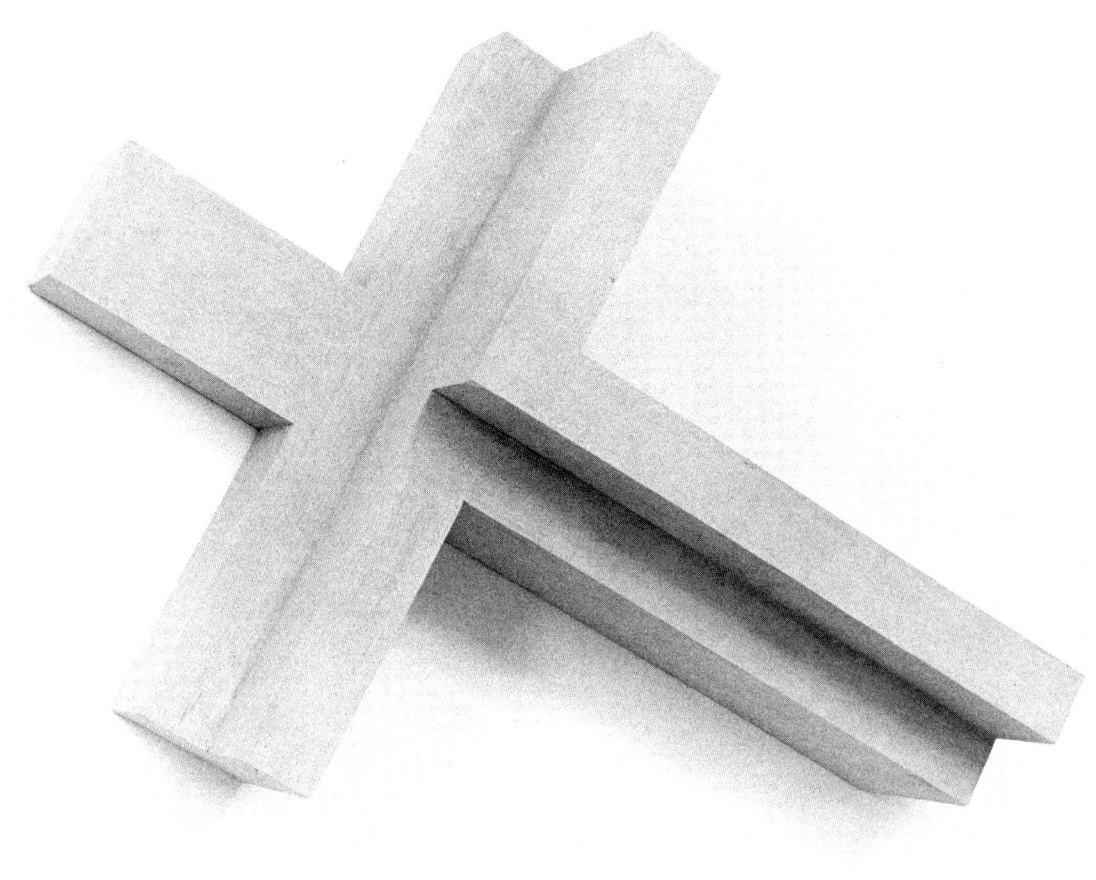

45.
One Hundred and Eighth Cross. 1979
Sirapite and acrylic on wood, 29½ x 38 x 11¼ "
Courtesy Rowan Gallery Ltd., London

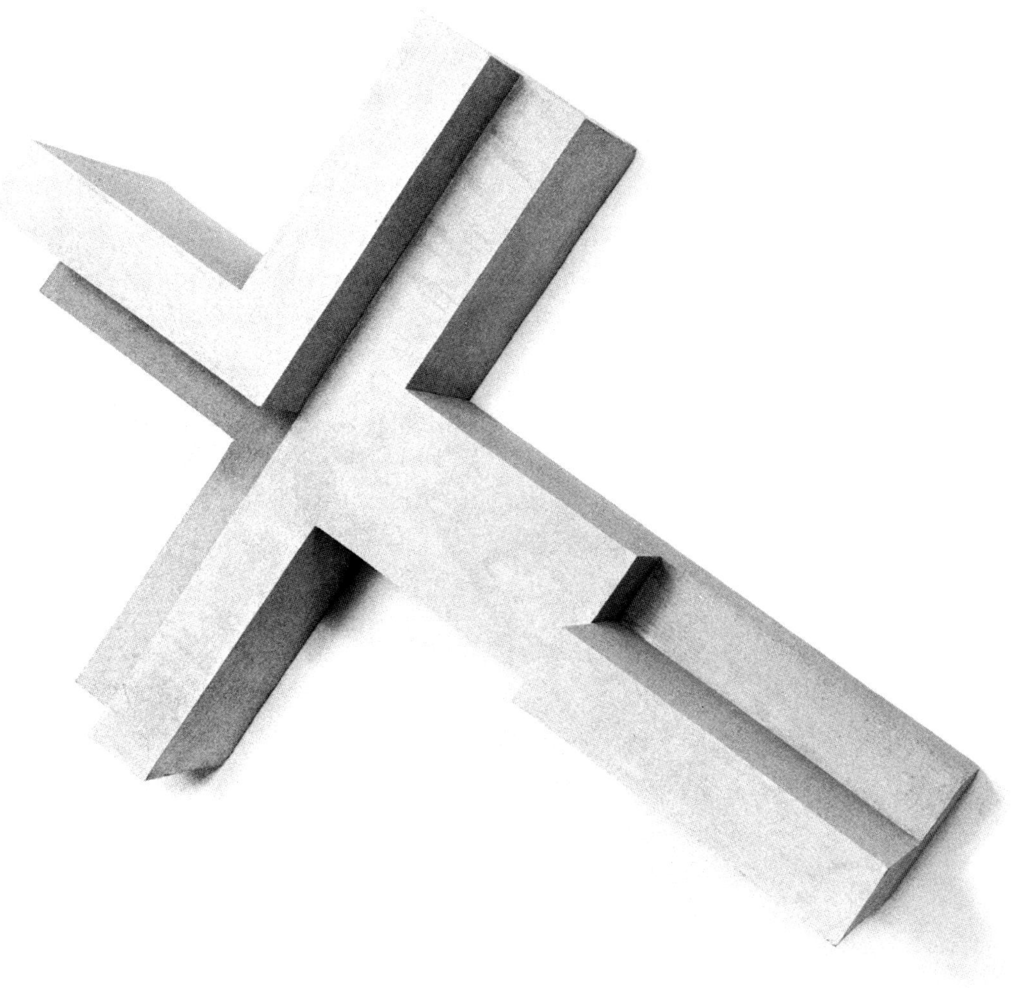

46.
One Hundred and Tenth Cross. 1979
Sirapite and acrylic on wood, 29½ x 38 x 11¼″
Courtesy Rowan Gallery Ltd., London

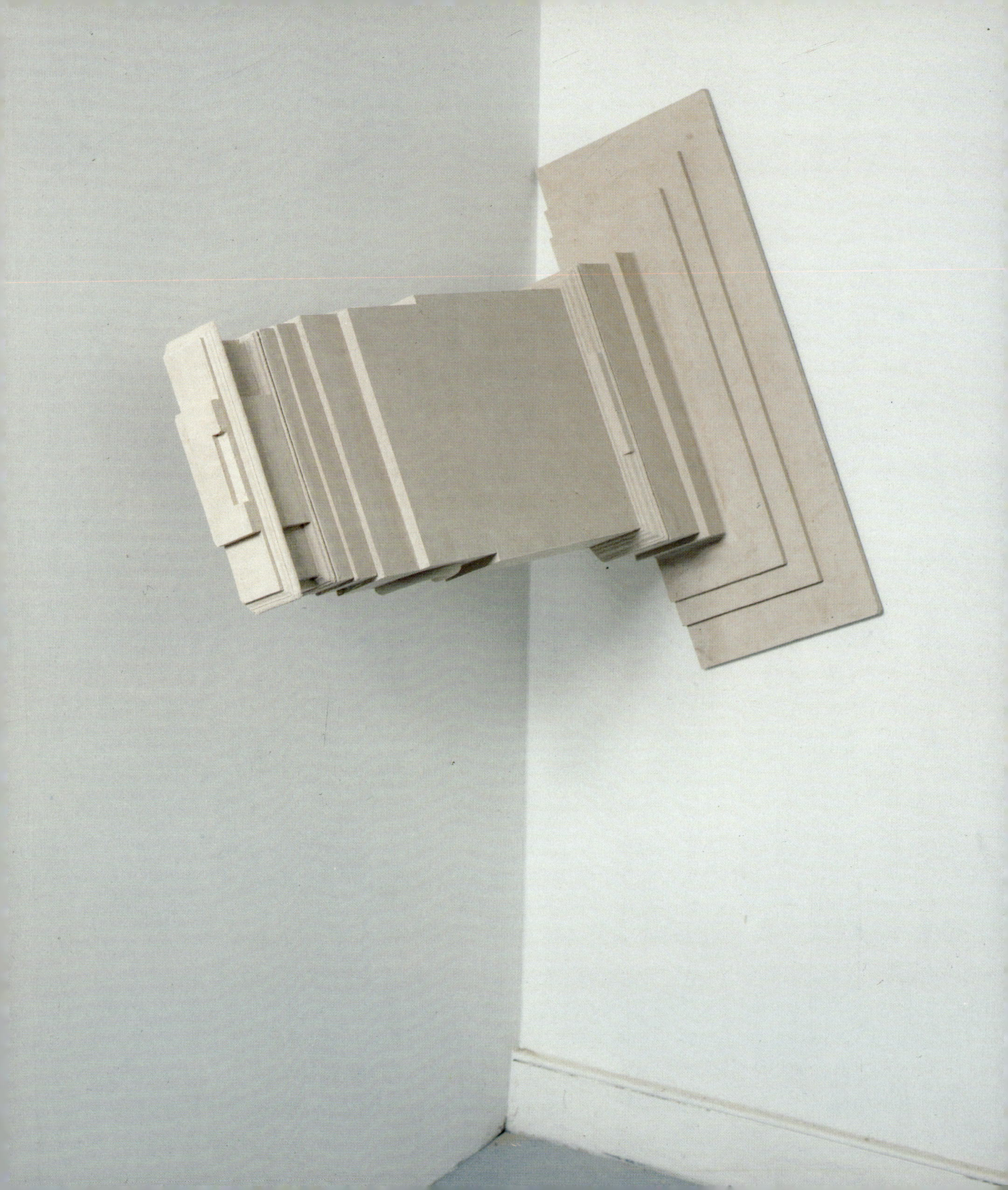

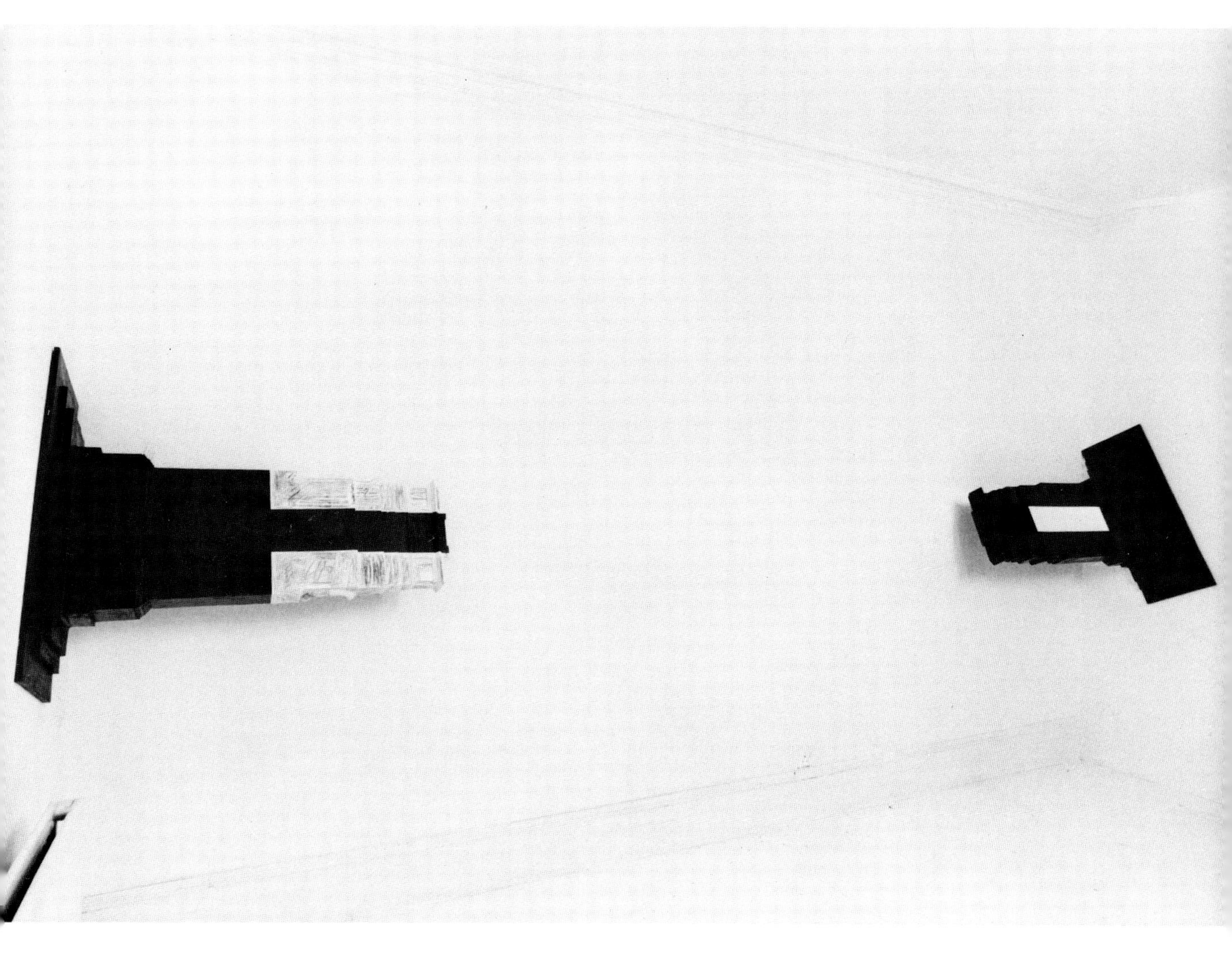

<table>
<tr><td>

47.

Detail of *First Cenotaph.* 1979

Sirapite and acrylic on wood, one of two sections, 37 x 43 x 26″

Courtesy Rowan Gallery Ltd., London

</td><td>

48.

Second Cenotaph. 1979

Oil and bronze powder, resin and fiberglas, each section, 37 x 43 x 26″

Courtesy Rowan Gallery Ltd., London

</td></tr>
</table>

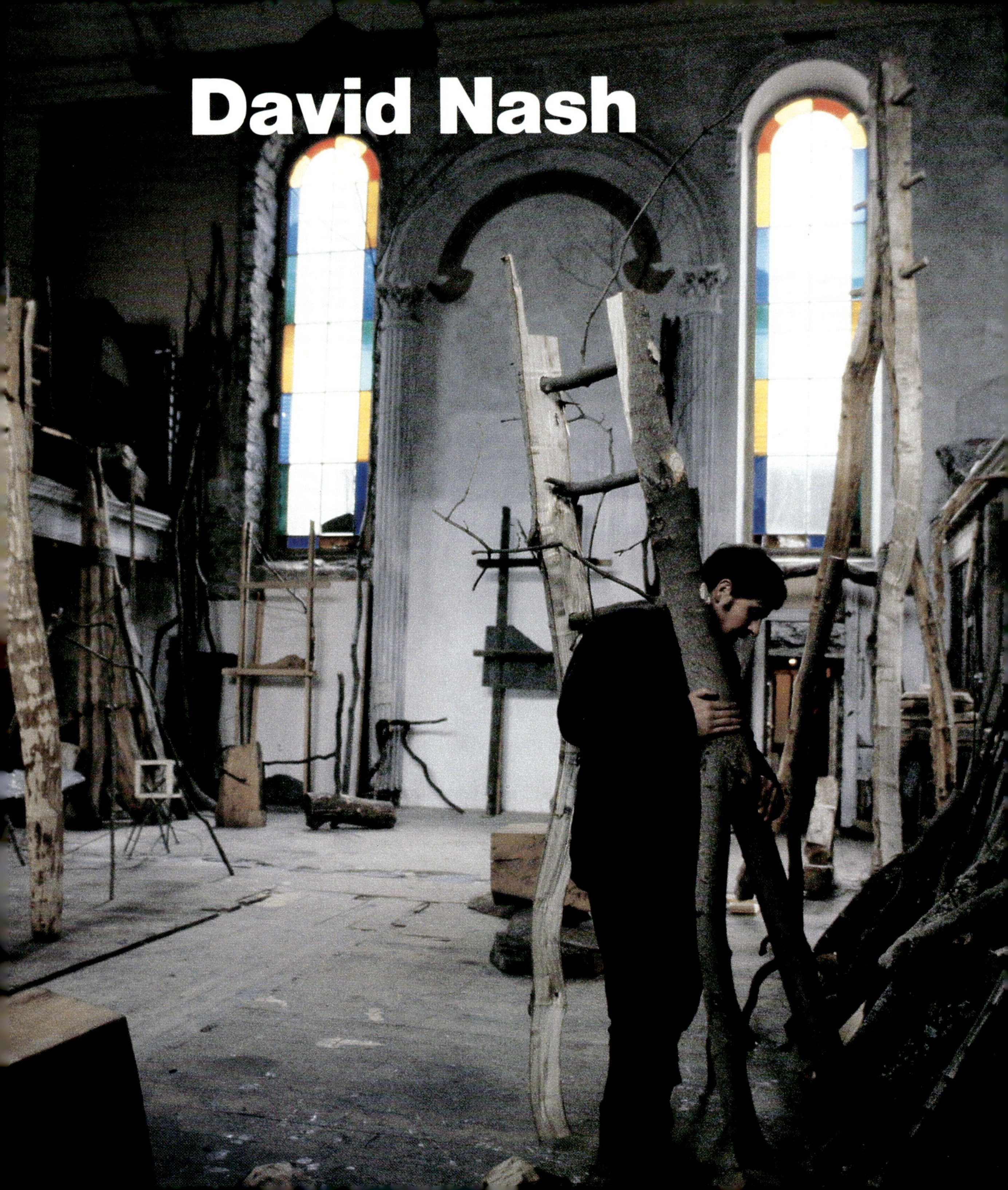
David Nash

David Nash came to Blaenau Ffestiniog, Wales, in 1967, directly after leaving college. His grandparents had lived nearby, his family often went there when he was a child. He chose virtual isolation in Wales because life in London was simply too expensive. Nash lived and worked initially in a pair of cottages and in 1969 bought the chapel he now occupies.

Blaenau is a grim grey village dominated by massive slate quarries that are no longer in use. Situated in a pocket in Northwest Wales where the rainfall averages one hundred and twenty inches a year, it is without a sound economic base, without amenities. Yet, just a short distance away, above the omnipresent slate-grey slag, loom the awesomely majestic Moelwyn mountains. Beneath the quarries spread lush valleys and the open expanse of the sea. In an environment of magnificent contrasts, Nash has found the major source of inspiration for his art.

Nash first worked with standard units of milled wood. Originally he was chiefly interested in painting the wood, in "putting colour into space. Wood was a convenient material to put colour onto. I loved putting big colour shapes high up into the air above me. I made a series of 30 ft. high towers of painted wood. I loved the engineering involved, the joints, the weight, the give to the wind."[1] Then he became dissatisfied with applying color to wood and tried to stain the wood; ultimately he recognized that he could utilize the wood's own color. "I was gradually being humbled by Nature. I realized wood has a special nature. The towers led me on. I began to understand Brancusi's *Endless Columns* and felt their humanity. I was drawn into his work and particularly his way of life. A way of life completely consistent with his work."[2] Nash did not attempt to emulate Brancusi's lifestyle but rather saw in it an inspiration for his own way of living. ". . . the immediate presence of Nature, the land and the weather, enables me to construct a life and a way of working that are so consistent that there is no separation. The family life, the teaching, the looking and the doing are intermingled in a continuous flow."[3]

As he allowed nature to enter into his daily existence, his disenchantment with the man-made shapes of the towers increased. Continuing to preoccupy himself with the upward thrust that the towers had conveyed, Nash turned to the tree as the natural equivalent of the tower. He made no attempt to refine the forms he cut from the trees. He abandoned applied color in favor of the color and surface qualities of the wood. His insistence upon absolute truth to materials led him ultimately to strip not only the artificial or architectural elements from his work but also to reveal his process by leaving the marks of the chisel or axe intact.

Because Nash incorporated undisguised, unaltered parts of trees into many of his pieces—grafting limbs or branches on tables, picture frames, ladders—he invited criticism for being too literal, for bringing nature indoors, for making artifacts rather than sculpture. Nash risked these pitfalls, however, because this new direction enabled him to disengage himself from his earlier work, to adopt a more direct, primitive means of expression and to experiment with the tree itself as a work of art.

Nash uses only fallen trees, preferring not to cut down living ones. From parts of trees he creates shapes which are drawn from characteristics inherent in his material. The cracking of wood inspired the clams and pods in *Three Clams on a Rack,* 1975, and a more recent and larger version of 1979 (cat. no. 62). "The crack penetrates to the center, right into the volume of the material. I need that. The cracks in the pods and balls are like smiles, revealing more about themselves. They are open rather than closed. With paint I just had a surface skin on a hidden substance, now I have the whole material and a sense of its interior."[4]

The aging process of wood affects Nash's choice of material: different kinds of wood crack at different times—beech, ash and oak the most, others like alder, horse chestnut and elm hardly at all. However indebted he is to Brancusi, Nash, like the Dadaists, enjoys the element of chance, which allows the personality of the material to reveal itself. However, he often goes further than the Dada artists—for chance, in the form of change, often

David Nash in his studio with 49. *Ash Ladder.* 1978, Ash, 112 x 33 x 22", Collection of the artist

comes into play as wood dries and cracks and alters shape well after Nash has completed his part in the making of the piece.

In addition to the clams and the pods, Nash has produced a series of tables, among them *Running Table* of 1978 (cat. no. 65), a group of tripods, for example *Tall Tripod* of 1976 (cat. no. 52), of Miróesque ladders (cat. no. 64) as well as objects, such as *Over the Brow, Holed Slate and Hazel,* 1977 (cat. no. 58), so singular as to defy classification. In addition to the more fanciful pieces, Nash has also produced a group of starkly simple structures such as *Wall Leaner—a Lazy Log,* 1976 (cat no. 55), which are almost Minimalist in their reduction. To some he has given fairly straightforward, descriptive titles; for others he has invented names which refer to the family context in which they were created. His humorous titles *(Up, Flop and Jiggle; Three Dandy Scuttlers; Elephant passing the window)* add a whimsical dimension to even the most rigorous works.

Nash works not only in his studio but in the woods around Blaenau and recently in the forest of Grizedale, Cumbria, a government trust in which he was allowed to work with fallen trees. He clearly sees the distinction between indoor and outdoor pieces: "An object made indoors diminishes in scale and stature when placed outside. The reverse happens when an object made outside is brought inside, it seems to grow in stature and presence. It brings the outside in with it. The object outside has to contend with unlimited space, uneven ground and the weather. The sculpture I show inside is meant to be seen inside, it relates to the limited space, the peculiar scale, and the still air."[5]

On five acres of scrubby, partially wooded hillside in Maentwrog, near Blaenau, Nash has set himself the task of making sculpture that is uniquely conceived for the site. In 1977 he planted a group of ash seedlings which will take at least thirty years to reach its intended configuration, a dome. Nash is cutting and pruning the dome, entitled *Fletched over Ash,* and intends to thoroughly document the course of its growth. The programmatic nature of this piece as well as its time span contrast sharply with Nash's more spontaneous, more rapidly executed indoor work. Among his other major landscape pieces is a *Wooden Boulder* (cat. no. 63). The boulder, cut from the bowl of an oak tree, has been placed in a nearby stream; pushed by water currents, it will eventually work its way downstream, aging in the process. This piece and *Running Table* (cat. no. 65), epitomize the extremely subtle alterations Nash makes in his work and reveal the balance he seeks to achieve between art and nature. He wishes to leave the barest imprint of his gesture upon nature, to touch it only enough to bring it to life.

Nash's use of landscape-based subject matter has prompted comparisons with Earthworks. Nash's art, however, is not ground-related, nor is it an outgrowth of the Minimalist movement which formed the basis for Earthworks. For he seeks neither primary symmetrical forms nor does he wish to impose his own geometry on nature. Rather, his work is anthropomorphic in its reference to nature and highly inituitive rather than doctrinaire in origin. He does not wish to make his pieces inaccessible but to place them in a one to one relationship with the viewer. Nash, like the Earthworks artists, thinks of his sculpture in terms of process, of space, of site. Yet his intimate, often linear and eccentric forms are full of wit and humor and thus differ radically from the vast, public, entirely sober, abstract and monumental Earthworks.

Elephant passing the window, 1977 (cat. no. 57), exemplifies Nash's intentions. The piece was directly inspired by an Indian stone carving in the British Museum. After seeing the carving, Nash spent two days drawing elephants at the London zoo. He chose materials from his immediate surroundings: the slate came from a tip behind the chapel, the oak from a frame used for growing roses, the alder from an abandoned sculpture. It came together easily and indicates a new direction. Nash contains the image within the frame, extends a portion of this image (the "elephant's trunk") from the two-dimensional picture plane into our space and uses slate to identify the wall and wood the floor. The sparse materials and extreme linearity endow his sculpture with the quality of a drawing in space. The result is a new combination of the pictorial and the sculptural.

By searching for his own identity and giving shape to what he finds meaningful, Nash has created a group of works in which nature intertwines with art and life. Not nature removed from life and sanctified, ritualized or romanticized, not nature objectified or given a strict aesthetic dimension, but nature accepted into the immediacy of everyday life and the context of art. The result is often playful, always engaging, arresting and highly original.

1. McPherson, Alan, "Interview with David Nash," *Artscribe,* no. 12, June 1978, p. 30
2. *Ibid.*
3. *Ibid.*
4. *Ibid., p. 32*
5. *Ibid., p. 33*

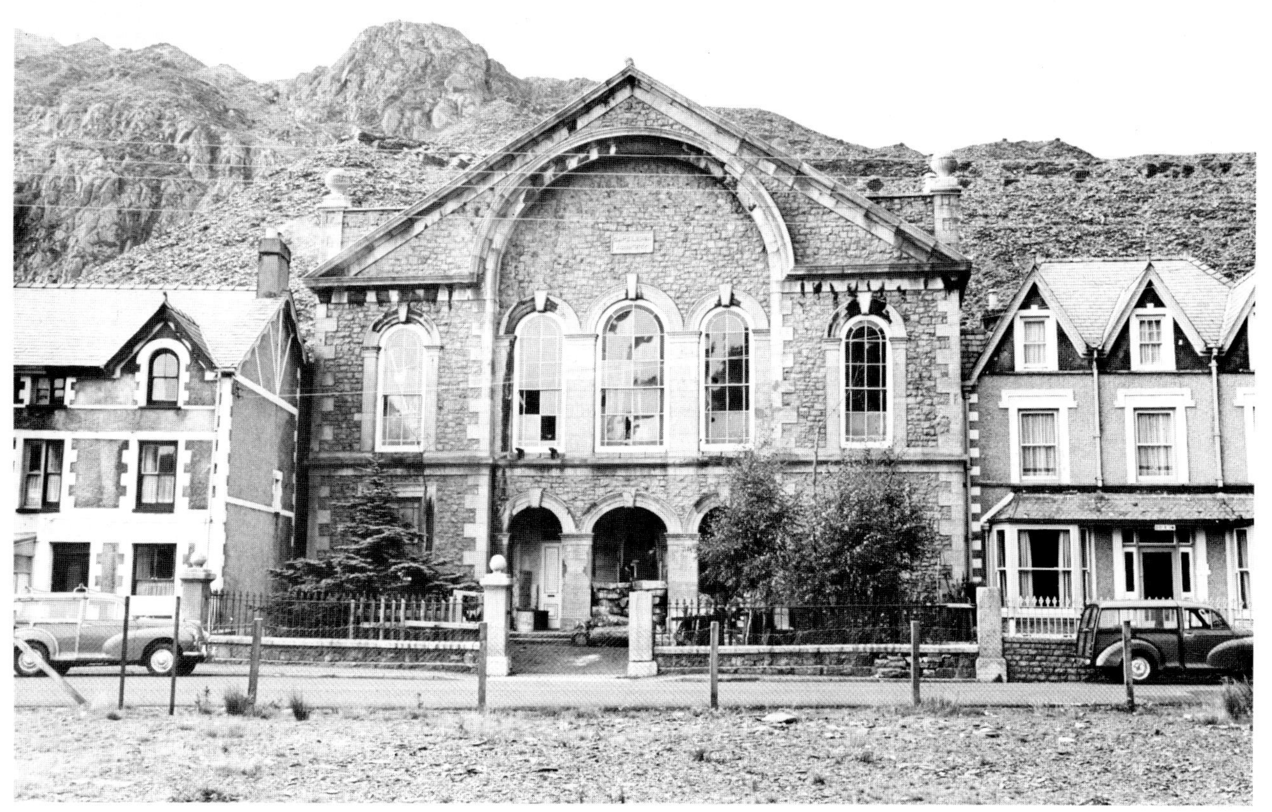

Capel Rhiw, Blaenau Ffestiniog, North Wales

David Nash

Born in Esher, Surrey, 1945

Kingston College of Art, Kingston upon Thames, Surrey, 1963-67

Visiting lecturer to art colleges and universities since 1967, including Newcastle Polytechnic, Newcastle upon Tyne; Royal College of Art, London; Newport College of Art, Wales; Dublin College of Art

Moves to Blaenau Ffestiniog, North Wales, 1967

Chelsea School of Art, London, 1969-70

Established field centre, Blaenau Ffestiniog (to enable visiting students to work with the space and elements of the land), 1973

Awarded Major Bursary, Welsh Arts Council, 1975

Resident Sculptor, Grizedale Forest, Spring 1978

Attended International Symposium of Sculpture, Macedonia, Yugoslavia, 1978

Planting Project Commission, larch and ash, Southampton University, 1979

Lives in Blaenau Ffestiniog

Selected Group Exhibitions

Hayward Gallery, London, *The Condition of Sculpture,* May-July 1975

Serpentine Gallery, London, *Summer Show 3,* July-August 1976

Welsh and Scottish Arts Council, Edinburgh, *From Wales,* March 1977

Arnolfini Gallery, Bristol, *On Site,* September-October 1977

Arts Council of Great Britain, London, *A Free Hand,* from January 1978. Traveled to Arts Centre Gallery, Chester; Ikon Gallery, Birmingham; Huddersfield Art Gallery; Great Yarmouth Exhibitions Centre; Leicester Polytechnic; Turnpike Gallery, Leigh

Ikon Gallery, Birmingham, *Sculpture = Furniture,* April 1979

Li Yuan Chia's Museum, Hadrian's Wall, Brompton, Cumbria, *Paul Neagu and David Nash,* August 1979

One-Man Exhibitions

York Festival, *Briefly Cooked Apples,* July-August 1973

Oriel Gallery, Bangor, North Wales, August-September 1973

Oriel Gallery, Bangor, North Wales, September 1976

Arnolfini Gallery, Bristol, *Loosely Held Grain,* October-November 1976. Catalogue with text and drawings by the artist

AIR Gallery, London, *Fletched Over Ash,* July 1978. Catalogue with text and drawings by the artist

Arts Centre Gallery, Chester, October 1978

Chapter Gallery, Cardiff, South Wales, November 1978

Arnolfini Gallery, Bristol [Documentation], February 1979

Selected Bibliography

By the artist

Loosely Held Grain, Arnolfini Gallery, Bristol 1976

Fletched Over Ash, AIR Gallery, London 1978

Periodicals

Jonathan Robertson, "David Nash," *Link,* no. 6, Winter 1976, pp. 8-9

Hilary Chapman, "New British Sculpture," *Arts Review,* vol. XXIX, February 4, 1977, p. 86

Ben Jones, "A New Wave in Sculpture: A Survey of Recent Work by Ten Younger Sculptors," *Artscribe,* no. 8, September 1977, pp. 14-20

Alan McPherson, "Interview with David Nash," *Artscribe,* no. 12, June 1978, pp. 30-35

John McEwen, "From Structure to surface," *The Spectator,* July 22, 1978, p. 25

Margaret Richards, "Going Along with wood," *Tribune,* July 21, 1978

William Feaver, "Paris Fashion," *The Observer,* July 23, 1978, p. 21

Marina Vaizey, "The Men who built our cages," *Sunday Times,* July 23, 1978, p. 35

Terence Maloon, "David Nash at AIR," *Artscribe,* no. 13, August 1978, p. 55

William Feaver, "Woodwork," *Observer Magazine,* November 19, 1978, p. 65

Hugh Adams, "The Woodman," *Art and Artists,* vol. 13, April 1979, pp. 44-47

Film

Woodman, directed by Peter Francis Browne, Arts Council of Great Britain, 1978

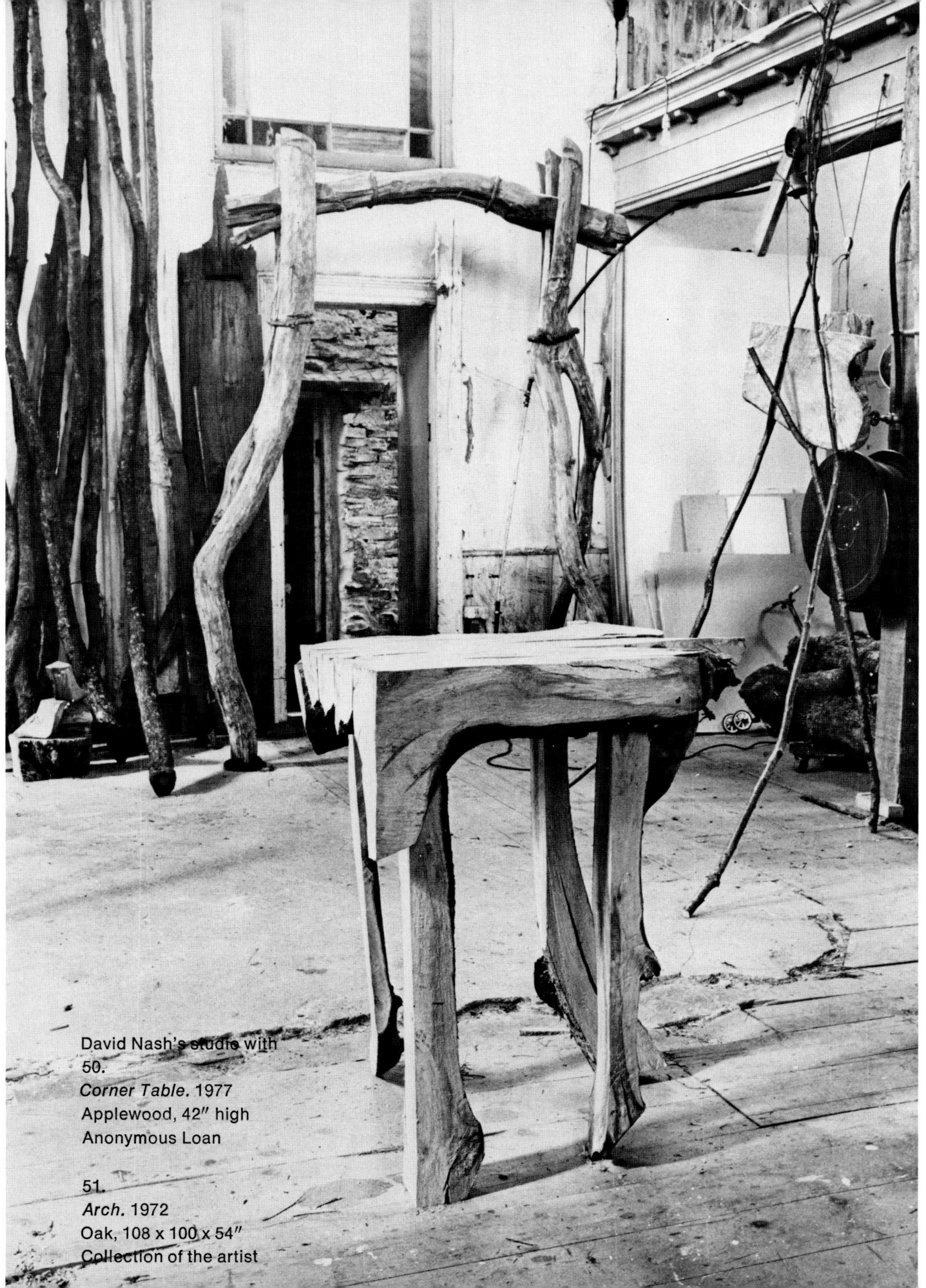

David Nash's studio with

50.
Corner Table. 1977
Applewood, 42″ high
Anonymous Loan

51.
Arch. 1972
Oak, 108 x 100 x 54″
Collection of the artist

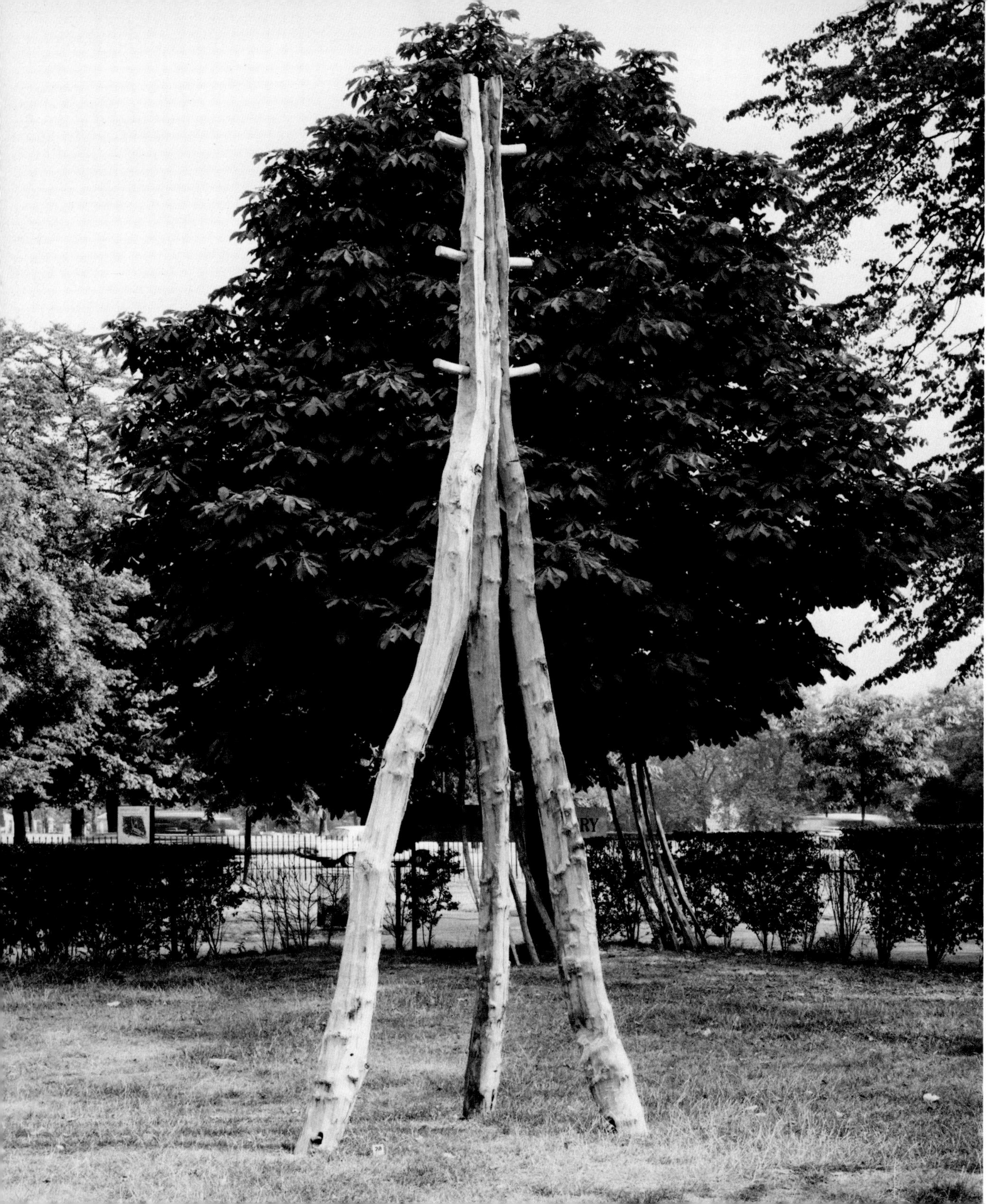

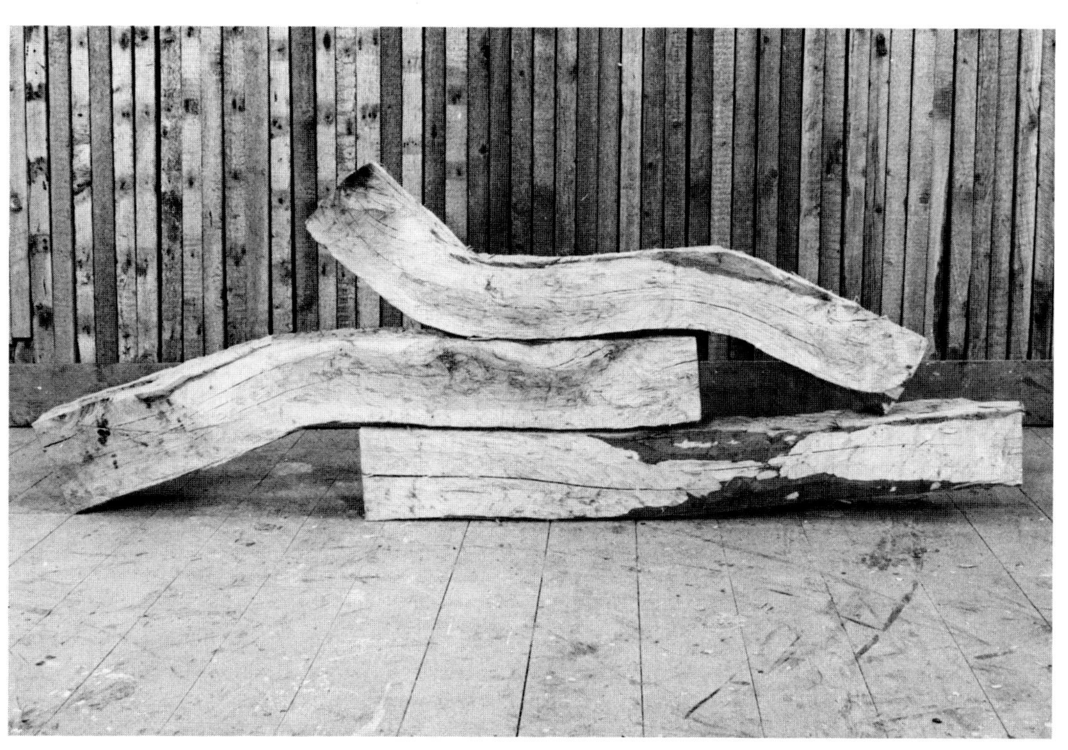

52.
Tall Tripod. 1976
Chestnut, 188 x 72 x 36″
Collection of the artist

53.
Up, Flop and Jiggle (Three Movements Through the Horizontal). 1976
Oak, 29 x 81 x 78″
Collection of the artist

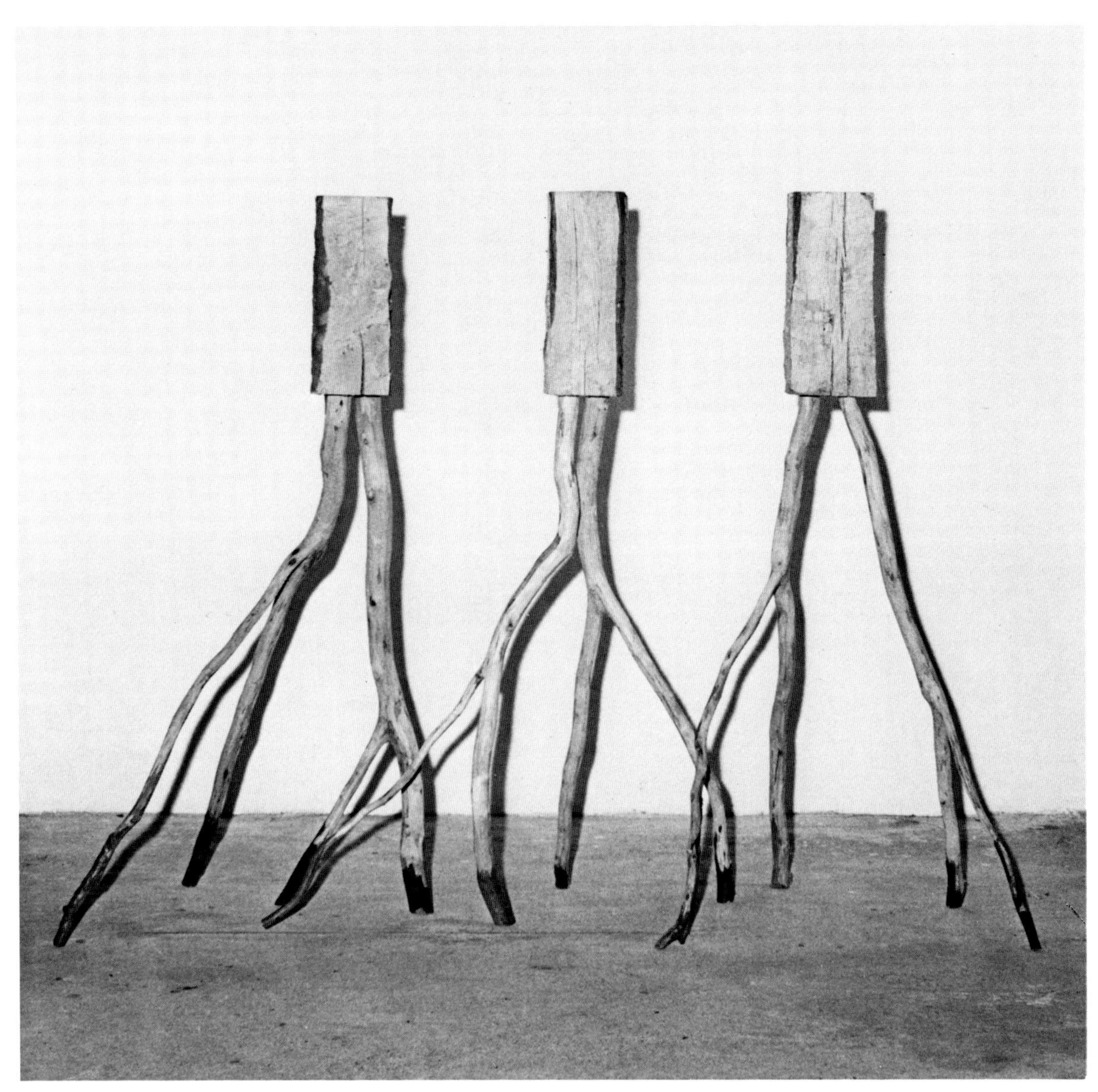

54.
Chorus Line (Three Dandy Scuttlers). 1976
Oak and beech, 63 x 30 x 96"
Collection of the artist

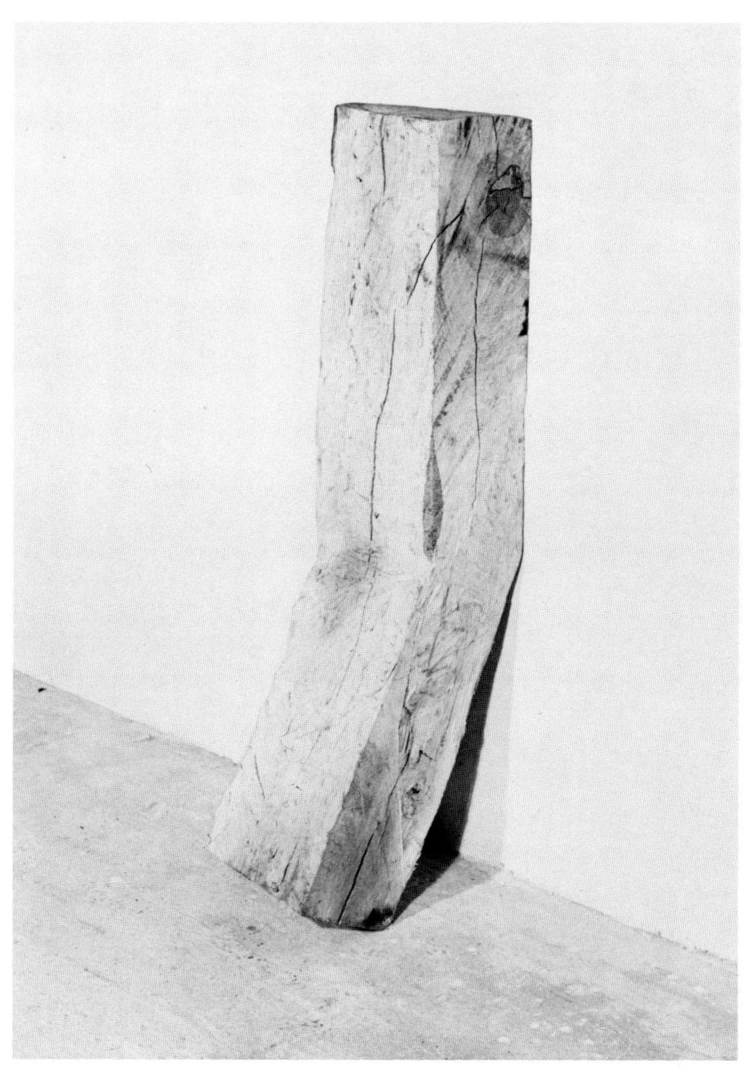

55.
Wall Leaner—A Lazy Log. 1976
 Oak, 54″ high
Private Collection, London

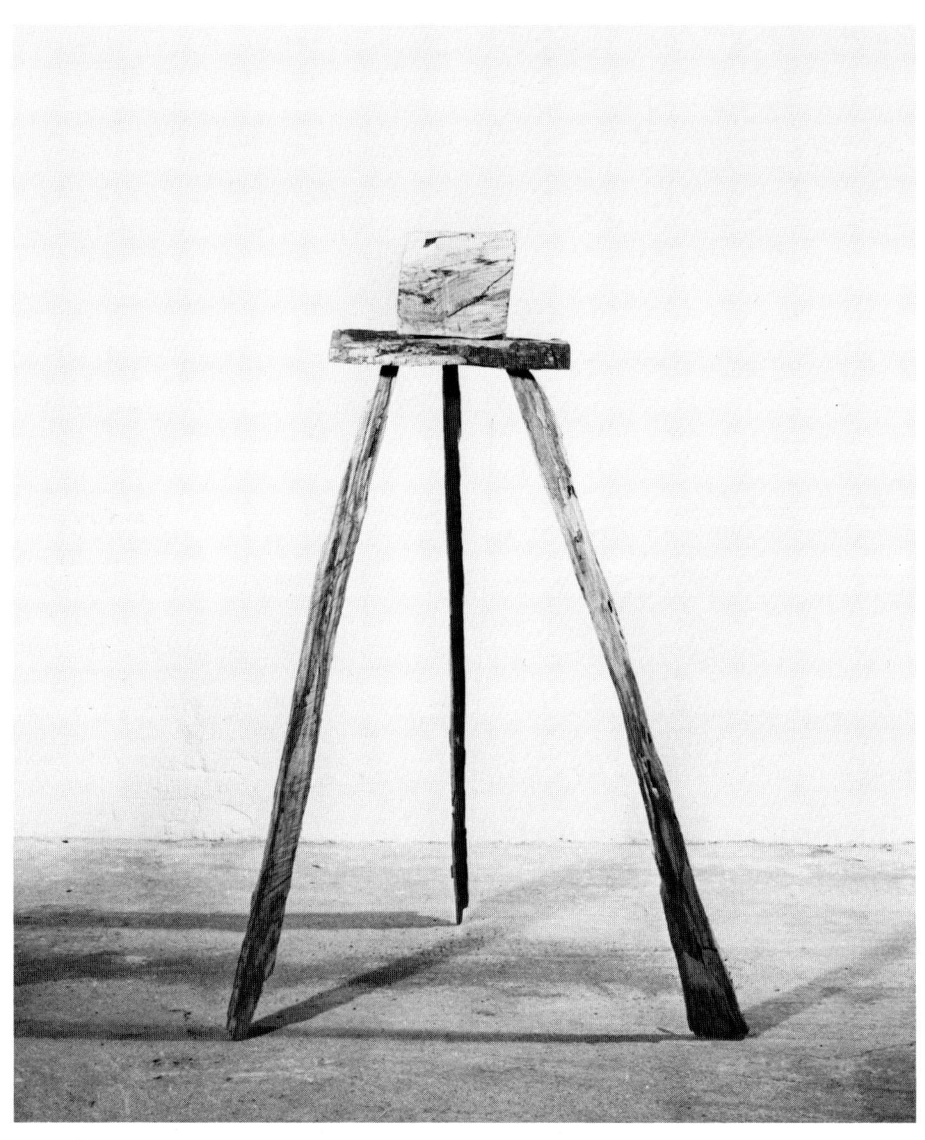

56.
Rough Cube. 1977
Sycamore and beech, 63 x 40 x 40″
Collection of the artist

David Nash's studio with
57.
Elephant passing the window. 1977
Slate, oak and alder, 126½ x 93¾ x 69″
Collection Rijksmuseum Kröller-Müller, Otterlo, The Netherlands

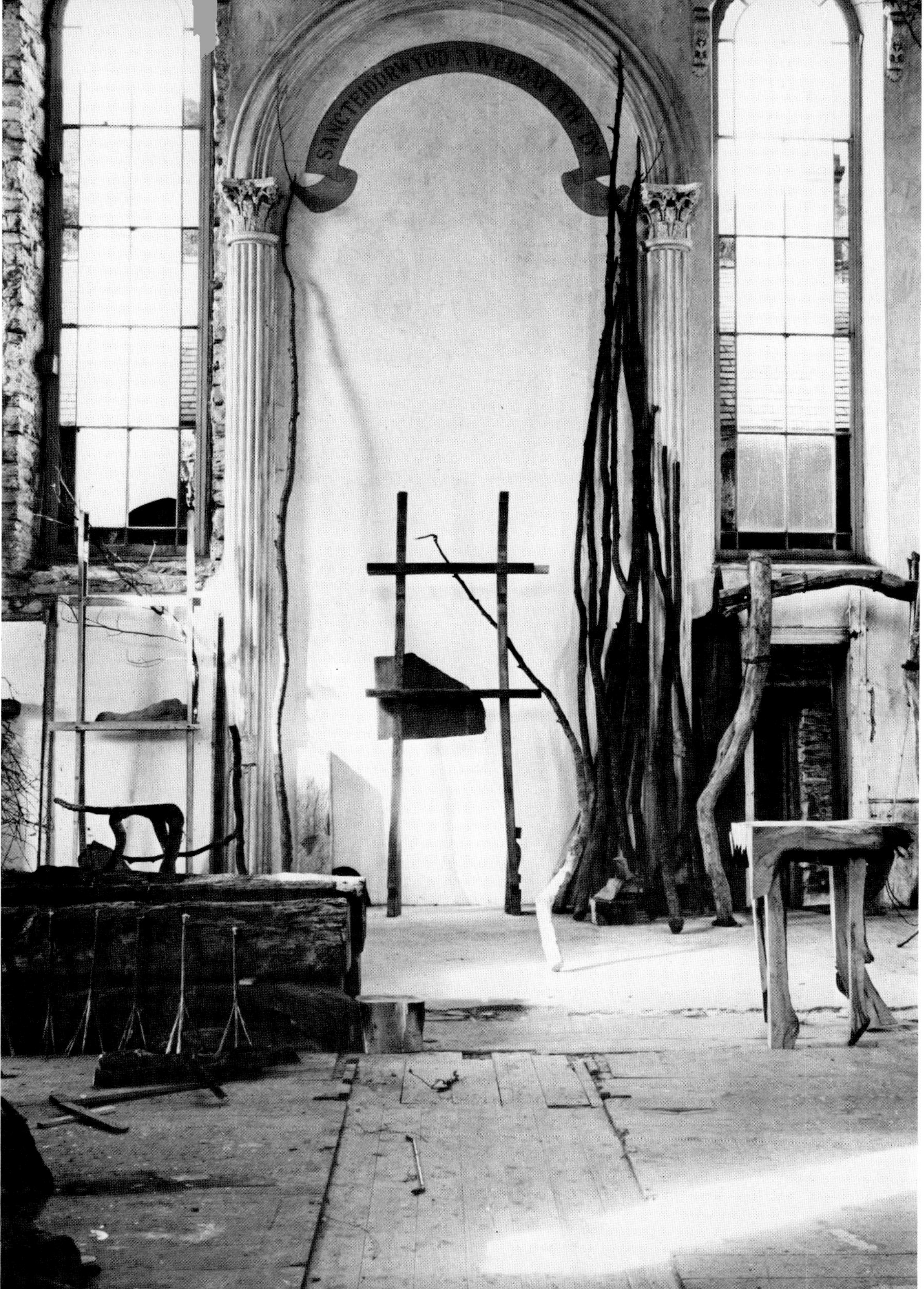
SANCTEIDDRWYDD A WEDDA I'TH DY

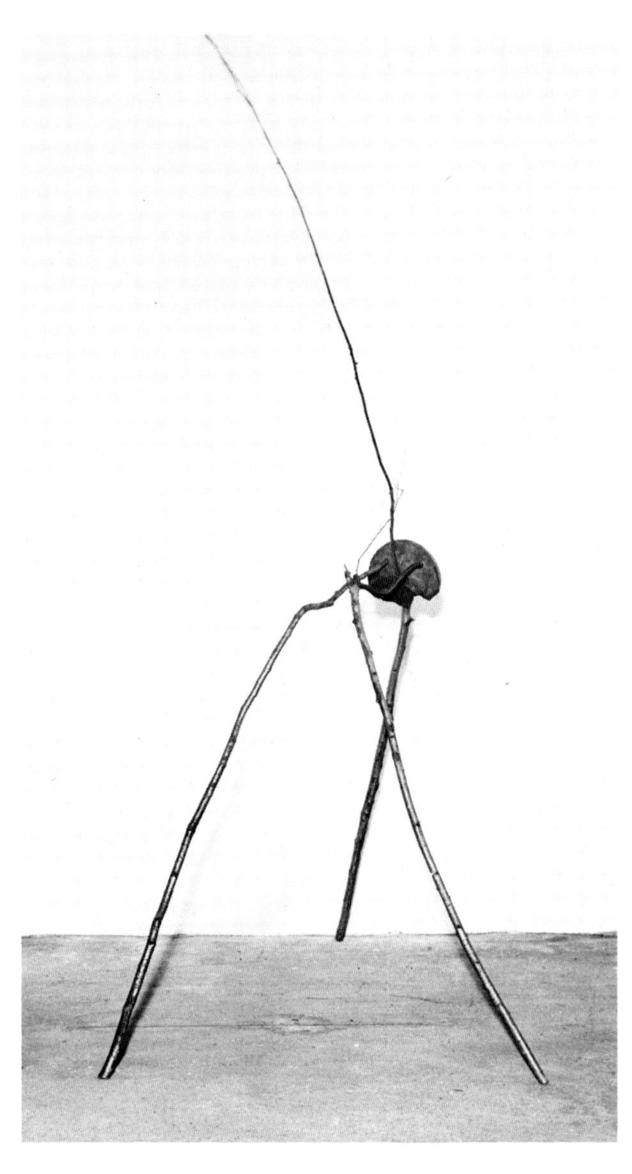

58.
Over the Brow (Holed Slate and Hazel). 1977
Slate and hazel, 124 x 69 x 49″
Collection of the artist

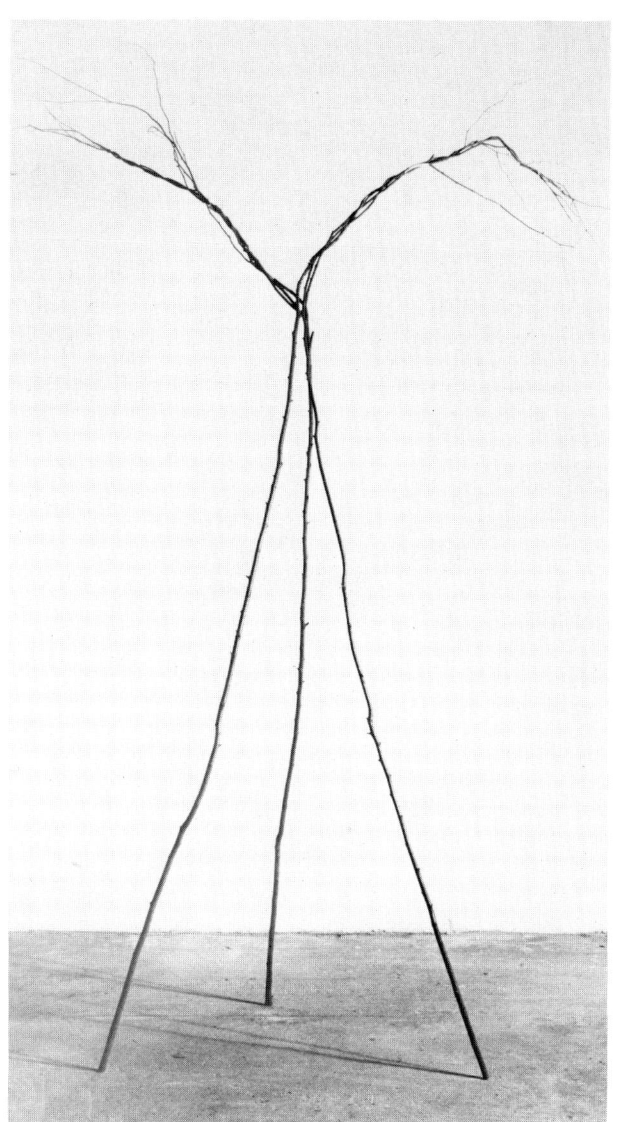

59.
Hazel Plaited Tripod. 1977
Hazel, 132 x 42 x 42″
Collection of the artist

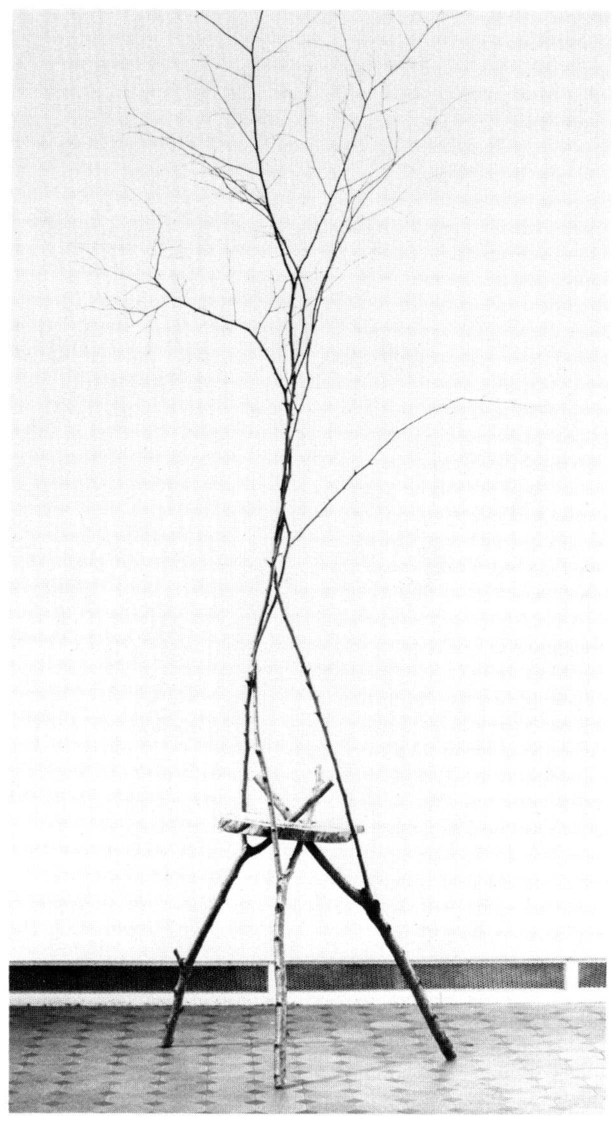

60.
An Awkward Stalk (Holed Oak and Hazel). 1977
Oak and hazel, 136 x 48 x 36″
Collection of the artist

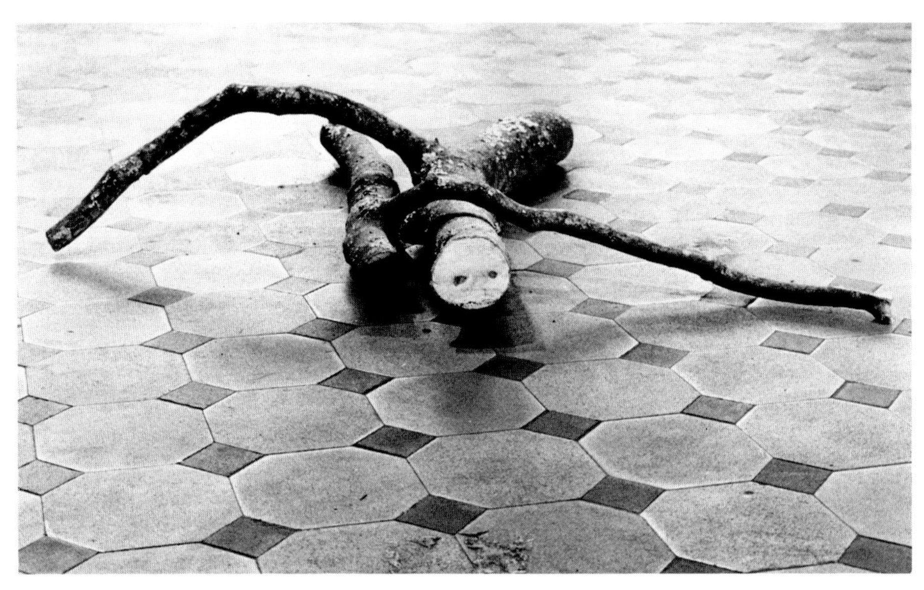

61.
Cuddling Branches. 1978
Sycamore, 8 x 34 x 36"
Collection of the artist

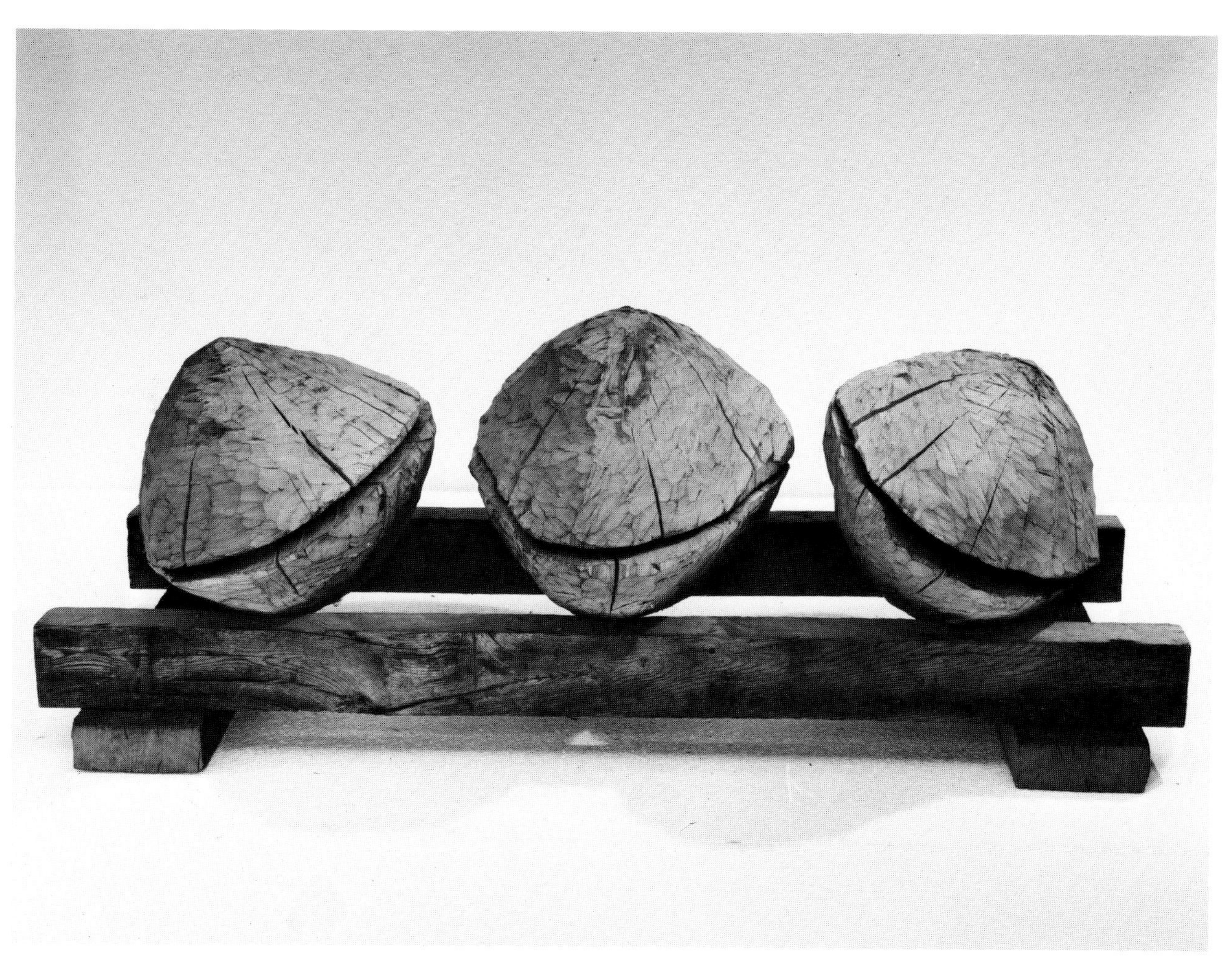

62.
Three Clams on a Rack. 1979
Beech and oak, 33 x 62 x 24″
Collection of the artist

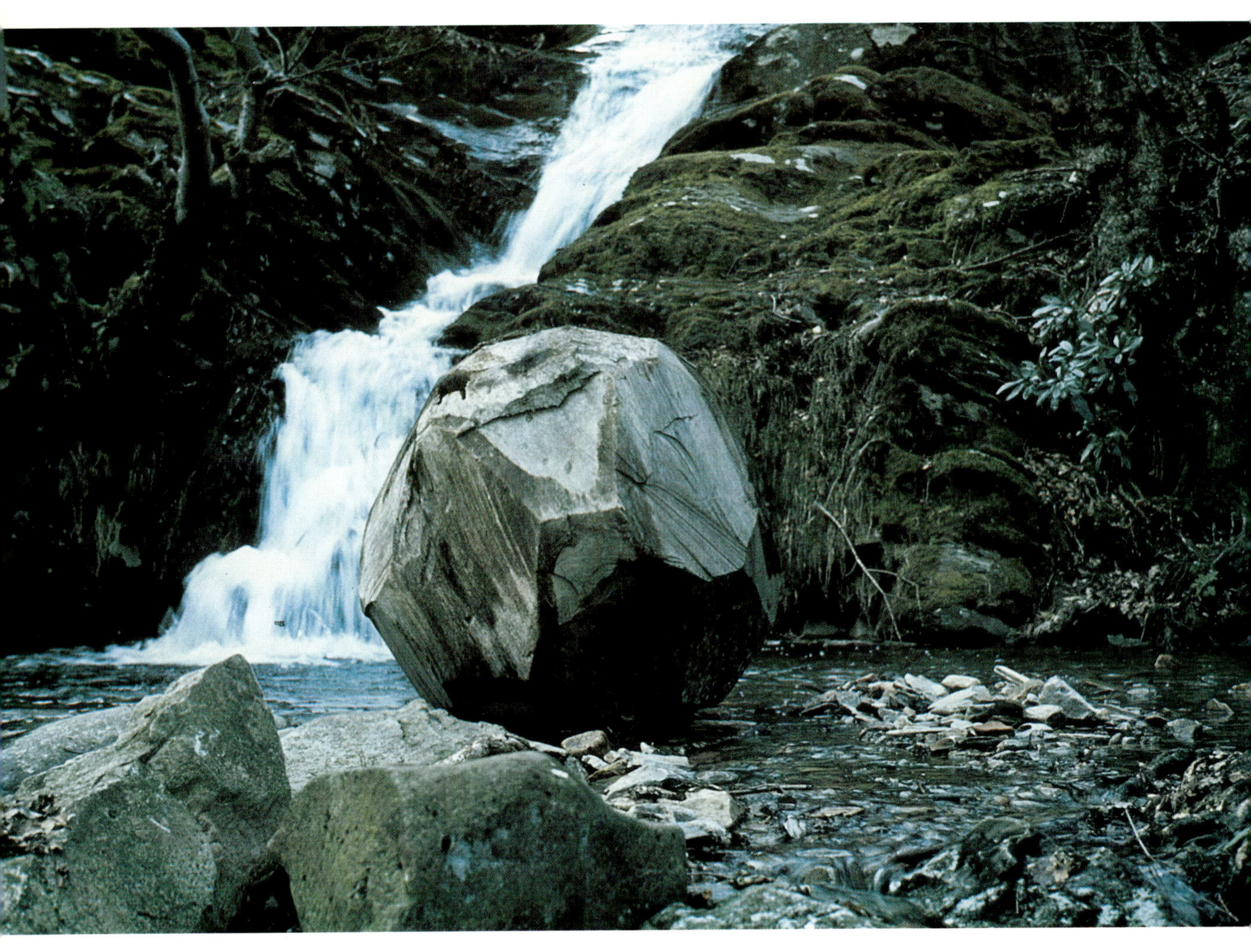

63.
Wooden Boulder, Maentwrog. In progress since
1978
48″ high, weight ½ ton
Collection of the artist

64.
Willow Ladder Taking Root. 1978
144″ high
Collection Grizedale Forest

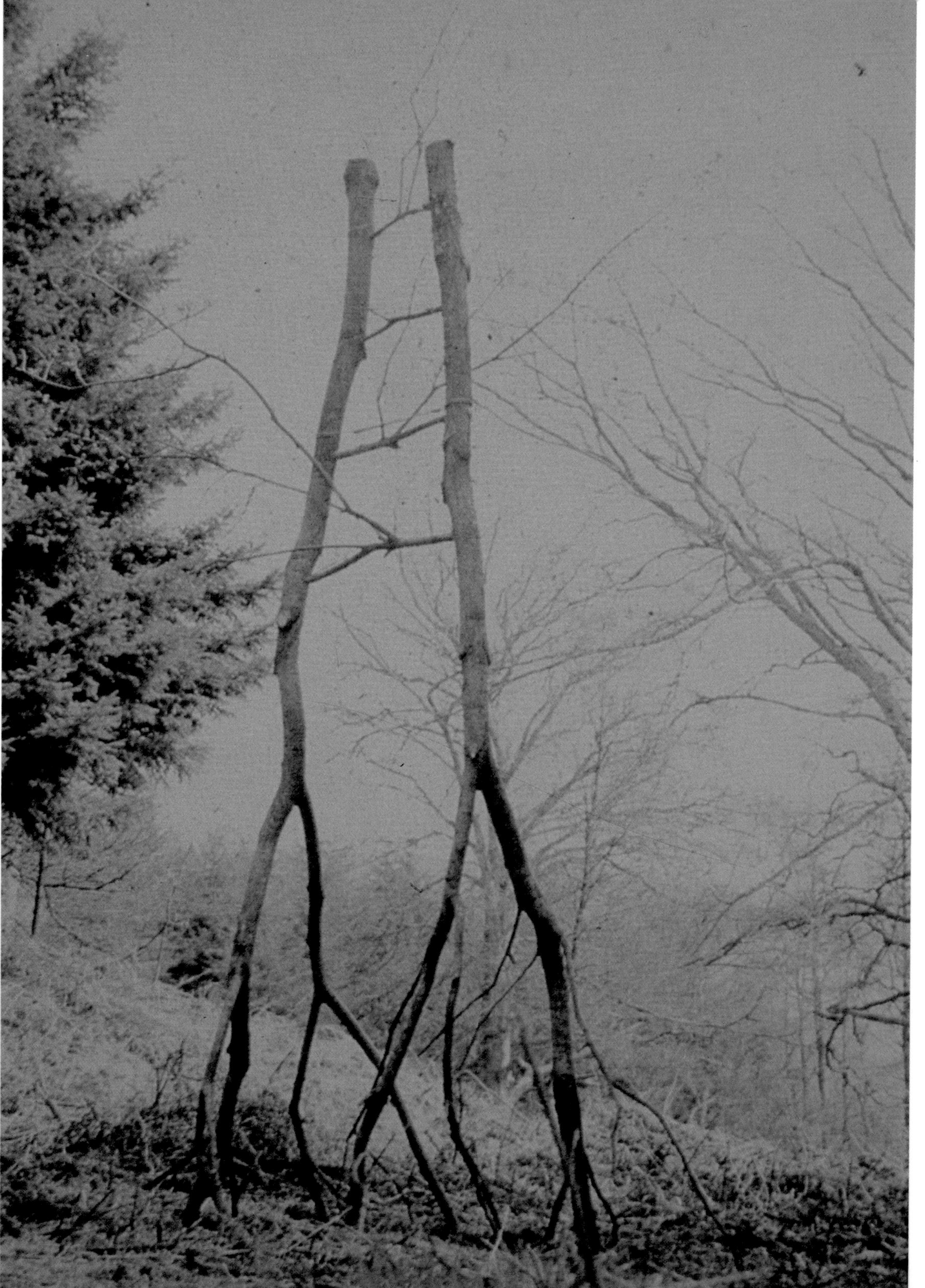

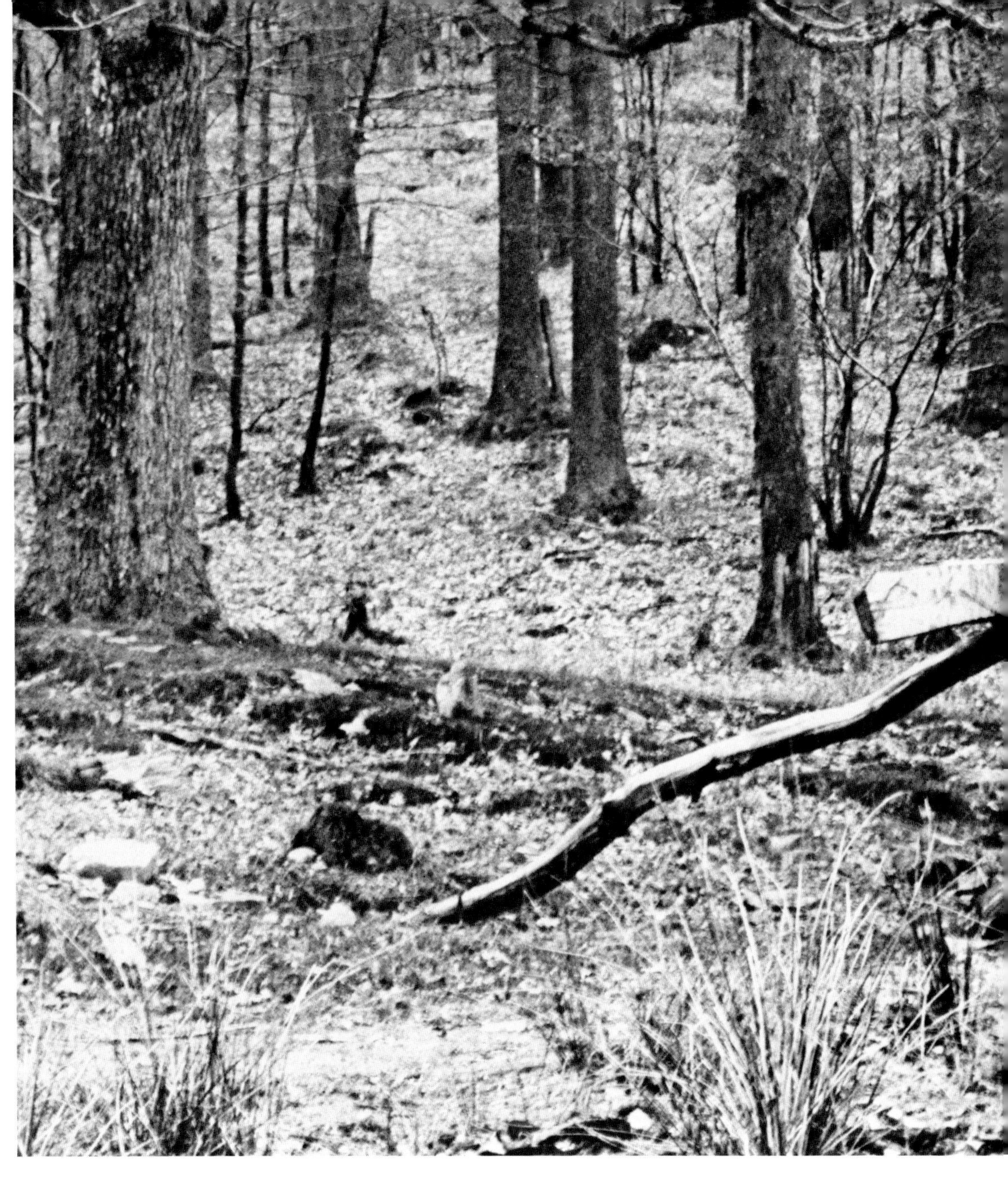

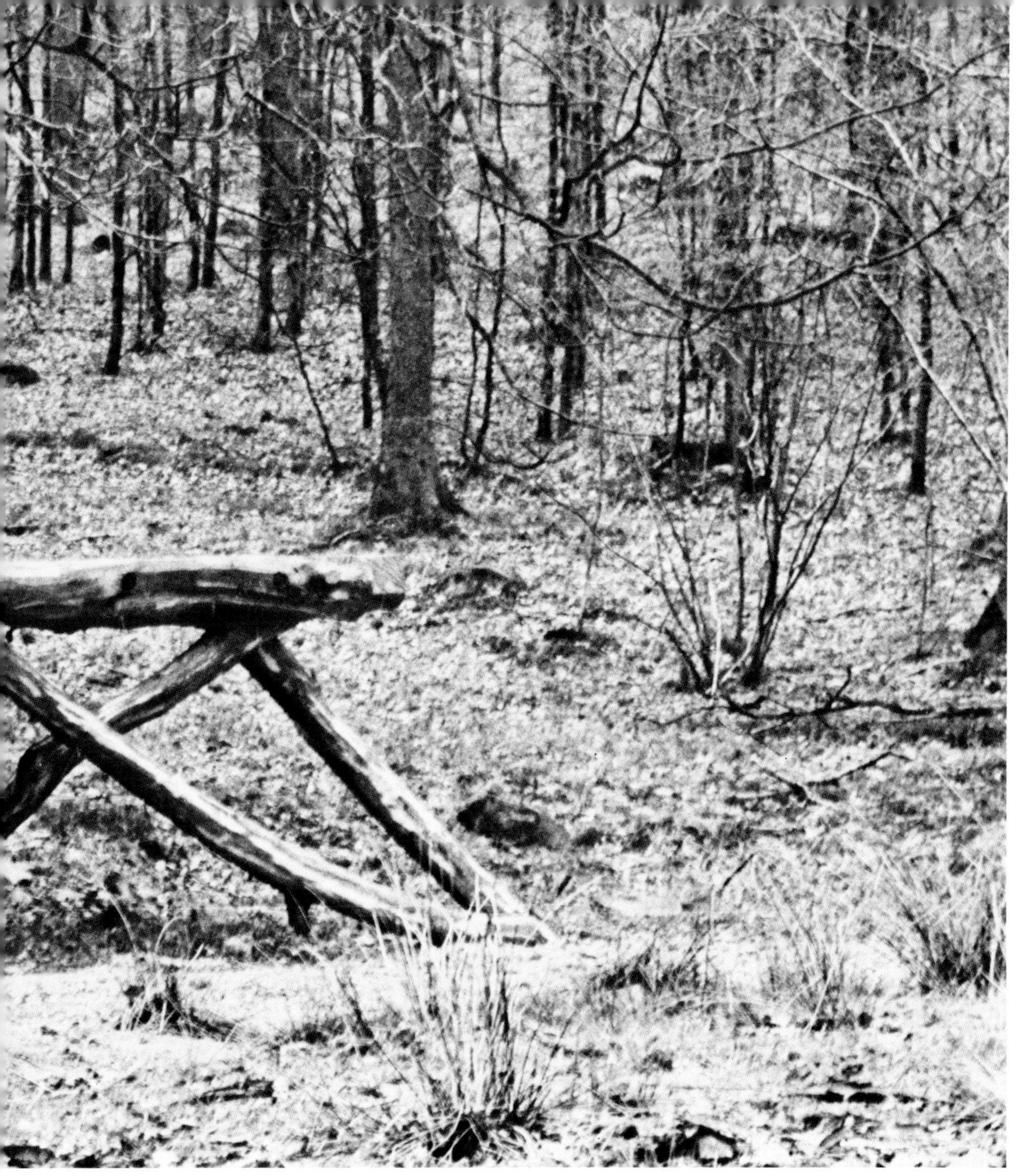

65.
Running Table. 1978
Oak, 60″ high
Collection Grizedale Forest

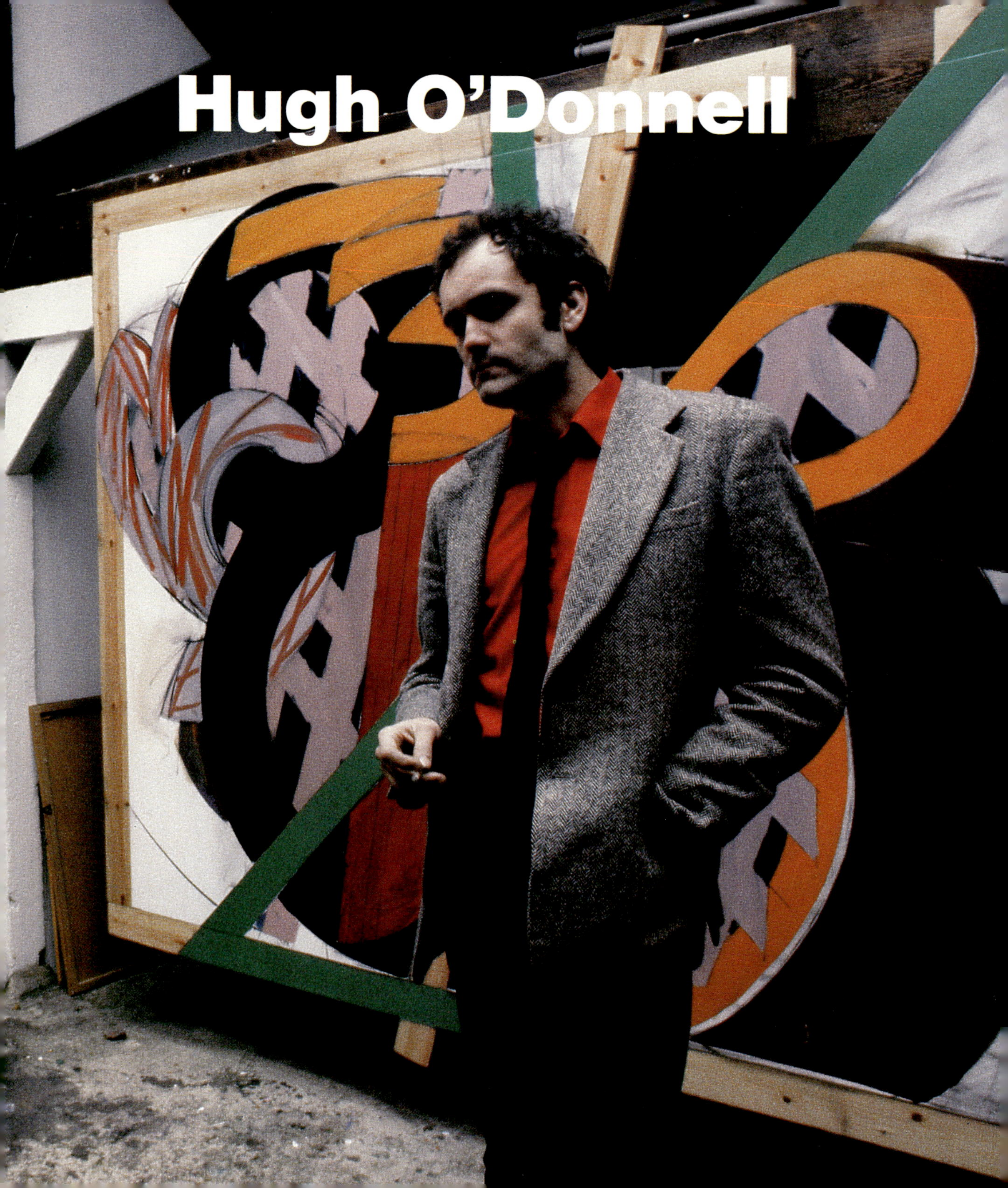

Hugh O'Donnell

At the age of nineteen, Hugh O'Donnell moved from London where he was born, to Falmouth, in Cornwall, to complete his undergraduate studies. Working close to the sea, he was increasingly affected by the blinding white light of the ocean and produced a series of paintings dominated by bold, sharp contrasts and vivid, high-key color. In 1972 he moved to Birmingham to complete his post-graduate work. His paintings underwent a dramatic change, impelled by the dark light of the Midlands. This luminosity, which suffused such paintings as *Stele Maris,* 1974 (cat. no. 66), gave his orientalized images their distinctive character. The amalgam of discrete image, amorphous field and architectonic structure became the basis for the next phase of O'Donnell's development. As O'Donnell's interest in Oriental art increased he decided to apply for a fellowship to Japan to study interior screen painting and its meaning as both the spiritual and structural foundation of the Japanese home.

O'Donnell received a scholarship from the Japanese government and moved to Kyoto in 1974. He began his study of screen painting and traveled extensively throughout the Japanese islands. Here, as in England, he was greatly moved by the varying qualities of light and landscape he encountered. He was equally impressed with the language of *Shime,* or binding, as a structural principle and with the proliferation of object making and ritual associated with Shintoism. O'Donnell participated in several shows in Japan, the most important of which was his first one-man exhibition at the Nishimura Gallery in Tokyo, where he showed the last of a series of drawings based on the concept of the discrete entity set within an expanded field. This formulation, in progress since its inception in Birmingham, now issued from the structural discipline of binding.

In 1976 O'Donnell returned to England via a short stay in Paris, where he visited an exhibition of Bulgarian icons. He was deeply impressed by the bold authority of these small works and the gold and non-naturalistic color familiar to him from the much larger screens of the Japanese Momoyama period. O'Donnell was attracted as well by their object quality and the flattened perspective which brought them close to the viewer. The hieratic, frontal nature of the images and their gilded surfaces imbued them with a spirituality at odds with their otherwise awkward homeliness. This combination of direct images, which seemed to burst from their frames, with extraordinary color and materials had a major impact upon the artist.

When O'Donnell moved to a new studio in Primrose Hill, London, he initiated a series of large canvases in which binding remained his primary structural language. Although the configurations grew larger and more dominant, they were still inhibited by the artist's need to separate figure and ground, usually by means of atmospheric washes or brushy paint handling. Not until O'Donnell began to disperse the figure within the field was he able to integrate these elements into a single entity. Ironically, he achieved this unity by emulating the Japanese screen, subdividing his canvas into a series of panels (*Barricade I,* 1978, cat no. 68); this allowed him to enlarge, fragment, compartmentalize and regroup his images into a new totality.

In 1978 O'Donnell moved to another studio at New Crane Wharf, Wapping, by the Thames. At this time, structure and strictly limited form rather than color continued to be his preeminent concerns. However, as he watched the boats on the Thames with their multicolored stripes, flags and emblems, O'Donnell began to think increasingly about enhancing the role of color in his painting without sacrificing the importance of form. This resolve was reinforced by a revelatory encounter with the work of Léger and Picasso during a visit to Paris in the summer of 1978. Upon returning to London, he began *Icon Enclosure* (now called *Barricade II,* cat. no. 69), incorporating in it the smooth full volumes and overlapping forms he had seen in Léger's canvases. He also introduced warm earthen colors and in later paintings increased the intensity of his palette by returning once more to the white ground he had employed nearly ten years before when he was a student at Falmouth.

The title *Icon Enclosure* was appropriate in terms of O'Donnell's clear attempt to integrate the flat, frontal, hieratic and object-like qualities of icons

Hugh O'Donnell with *Palaestra* in progress

with his Japanese-inspired concepts of binding and structural constraint. Yet *Barricade II* is an equally apt title for this transitional work which is essentially contained in comparison with the open, multi-faceted, dynamic volumes and shifting planes of his subsequent paintings.

From August to October of 1978, O'Donnell worked on *Trojan* (cat. no. 71). To enhance the physicality of his painting, he introduced the wooden frame as an active constituent of the image, a device which also figures prominently in paintings such as *Palaestra* and *Waltzer* of 1979 (cat. nos. 74 and 75). The wooden enclosure became increasingly dynamic, functioning both as frame and as part of the interior configuration, finally slicing into the rectangle of the canvas itself. O'Donnell played upon the double nature of the frame by means of trompe l'oeil techniques, painting parts of the canvas to look like wood and painting other areas to read as color. Although O'Donnell on the one hand treats his painting as object by introducing wooden elements, he goes to great lengths to avoid building out from the surface in the manner of Stella or Johns. He uses wood not primarily to call attention to the object quality of his painting but to stress the material's organic nature, in the tradition of Oriental art and architecture.

In paintings like *Trojan* and *Barcarole* of 1978 (cat. no. 72), large black and white areas cut the canvas almost in two. O'Donnell offsets this compartmentalization by countering his black and white forms with wedge-shaped, highly irregular blocks of color. These color areas appear to jut forward from the canvas, but their powerful thrust is contained by the equally strong but less volumetric black and white bands and finally by the actuality of the wooden frame.

O'Donnell relies less upon this kind of division and places more emphasis on heightened color in subsequent works such as *Waltzer and Palaestra*. Candied pinks and oranges, electric blues and cool lime greens generate more of the energy, as O'Donnell begins to open up and attentuate his forms. Still curved but much flatter, his shapes look almost like paper cutouts, collage-like in effect but without the sense of relief that collage entails. The insistent curves juxtaposed with straight edges and diagonals create a dynamic thrust which O'Donnell contains through a very skillful balancing of shapes. Certain shapes resemble forms drawn with the aid of a straight edge or draftsman's triangle, others look like letters of the alphabet. Comparisons may be drawn with the protractors and French curves in Stella's paintings and the graceful arabesques, brushwork and allover marks of Johns.

As the forms lose their bulk and density and become even more curved, they seem to spin like pinwheels. The heightened intensity of the forms, patterning and color of a work like the recent *Laocoon (cat. no. 79),* generates a sense of centrifugal force and blinding speed that recalls the velocity of vorticist and futurist painting. Yet each pictorial component is extremely tangible, and the cumulative effect is breathtaking in its forcefulness. As O'Donnell has said, ''I want the paintings to be a celebration. In this sense they are emotional, they are an amplification of feeling. I like them to go off like a fanfare.''[1]

O'Donnell has exploited both the delicacy of Eastern tradition and the most direct and forthright —one hesitates to say brutal, for brutality is not in the artist's vocabulary—vitality of Western European art. The interaction of passive and dominant forms, the contradictory play of volume and heightened, flat color, the use of framing elements which cut into the picture surface yet do not transform the painting into an object—in short, the dialogue between the flat picture plane and the three-dimensional nature of what is presented—all contribute to the intricate and compelling language of O'Donnell's art.

1. Kelly, Moira, ''Hugh O'Donnell,'' Ikon Gallery, Birmingham, June 1979, n.p.

Hugh O'Donnell

Born in London, 1950

Camberwell College of Art, London, 1968-69

Falmouth School of Art, 1969-72

Ceramic Installation for Artists Constructor, Wrington, Somerset, 1972

Birmingham School of Art, 1972-73

1st Prize, Sir Whitworth Wallace Trust, Birmingham, 1973

Fellowship to Gloucestershire College of Art, 1973-74

Japanese Government Scholarship to Kyoto University of Arts, 1974-76

Arts Council Award, 1978

Visiting Lecturer to art colleges and universities since 1976, including Falmouth School of Art; Birmingham Polytechnic; Reading University; Bath Academy of Art, Corsham; Wimbledon College of Art; Croydon College of Art, London

Lecturer at Brighton Polytechnic, 1978-present

Installation Commission for Bognor Regis Arts Centre, 1979

Lives in London

Selected Group Exhibitions

Newlyn Society, Penzance, Cornwall, May-June 1972

Ikon Gallery, Birmingham, June 1973

Museum of Modern Art, Oxford, *The Platform,* July-October 1973

DM Gallery, London, September-October 1973

Cheltenham College of Art and Stroud Museum, Stroud, Gloucestershire, *Cheltenham Fellowships Exhibitions,* July-August 1974

Iteza Gallery, Kyoto, *Documentation,* September 1975

Museum of Modern Art, Kyoto, September 1975

Artists Market, London, October 1976; October-November 1977; December 1978

DM Gallery, London, September 1977

Gulbenkian Gallery, Royal College of Art, London, *London Group,* September 1978

Walker Art Gallery, Liverpool, *John Moores Liverpool Exhibition II,* November 1978-February 1979

AIR Gallery, London, December 1978

Newcastle upon Tyne Polytechnic Art Gallery, December 1978

Selected One-Man Exhibitions

Nishimura Gallery, Tokyo, February 1976

AIR Gallery, London, October 1977

Ikon Gallery, Birmingham, June 1979. Catalogue with text by Moira Kelly

Selected Bibliography

Richard Walker, "Young Painters," *Arts Review,* vol. XXV, September 22, 1973, p. 630

Piero de Monzi, "Interior Painting in Installation," *Harpers & Queens,* July 1975, p. 74

Marina Vaizey, "Artists Market," *Arts Review,* vol. XXVIII, September 17, 1976, p. 478

William Packer, "Summer Mixtures," *Financial Times,* August 8, 1978, p. 11

William Packer, "The 11th John Moores," *Financial Times,* December 5, 1978, p. 17

John McEwen, "John Moore's exhibition review," *The Spectator,* December 8, 1978

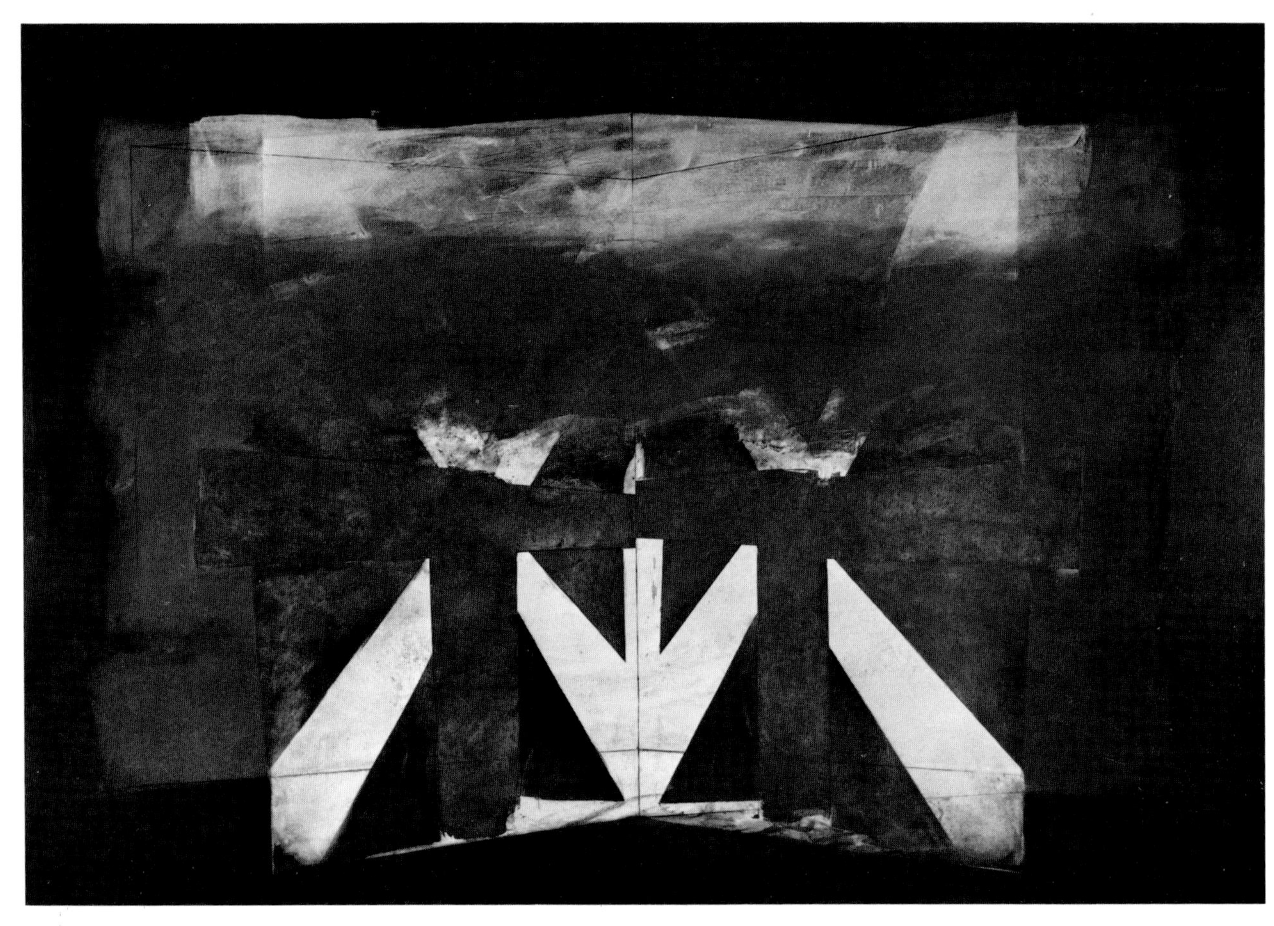

66.
Stele Maris. 1974
Oil on canvas, 84 x 108″
Collection of the artist

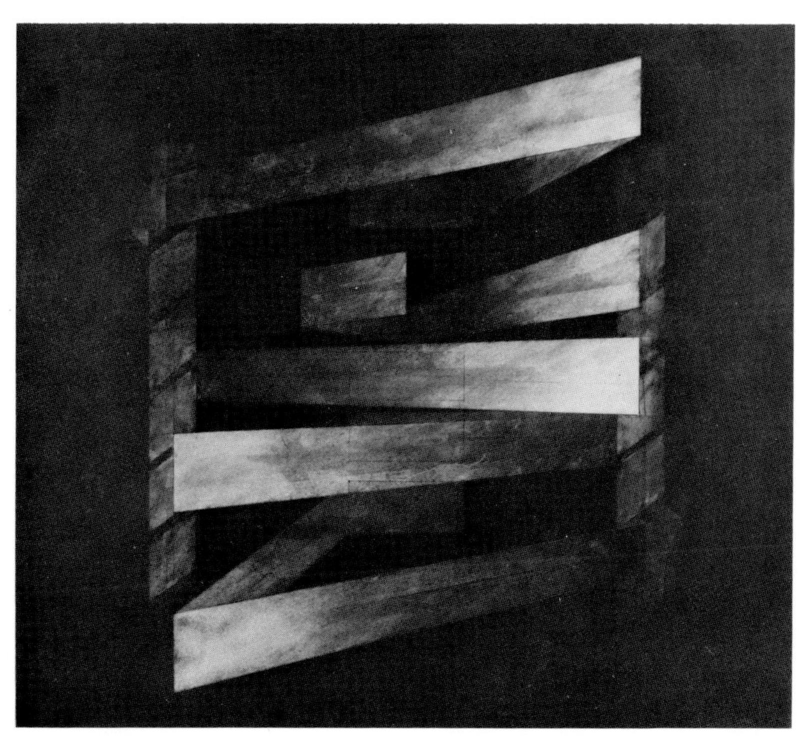

67.
To Inzanagi. 1976
Graphite and pastel, 36 x 36″
Collection Peter Tunnard, London

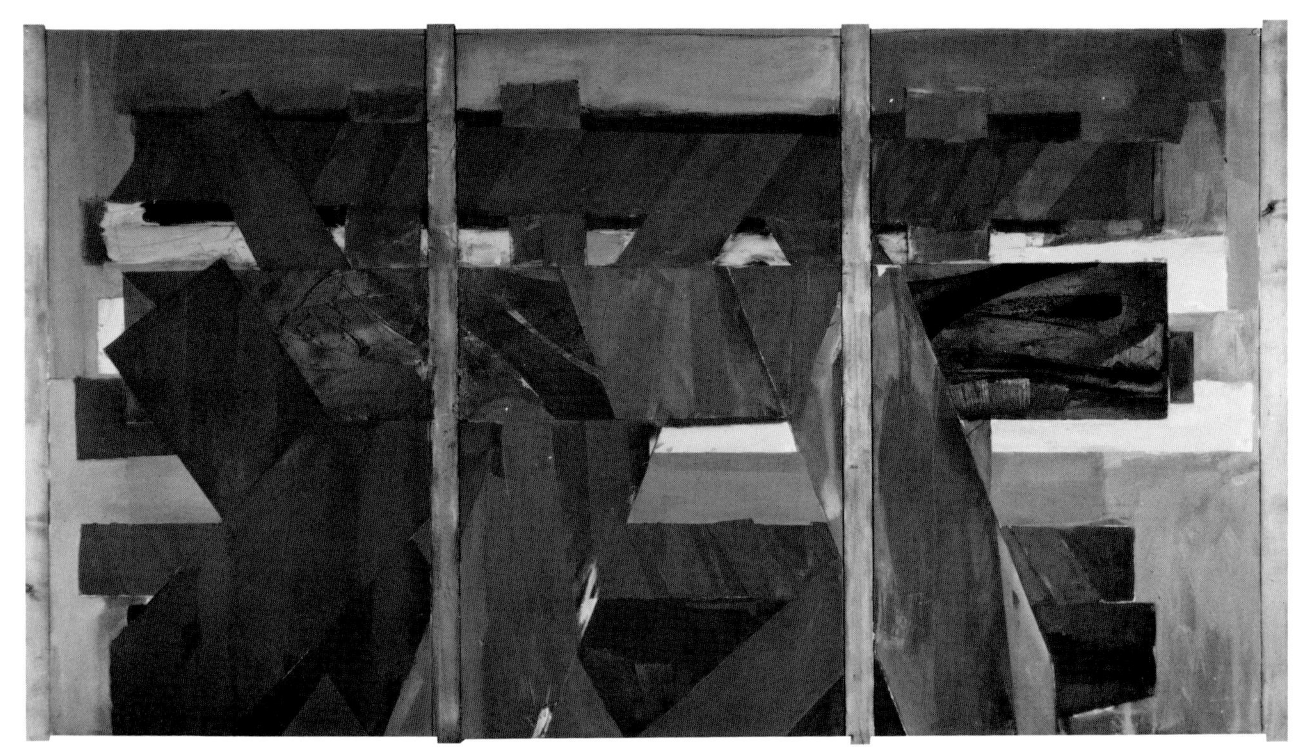

68.
Barricade I. 1978
Oil on canvas and wood, 84 x 132″
Collection of the artist

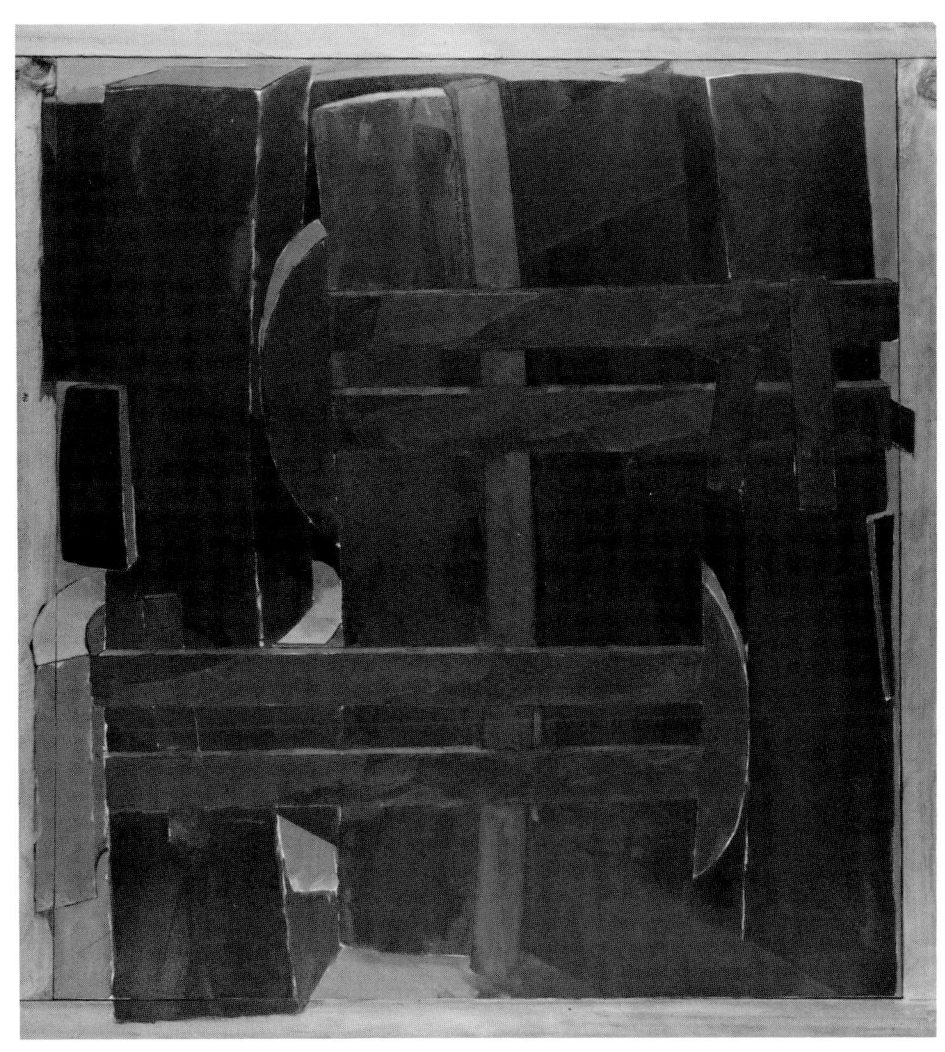

69.
Barricade II. 1978
Oil on canvas and wood, 80 x 72″
Collection of the artist

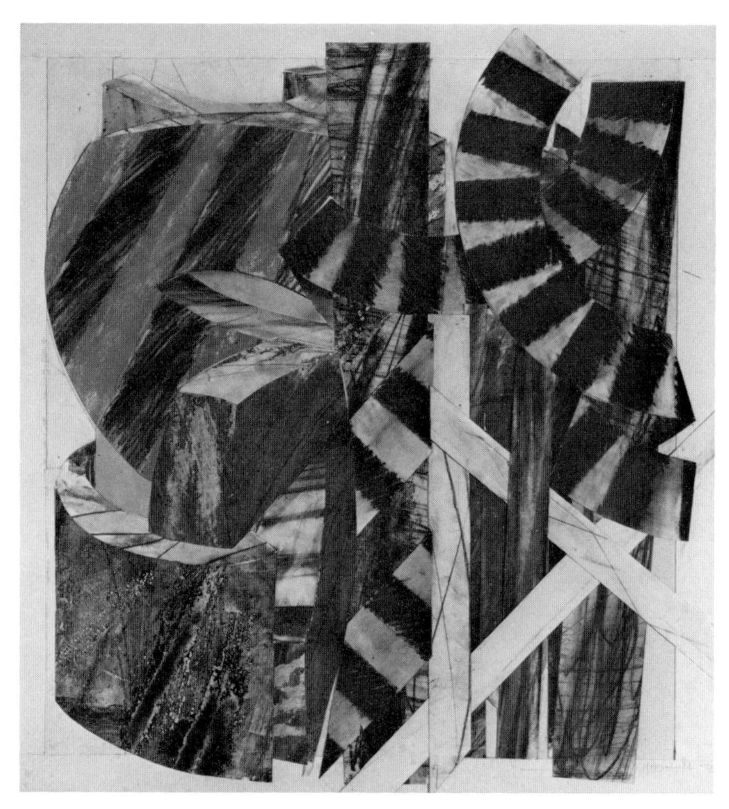

70.
Study for Trojan. 1978
Mixed media, 30¾ x 28¾ ″
Anonymous Loan

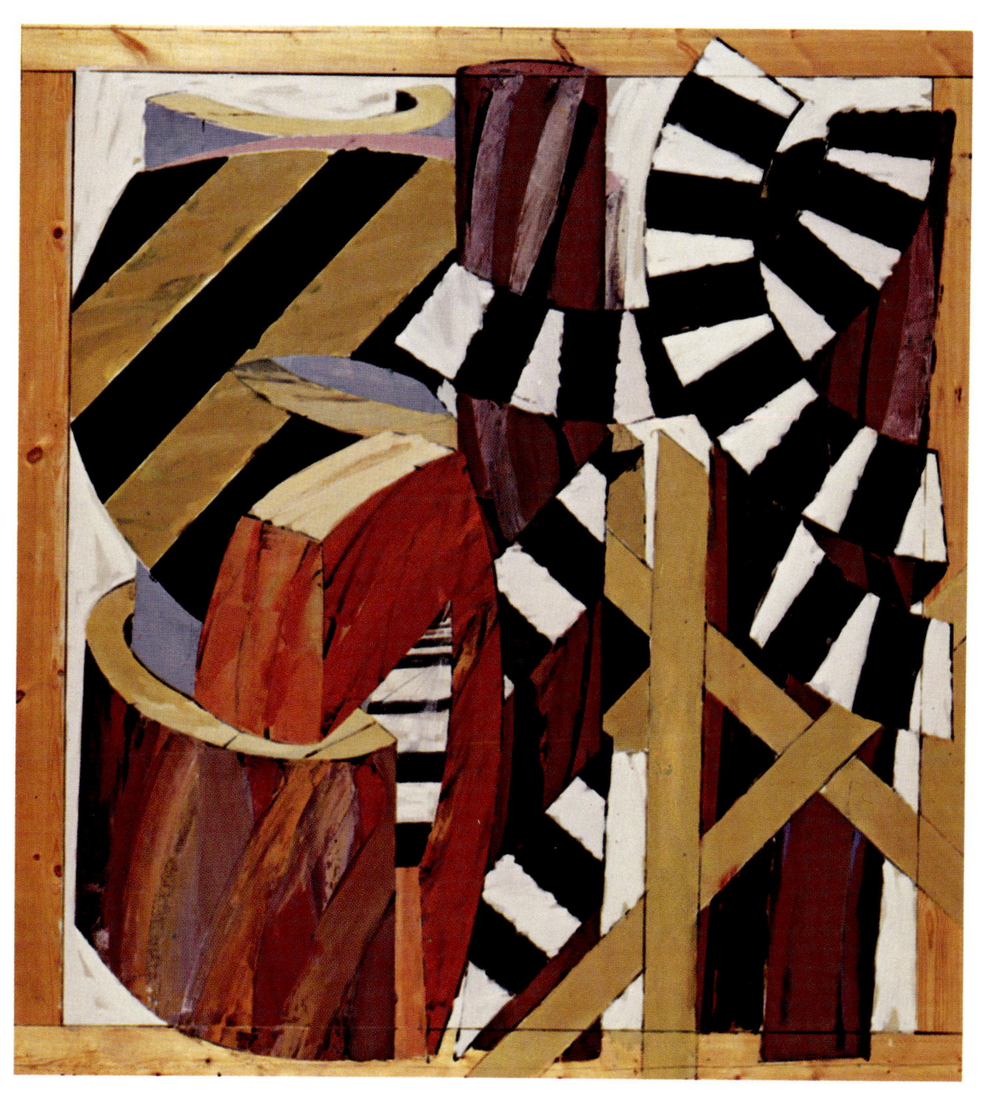

71.
Trojan. 1978
Oil on canvas and wood, 80 x 72"
Anonymous Loan

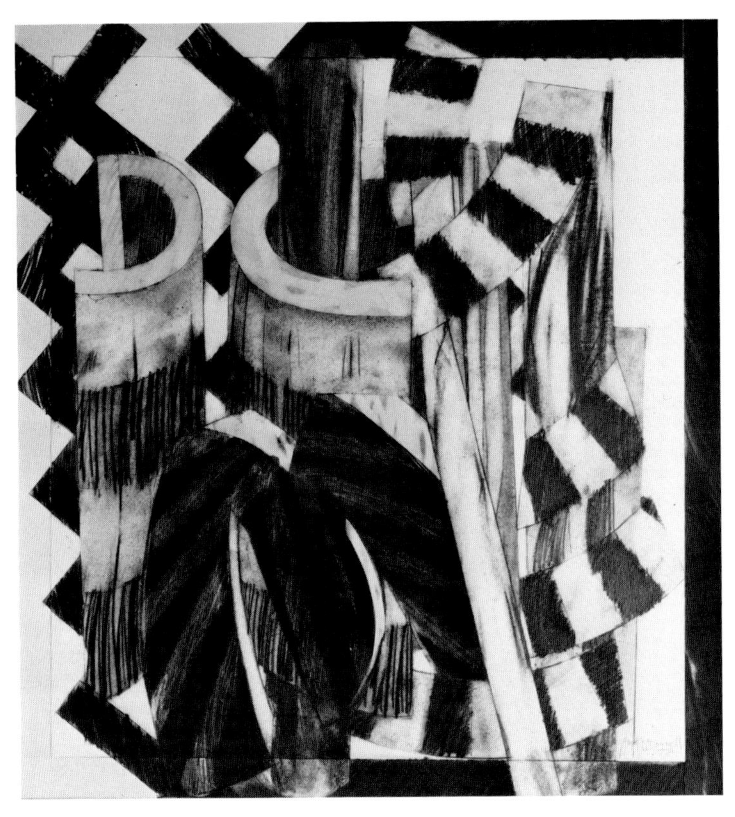

72.
Study for Barcarole. 1978
Graphite on paper, 30¾ x 28¾ ″
Collection of the artist

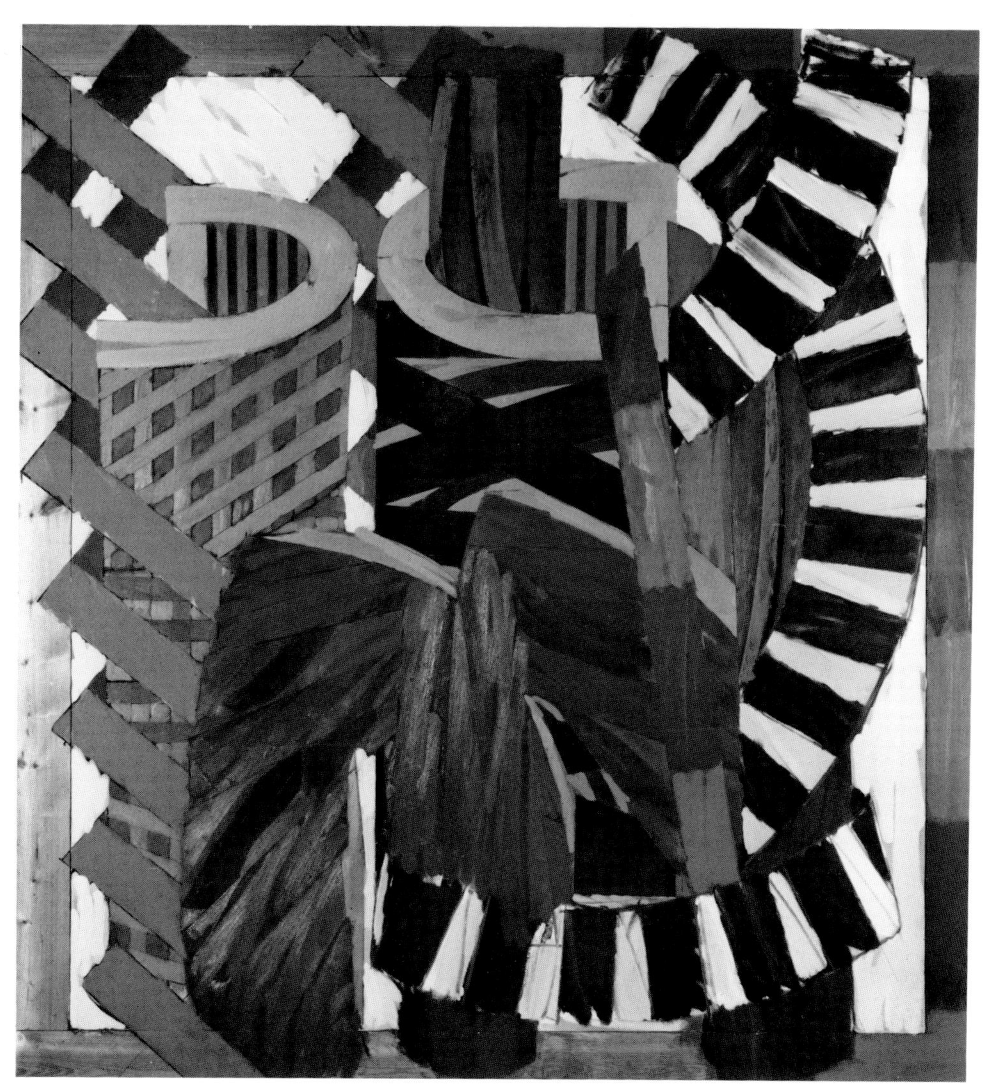

73.
Barcarole. 1978
Oil on canvas and wood, 80 x 72"
Collection The Arts Council of
Great Britain, London

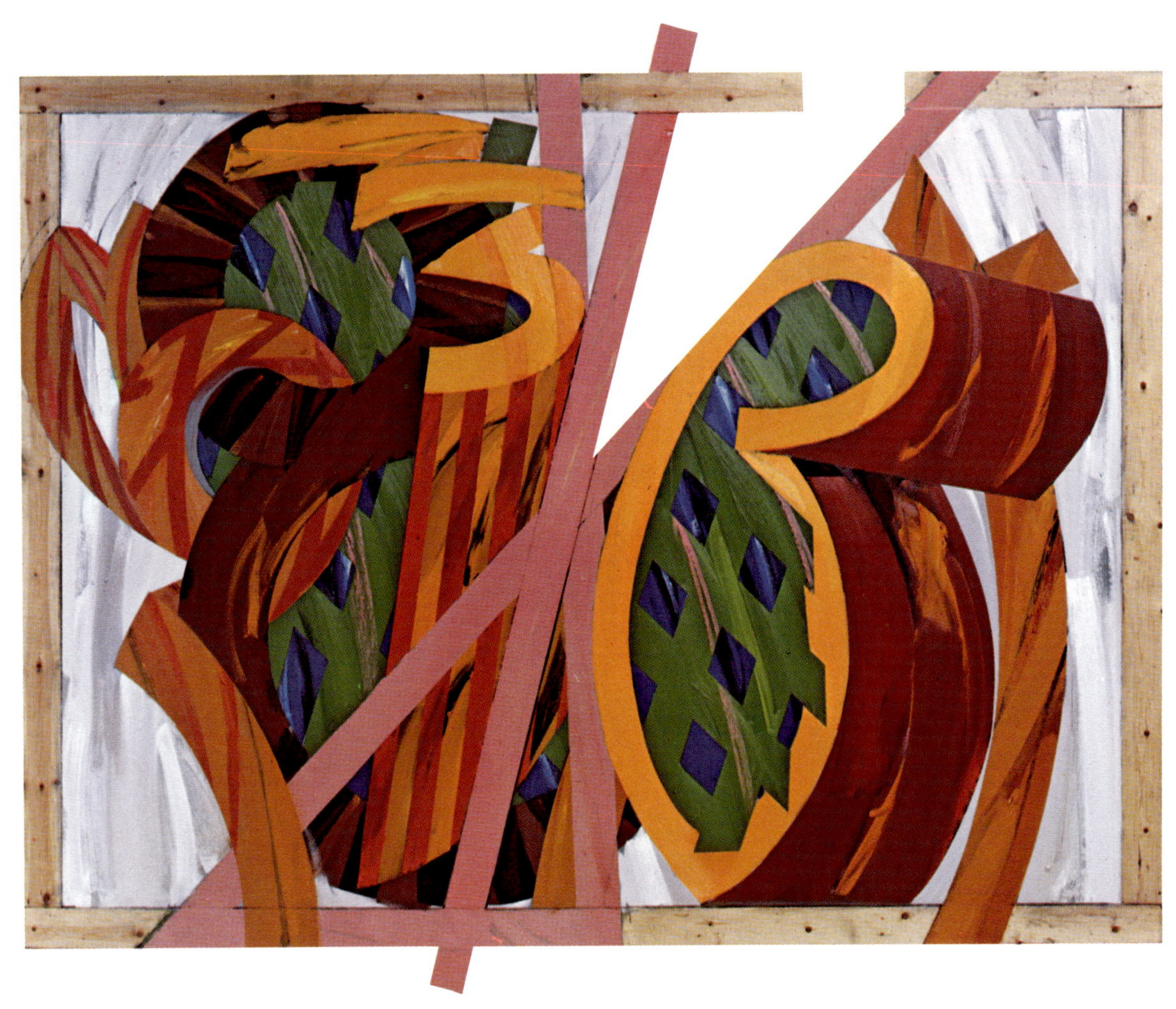

74.
Palaestra. 1979
Oil on canvas and wood, 79 x 103"
Collection of the artist

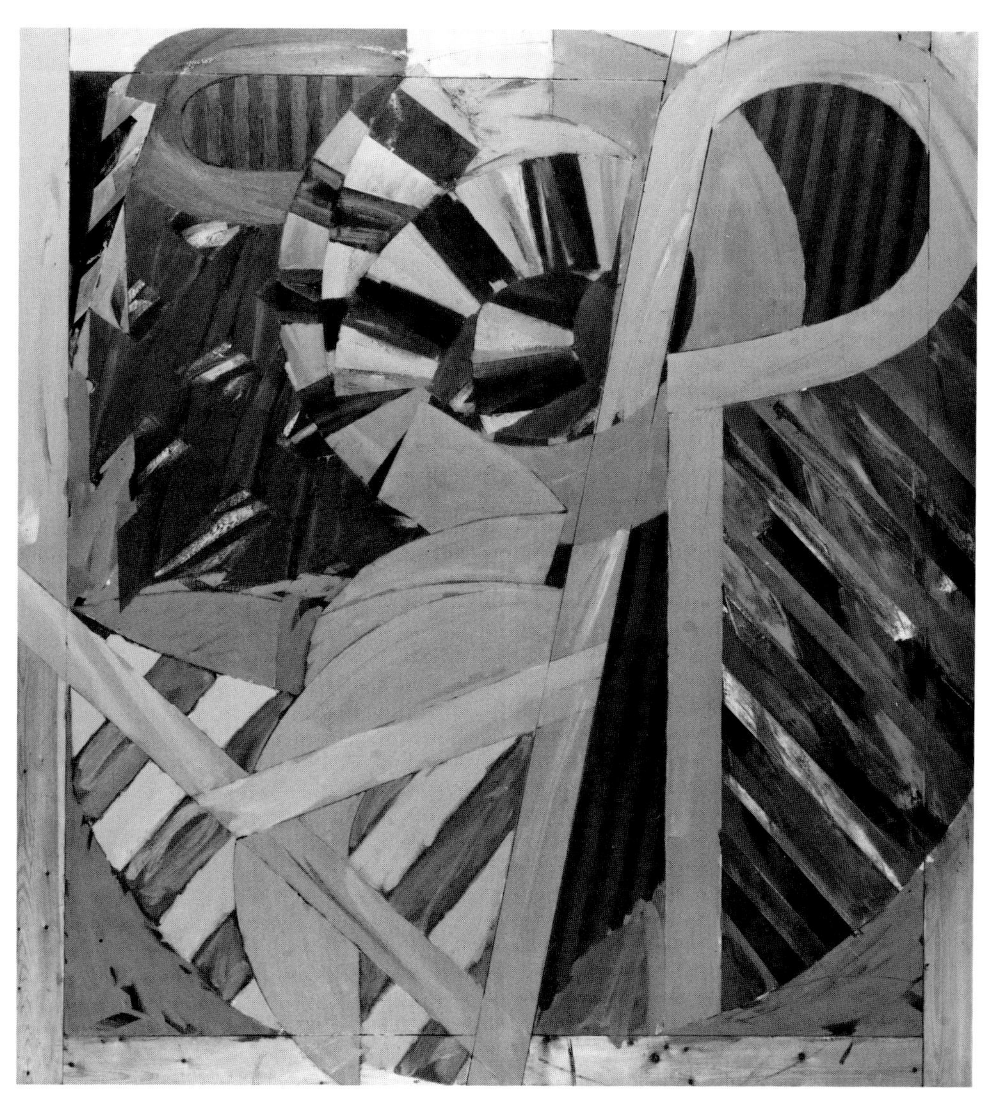

75.
Waltzer. 1979
Oil on canvas and wood, 80 x 72″
Anonymous Loan

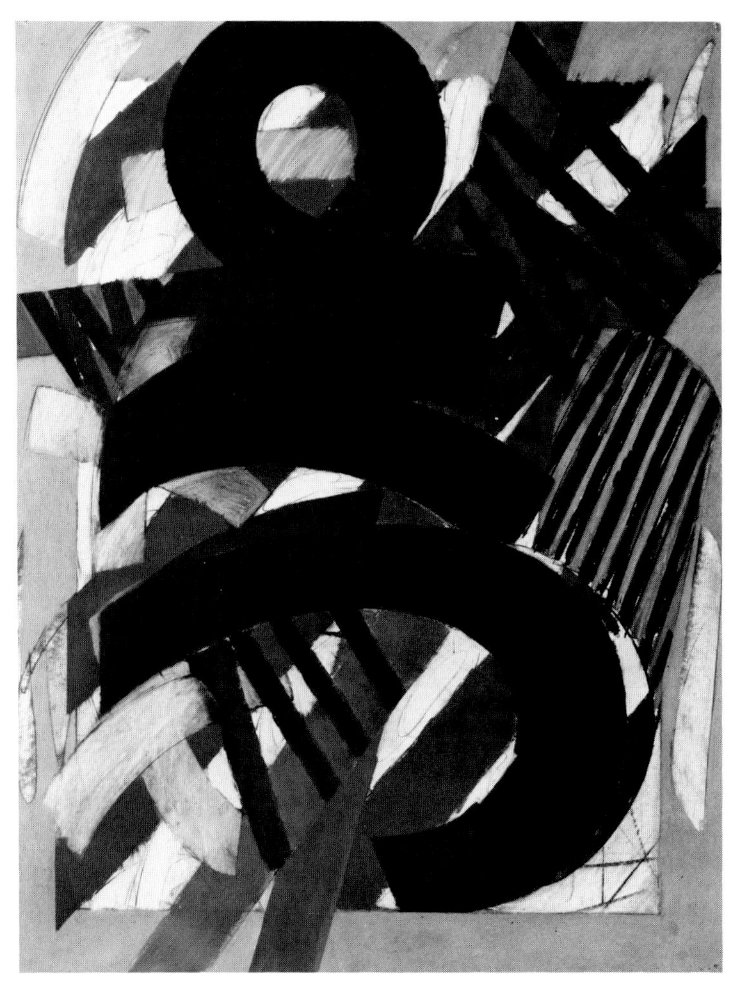

76.
Untitled I. 1979
Chalk on paper, 54 x 40″
Collection of the artist

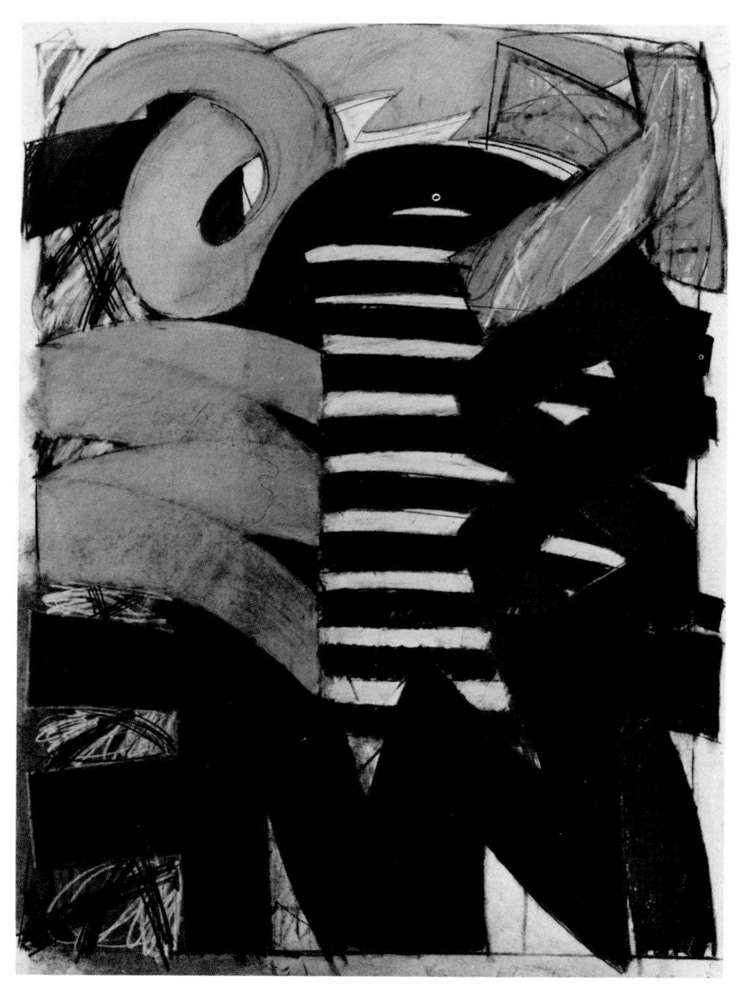

77.
Untitled II. 1979
Chalk on paper, 54 x 40"
Collection of the artist

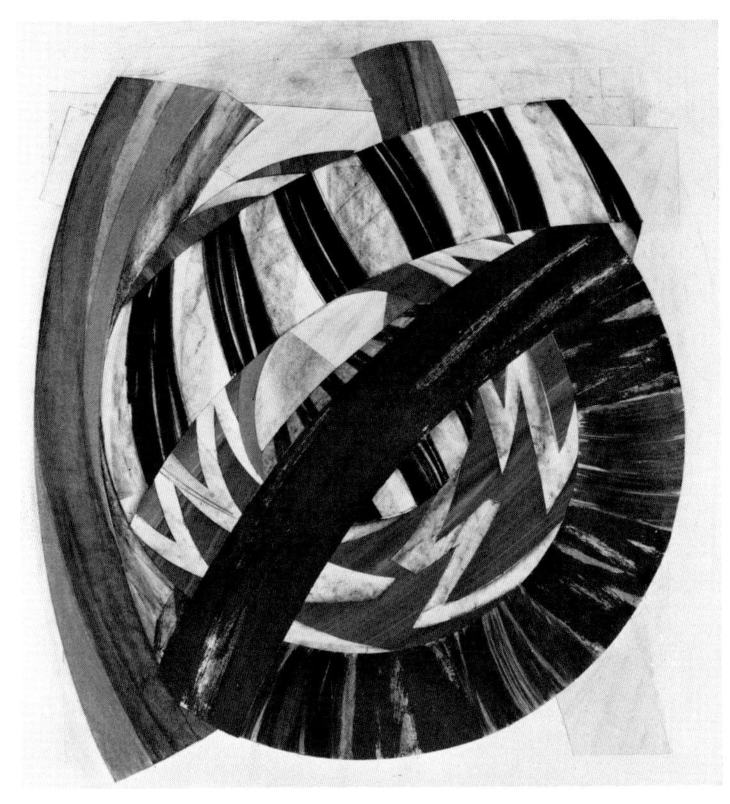

78.
Belatrix I, Study for Bognor Regis Center Installation. 1979
Mixed media and collage on paper, 44 x 40″
Collection of the artist

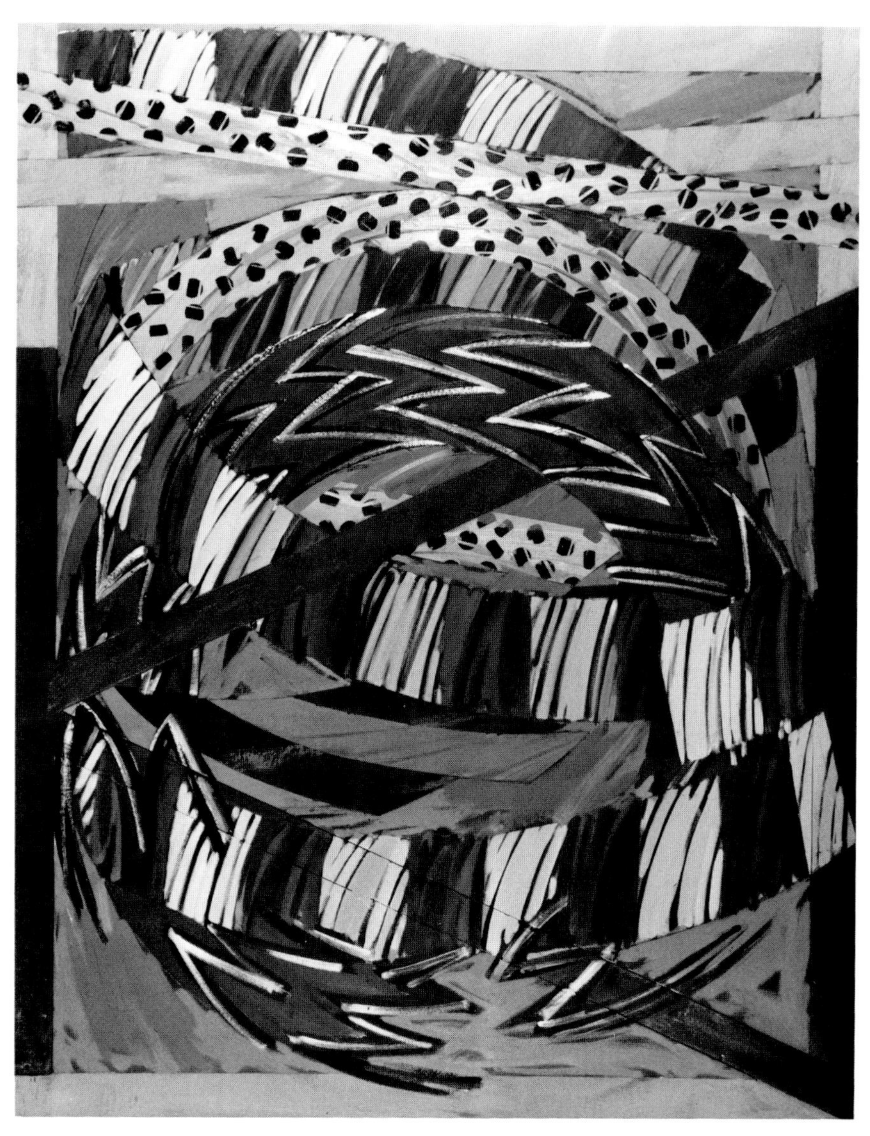

79.
Laocoon. 1979
Oil on canvas and wood, 96 x 72″
Collection of the artist

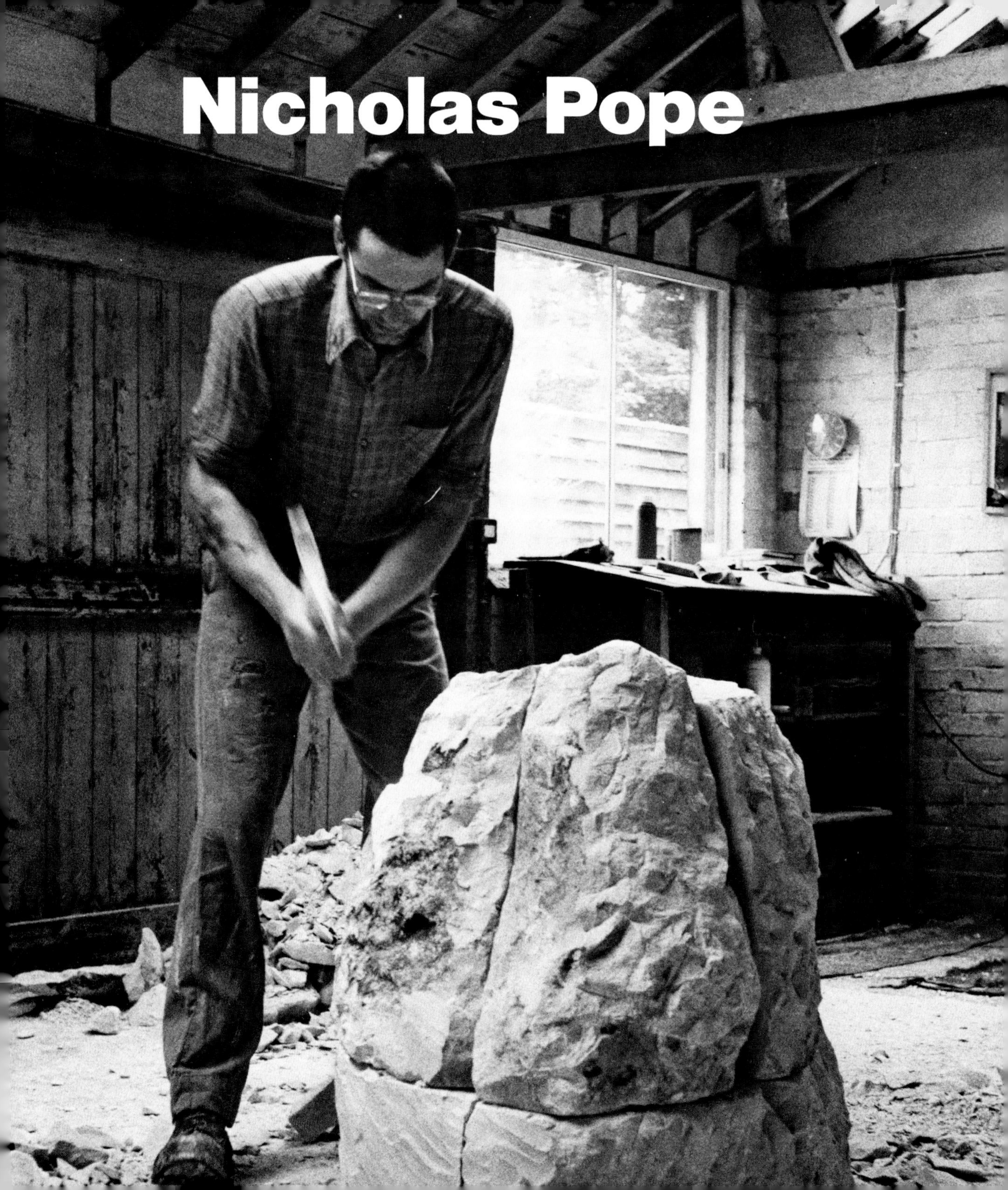

Nicholas Pope

The quaint hamlet of Acton, in Hampshire, where Nicholas Pope lives and works is but a scant two hours from London. Yet it has afforded him a sense of isolation, timelessness, permanence, tradition and craft difficult to maintain in the fast-moving atmosphere of London. The idyllic Hampshire countryside appears to have reinforced Pope's resolve to reject topical content and encouraged his use of time-honored, conventional materials through which he at once acknowledges the past and addresses the present.

Like David Nash, Nicholas Pope has focused much of his attention recently on working in wood. He is, similarly, an admirer of Brancusi and had ample opportunity to study the master at first hand in the course of fellowships to Rumania in 1974-75 and again in 1977. While it would be tempting to discuss the work of Nash and Pope in the light of a shared aesthetic, they are, in fact, confronting very different issues and achieving very different results. Pope's original point of departure was wood, which he continues to use, but he also works with Bath-stone (he studied at the Bath Academy of Art from 1970-73), clay, chalk, terra-cotta and lead. The color, mass, density, tactility and texture of these materials are very different from those of wood. Pope has been guided by the inherent properties of each medium to produce a series of refreshingly varied sculptures.

Pope's exploration of the innate properties of his materials is augmented by his concern for structure, mass, density, balance, stacking, butting and compression. Much of his recent work is modest, even diminutive, in scale, although a few pieces approach life-size. For the most part they are ground-related rather than anthropomorphic or architectonic. The sculpture is quietly contained, exquisitely proportioned and deceptively simple. The wooden stacks, stone slabs or chalk blocks are assembled with care, yet they possess an air of fragility and a delicate, precarious balance. This tenuous equilibrium evokes a sense of their ephemeral nature and an apprehension of chaos and disorder beneath the surface of an ordered reality. In some ways Pope's sculptures are reminiscent of Serra's prop pieces but their balance is not as threatening as Serra's nor are the forms, held in tenuous equilibrium, as densely organized. Pope, unlike Serra, often emphasizes the spaces between the individual units of the sculpture, so that internal relationships and the total presence of the piece are more important than the seeming randomness of its parts. Whether Pope deploys his forms laterally, as in *Three Stone Slabs* or *Seven Odd Chalks* of 1978 (cat. nos. 83, 84), he is equally intent upon defining the overall configuration of his work. He occasionally refines the contours of pieces, securing them with pins or dowels, as they are installed, to adjust them to the setting.

Pope eschews both the grand or heroic gesture of fifties sculptors and the rational, analytic approach of the Minimalists of the sixties. While related to Minimalist sculpture in its coolness, Pope's use of natural materials such as wood or stone rather than prefabricated industrial units and his emphasis upon craft set him apart from these earlier aesthetics. He is far less concerned with place, so central to the Minimalist concept, with making marks upon nature like the Earthworks artists, or with producing sculpture for particular sites than he is with the value of the unique object.

Like Nash, Pope refers to nature in his use of organic forms and materials. However, Pope's wooden sculptures are totally abstract, without allusion to the specific forms of nature, without literary or other extra-pictorial reference. The emphasis here is upon nuance created by the careful positioning of forms, the delicate chiseling of the edge, the graceful torsion of shapes. Pope exploits the extraordinary beauty of the inherent properties of his medium, using the knots, the grain, the texture, the silveriness, the blondness, the sheen, almost as a painter would. The modest size of these works engenders intimate contact between the spectator and the piece, drawing him into it, inviting him to examine every mark on the surface.

Pope is a classical sculptor in the sense that the beauty of ideal form rather than its theoretical premise most intrigues him. While his origins as a woodcarver remain apparent, especially in his respect for materials, it is through subordinating craft

Nicholas Pope in his studio working on chalk piece, 1979

to the definition of form that Pope has attained his innovatory contribution. Pope subscribes to no other doctrine than the need to achieve a direct and simple statement of clarity, expressive of both the inherent nature of sculpture and its potential for individual human expression.

What sculpture is for and how I evaluate it must be very close. Sculpture is that which I can welcome intelligently and learn from. However I do not think it should infringe on other walks of life. I think that artists and therefore sculptors are most moving when they use the simplest language of the heart; direct utterance is a quality that I admire. When this is marred by political or sociological overtones this directness is lost. Material experimentation, political comment and the many other diversions are all very well but they are not and have never been sculpture. Sculpture is for conveying, through the sculptor's chosen medium, straightforward, whole-hearted emotion.[1]

Pope confronts many of the central issues of sculpture in the twentieth century; in avoiding a didactic or theoretical approach he has succeeded in producing a group of works that are ambitious and engaging, intelligent and personable. They are the result of a process by which Pope has managed to effectively balance the intellectual process, "the clarity of construction and technical control" with "an emotional aliveness which I could not begin to describe, but which I can begin to see in all great sculptures."[2]

1. Pope, Nicholas, "Sculptors Replies," *Artscribe*, no. 3, Summer 1976, pp. 9-10
2. *Ibid.*

Nicholas Pope

Born in Sydney, 1949

Bath Academy of Art, 1970-73

Awarded Southern Arts Association Bursary, 1974

Rumanian Government Exchange Scholarship, 1974-75

Calouste Gulbenkian Foundation Visual Arts Award, 1976

British Council Visitor to Rumania, 1977

Commonwealth Games Commission, Edmonton, Canada, 1978

Australian Council Visitor to Australia, 1979

Lives in Alton, Hampshire

Selected Group Exhibitions

Festival Gallery, Bath, October-November 1973

Portsmouth and Southsea, *City Art Project*, August-September 1974

Garage Gallery, London, March 1975

Hayward Gallery, London, *The Condition of Sculpture*, May- July 1975

Serpentine Gallery, London, *Summer Show 3*, July-August 1976

Hayward Gallery, London, *Arts Council Collection Exhibition 1975-76*, August 1976

Southampton Art Gallery, *Stephenie Bergman and Nicholas Pope*, February-March 1977

Brighton Festival, *Carving*, June 1977

Arnolfini Gallery, Bristol, *On Site*, September-October 1977

Battersea Park, London, *Silver Jubilee Sculpture Exhibition*, September 1977

Mappin Art Gallery, Sheffield, *Stephenie Bergman and Nicholas Pope*, October 1977

ICA Gallery, London, *A Critic's Choice*, September 1978

Arts Council of Great Britain, London, *A Free Hand*, from January 1978. Traveled to Arts Centre Gallery, Chester; Ikon Gallery, Birmingham; Huddersfield Art Gallery; Great Yarmouth Exhibition Centre; Leicester Polytechnic; Turnpike Gallery, Leigh

Taranman Gallery, London, October 1978

Fitzwilliam Museum, Cambridge, *Tolly Cobbold/ Eastern Arts Association 2nd National Exhibition,* from April 1979. Traveled to Castle Museum, Norwich; Christchurch Mansion, Ipswich; Camden Arts Centre, London; Graves Art Gallery, Sheffield

Kunsthalle, Nuremberg, *1 Internationale Jugendtriennale der Zeichnung,* June-October 1979

Arnolfini Gallery, Bristol, *Style in the Seventies,* from July 1979. Organized by *Artscribe*

Mappin Art Gallery, Sheffield, *The British Art Show,* from December 1979. Will travel to Laing Art Gallery, Newcastle upon Tyne; Hatton Gallery, University of Newcastle; Arnolfini Gallery, Bristol; Royal West of England Academy. Catalogue with text by William Packer

Selected One-Man Exhibitions

Garage Gallery, London, March 1976

City of Portsmouth Museum and Art Gallery, *Nicholas Pope Sculpture 1973-1976,* September-October 1976

Anthony Stokes Gallery, London, February-March 1979

Art and Project, Amsterdam, May 1979

Gallery 'A,' Sydney, November 1979

Selected Bibliography

By the artist

"Sculptors Replies," *Artscribe,* no. 3, Summer 1976, pp. 9-10

On the artist

Marina Vaizey, "Object Lessons," *Sunday Times,* March 7, 1976, p. 35

Caroline Tisdall, "Rumanian Rich," *The Guardian,* March 12, 1976, p. 10

William Packer, "Nicholas Pope and Patrick Hughes," *Financial Times,* March 15, 1976, p. 3

Ben Jones, "Review," *Artscribe,* no. 2, Spring 1976, p. 10

Fenella Crichton, "Nicholas Pope," *Studio International,* vol. 191, May/June 1976, p. 299

Ben Jones, "A New Wave in Sculpture. A Survey of Recent Work by Ten Younger Sculptors," *Artscribe,* no. 8, September 1977, p. 15

William Packer, "4 Artists of the 80's," *Vogue,* March 15, 1978, p. 126

John McEwen, "Aspects of British Sculpture," *Artforum,* vol. XVI, April 1978, pp. 27-31

William Packer, "Silver, Dante and wood," *Financial Times,* February 6, 1979, p. 15

John Glaves Smith, "Nicholas Pope," *Art Monthly,* no. 24, March 1979, p. 21

James Bustard, "Nicholas Pope," *Art Log,* no. 4, 1979

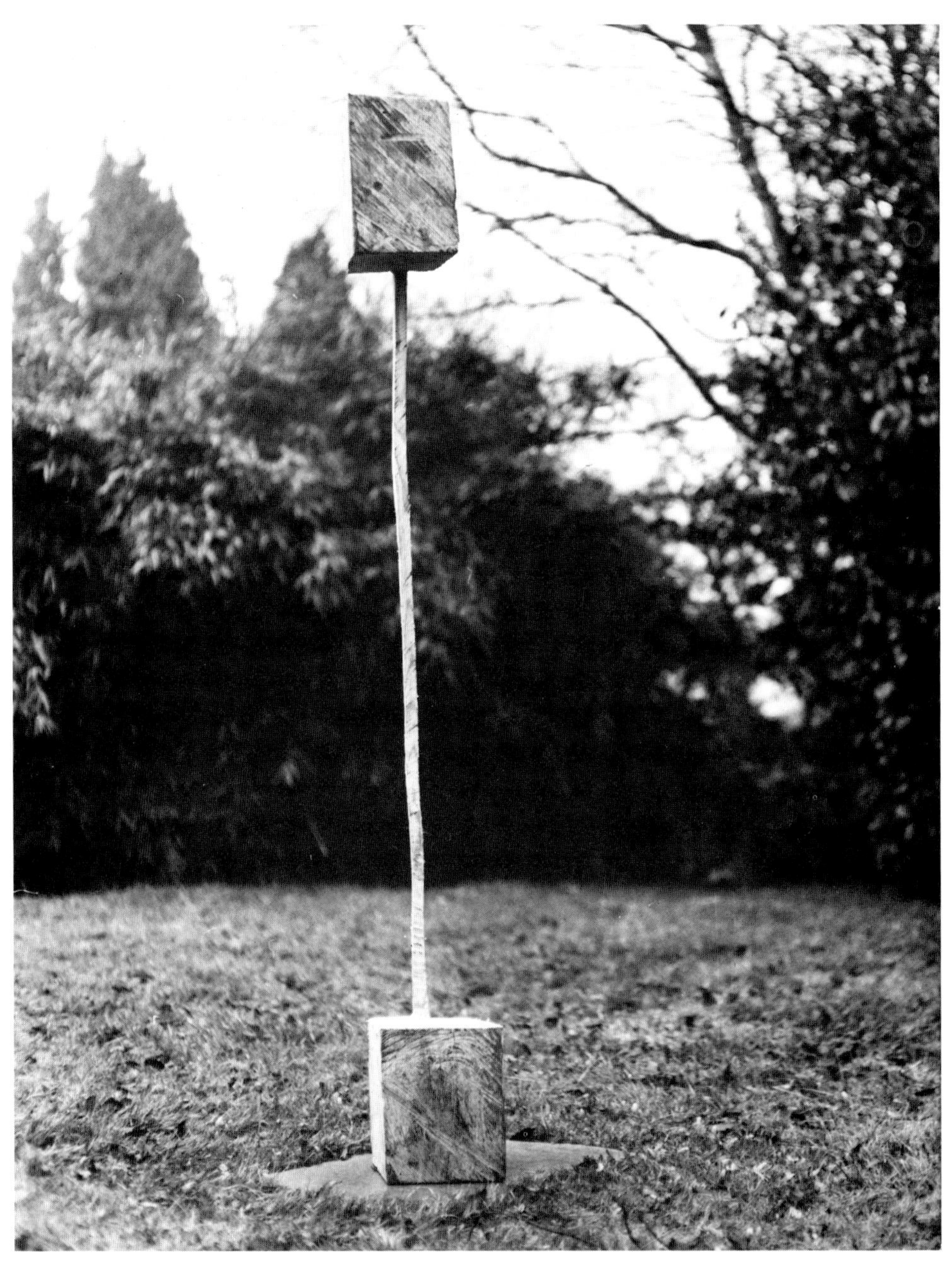

80.
Oak Wood Column. Winter 1973
Oak wood, 60″ high
Collection John Cox, Greenwich, England

81.
Stone Pile. Summer 1976
Bath stone, 47¼″ high
Collection Frits and Agnes Becht, Naarden, The Netherlands

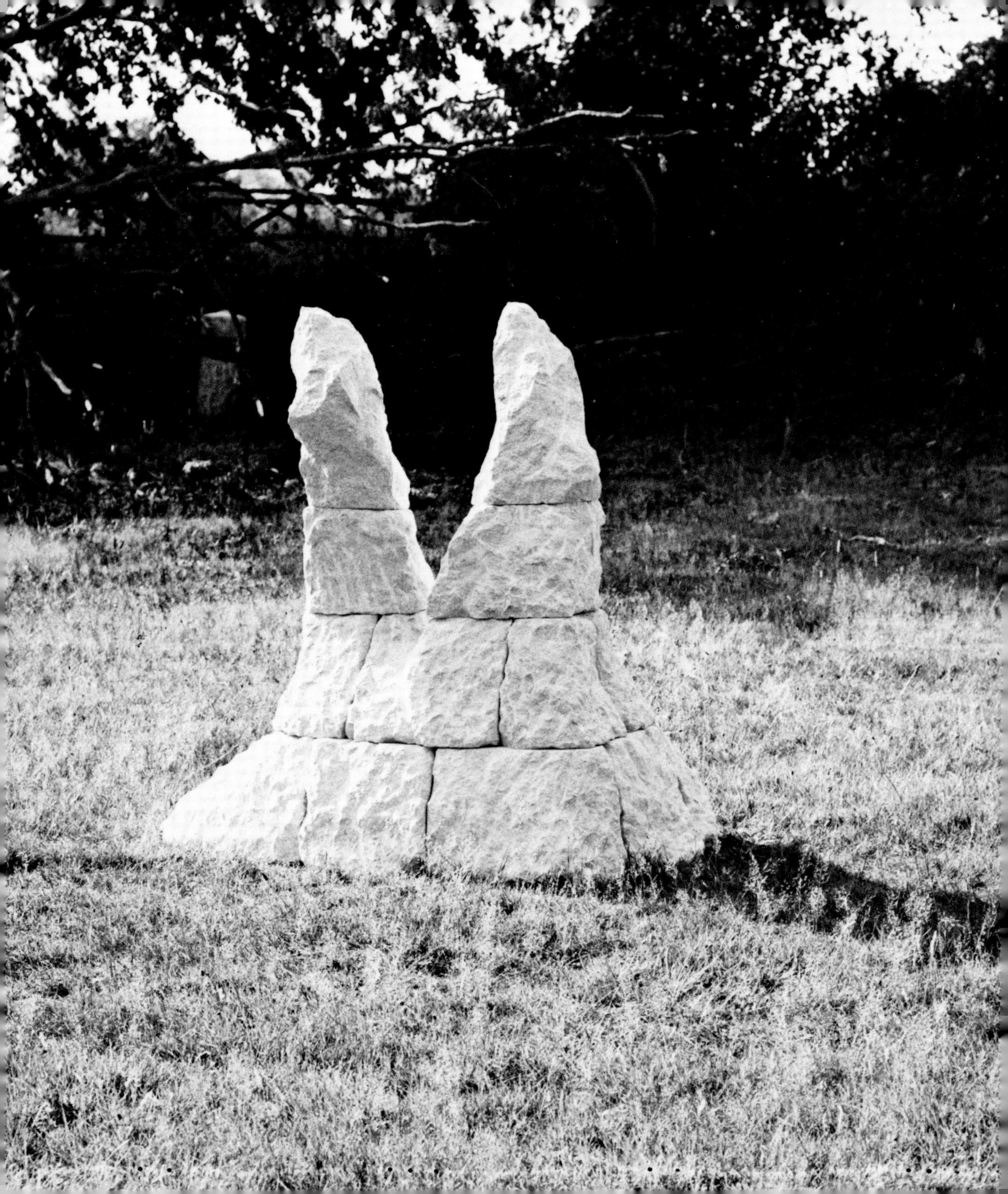

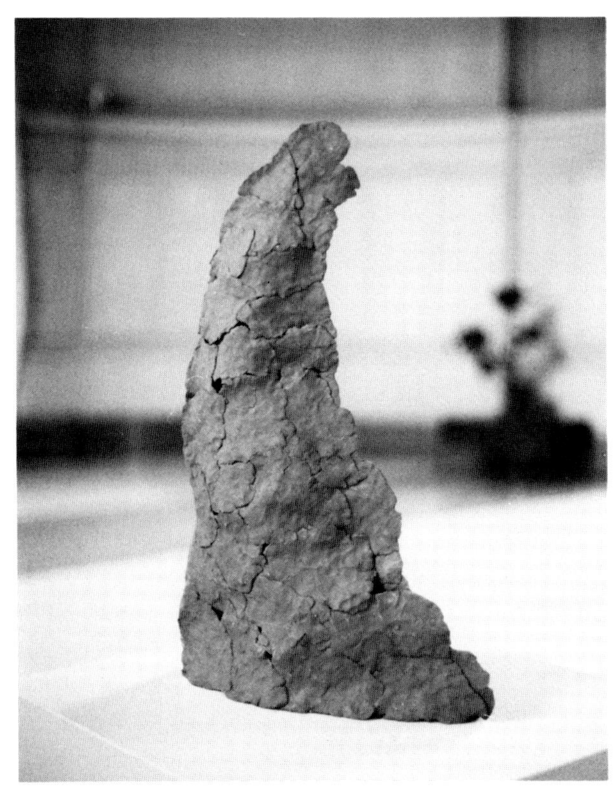

82.
Large Terra-cotta Pile. 1976-77
Fired clay, 26½″ high
Collection Paula and Hans-Eugene Bisson-Millet,
Heidelberg, West Germany

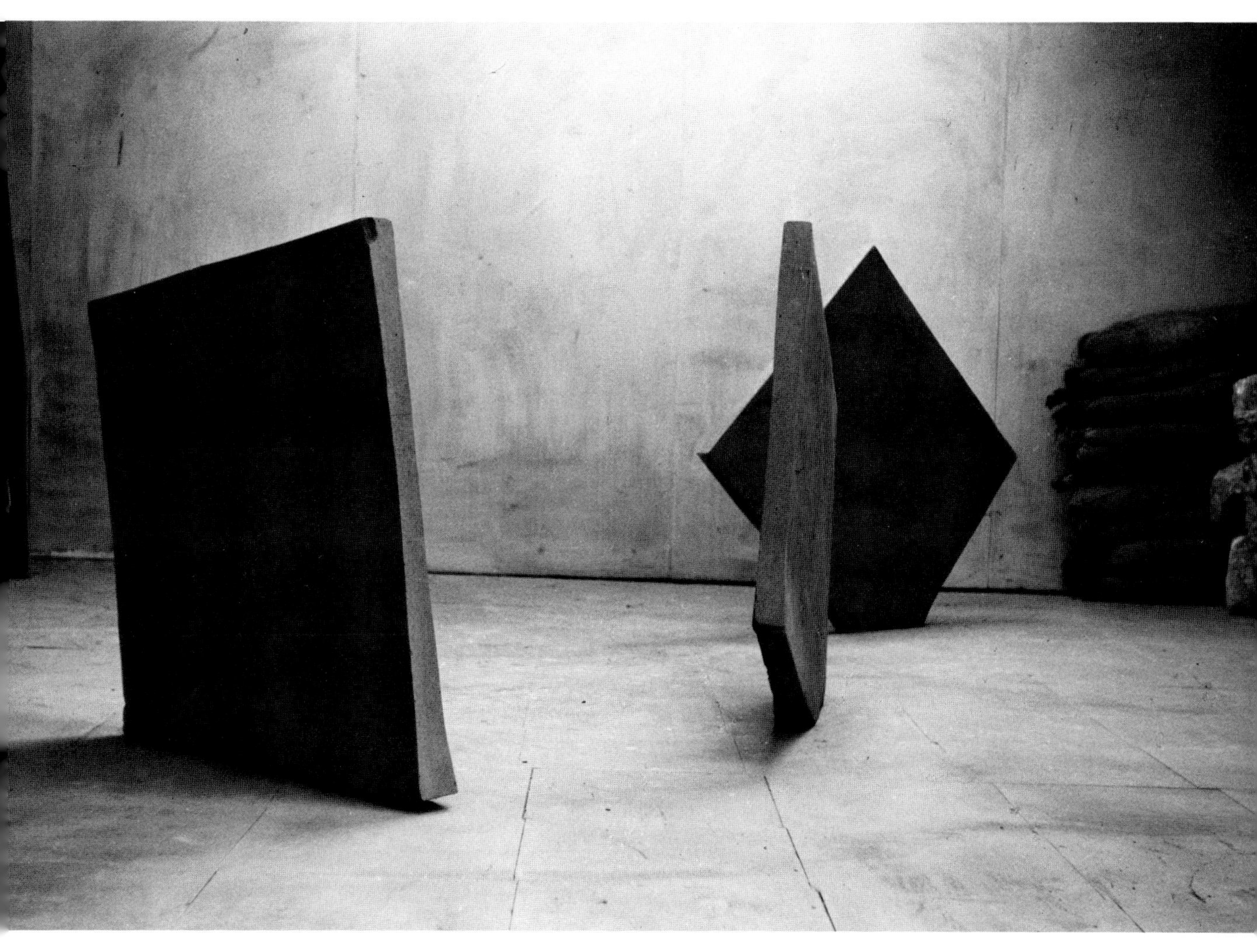

83.
Three Stone Slabs. 1978
Forest of Dean Stone, 47¼ x 173″ overall
Collection Rijksmuseum Kröller-Müller, Otterlo,
The Netherlands

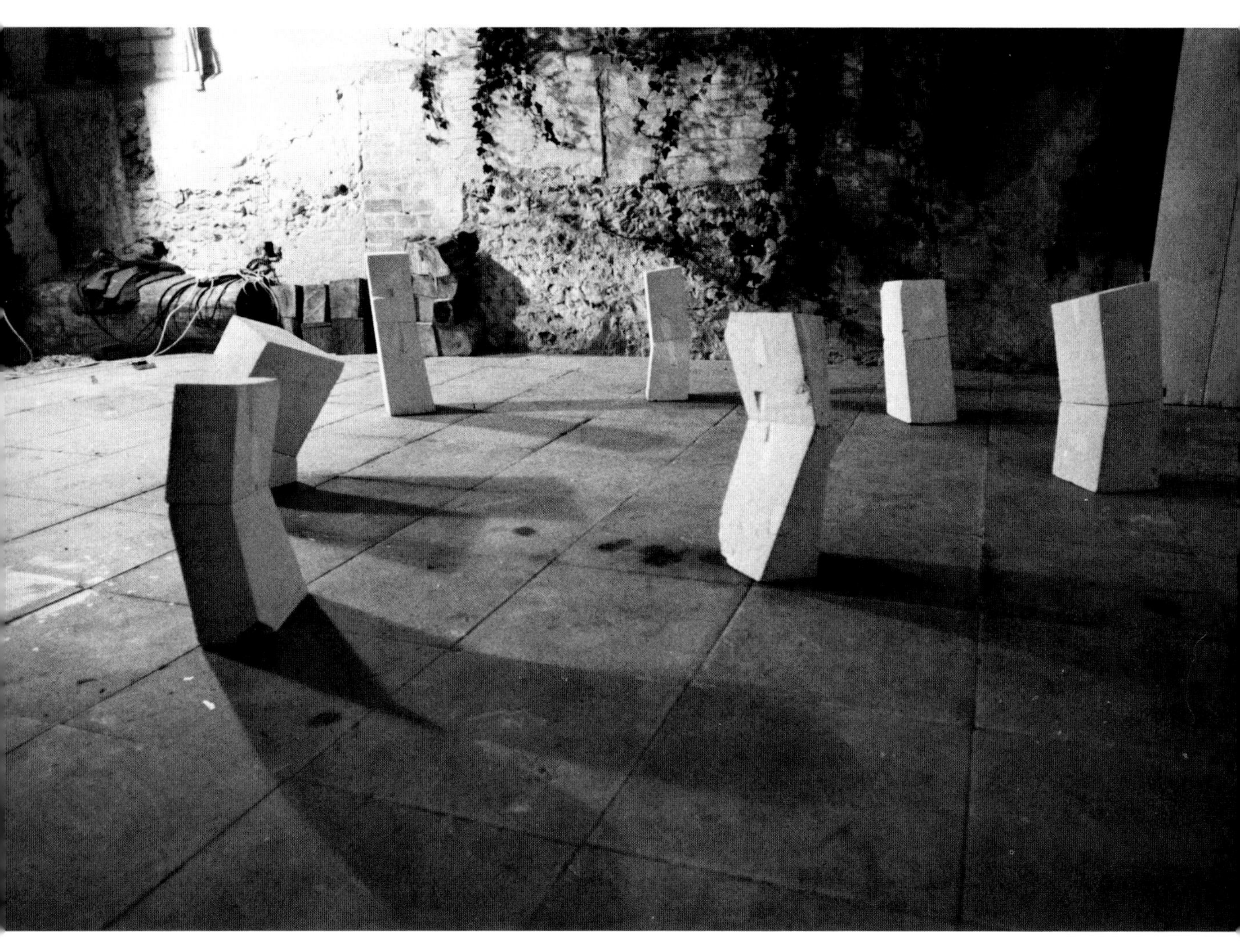

84.
Seven Odd Chalks. 1978
Chalk, 31½ x 106¼″ overall
Courtesy Art and Project, Amsterdam

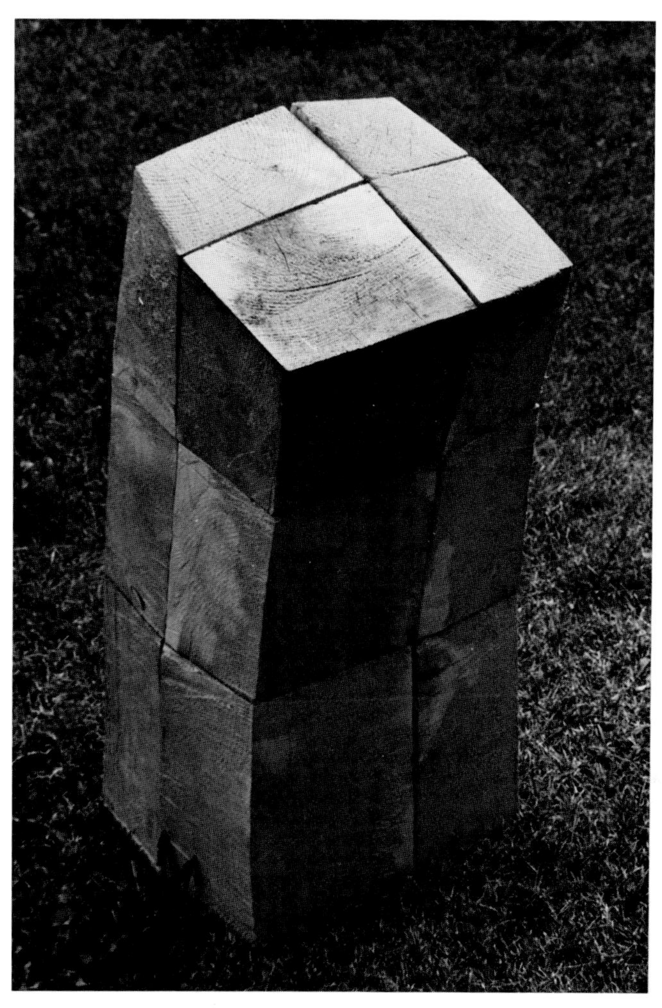

85.
Twelve Wood Block. Summer 1978
Pine wood, 30½ x 12 x 12½ ″
Collection Lucille Schmidt, Edmonton, Canada

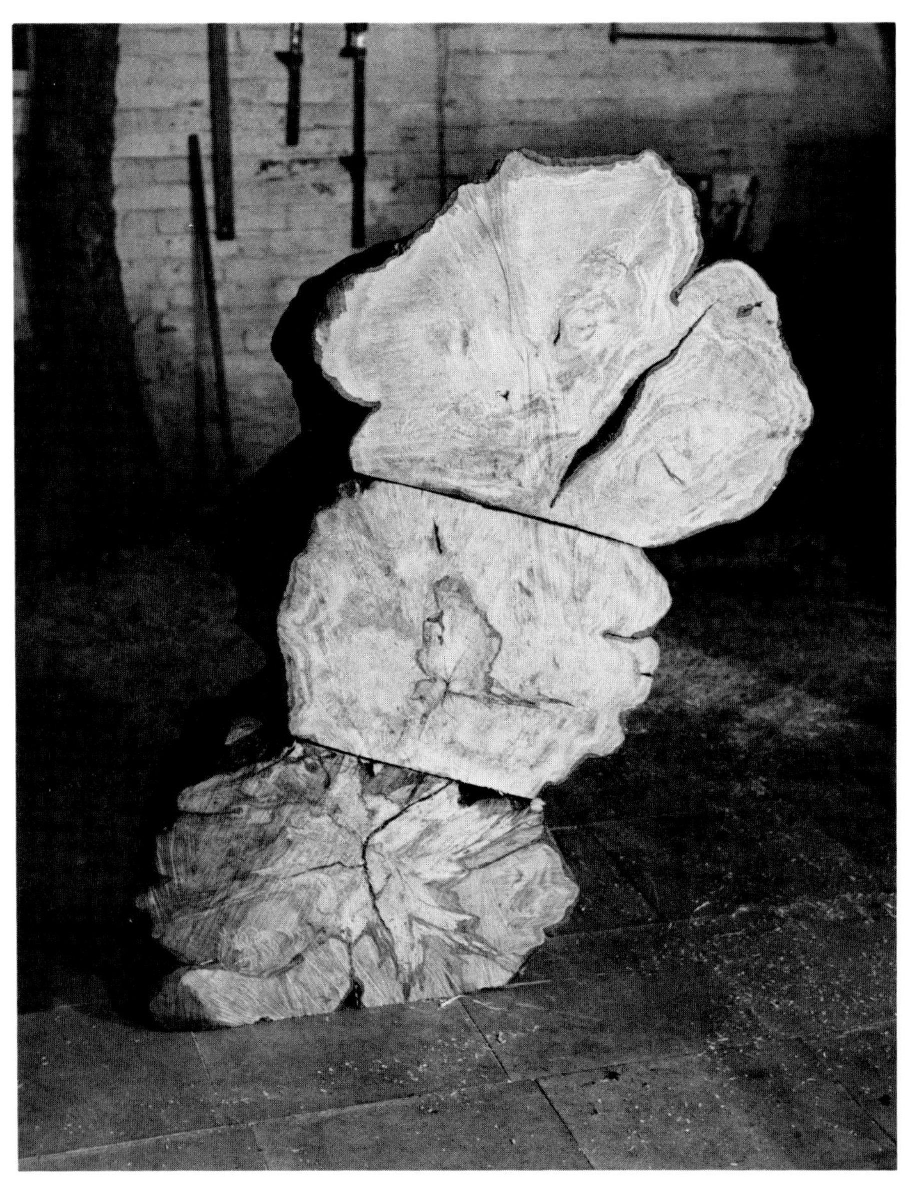

86.
Three Wood Block. Autumn 1978
Hornbeam wood, 55⅛″ high
Collection The Arts Council of Great Britain, London

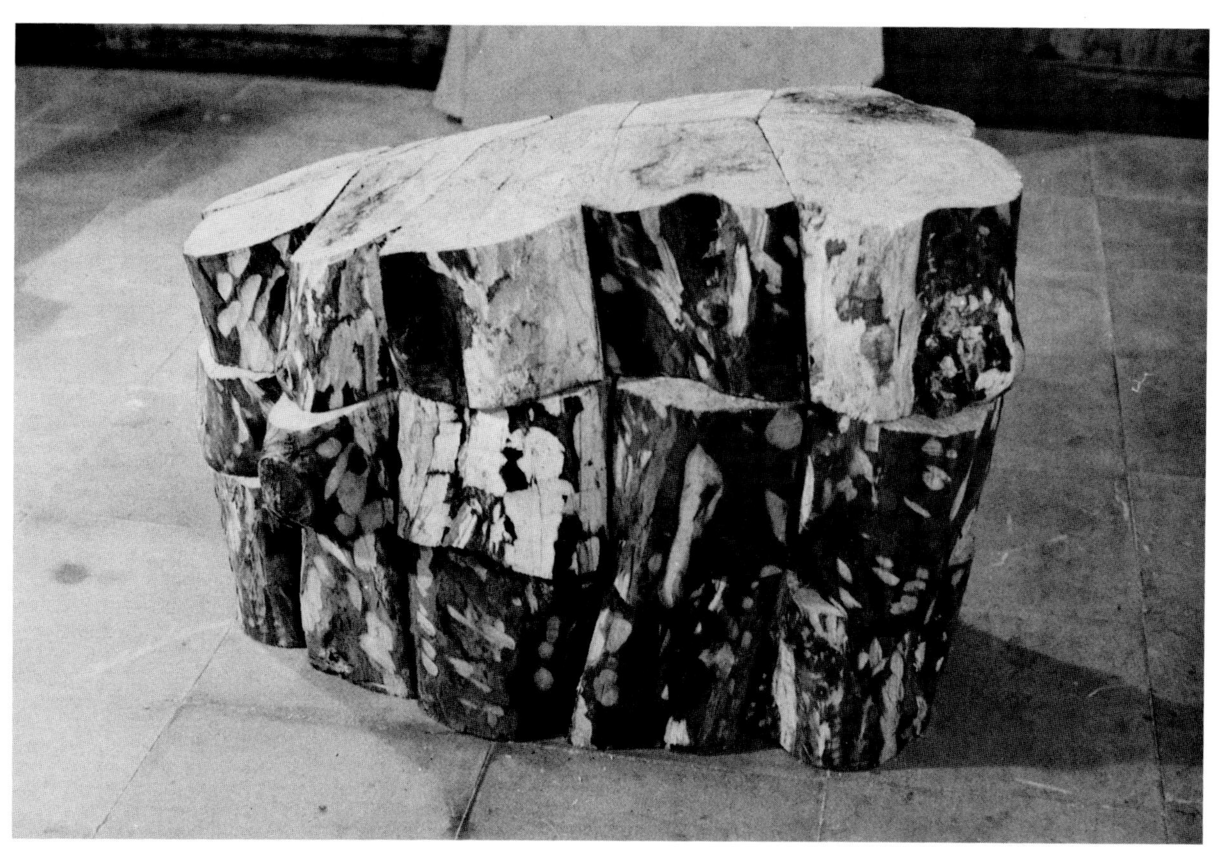

87.
Thirty Wood Block. 1978
Silver birchwood, 39⅜″ high
Collection Frits and Agnes Becht, Naarden, The
Netherlands

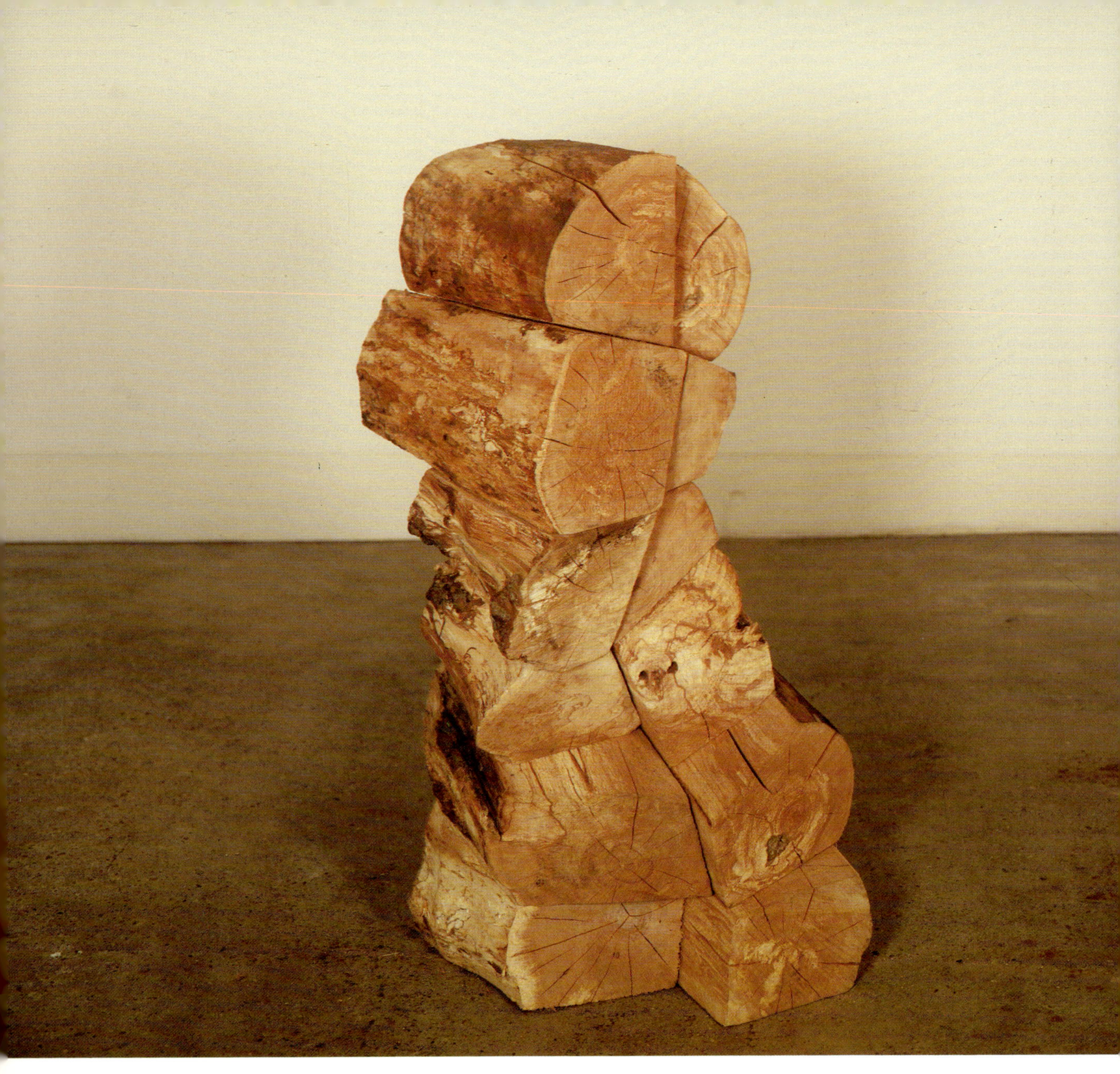

88.
Apple Pile. 1979
Applewood, 35″ high
Courtesy Anthony Stokes Gallery, London

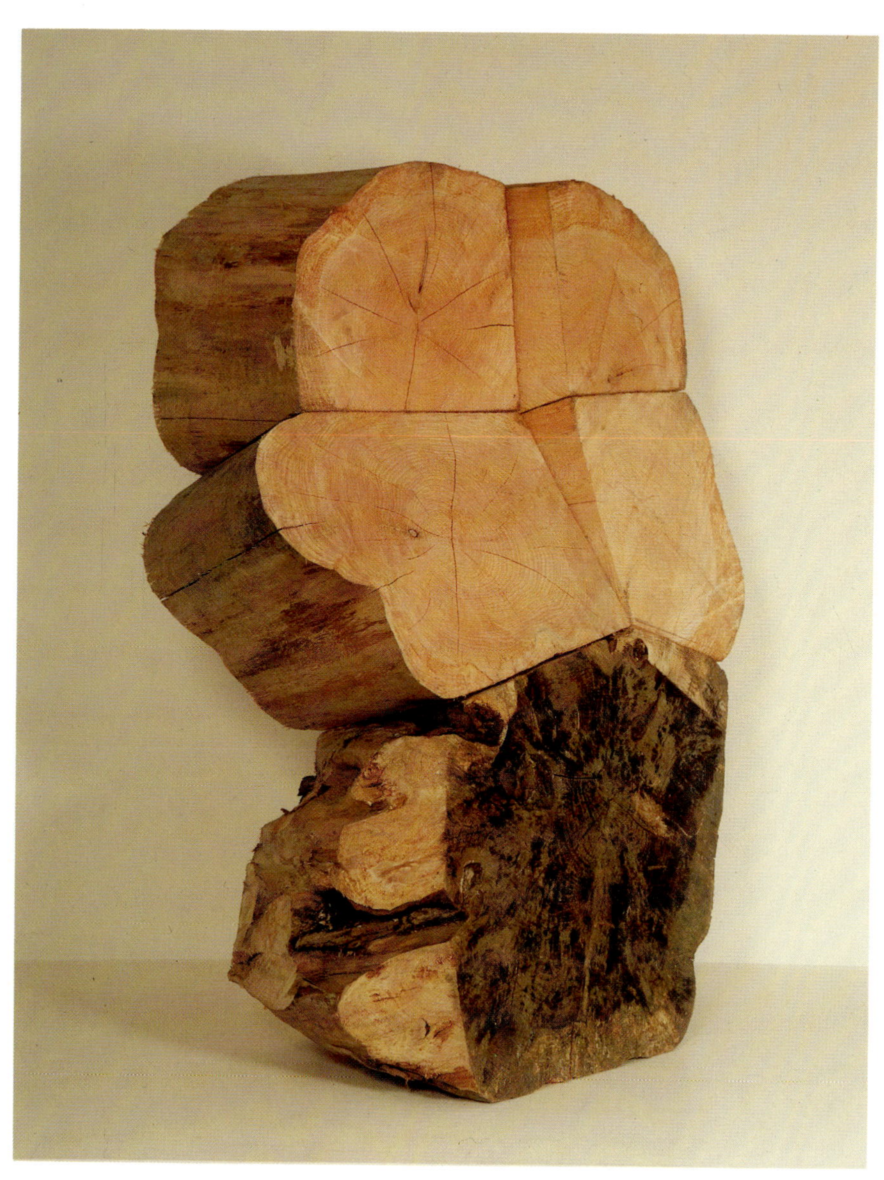

89.
Round Pile. 1978
Cypress wood, 44″ high
Collection The British Council, London

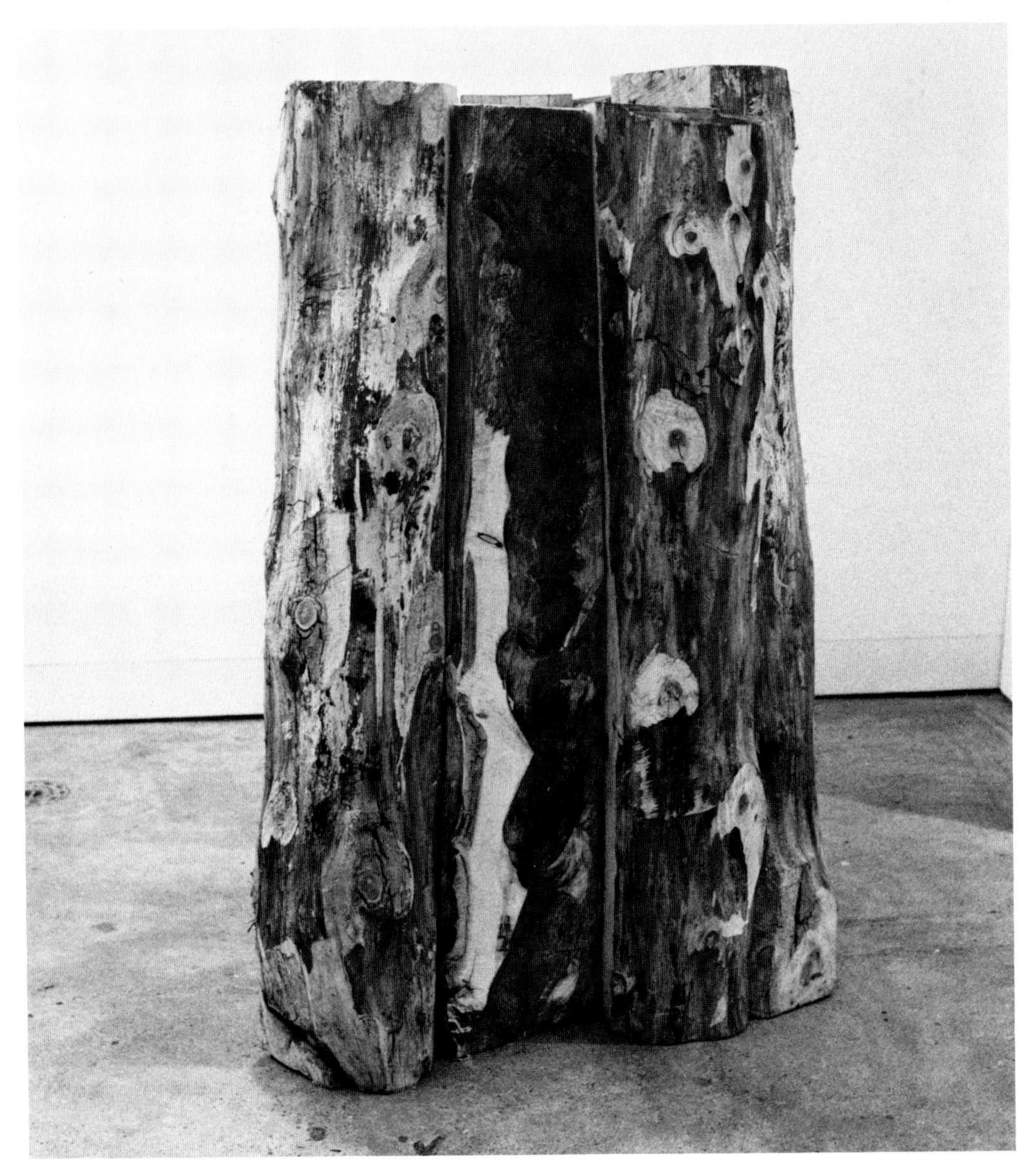

90.
Tall Block. 1978
Cypress wood, 63″ high
Anonymous Loan

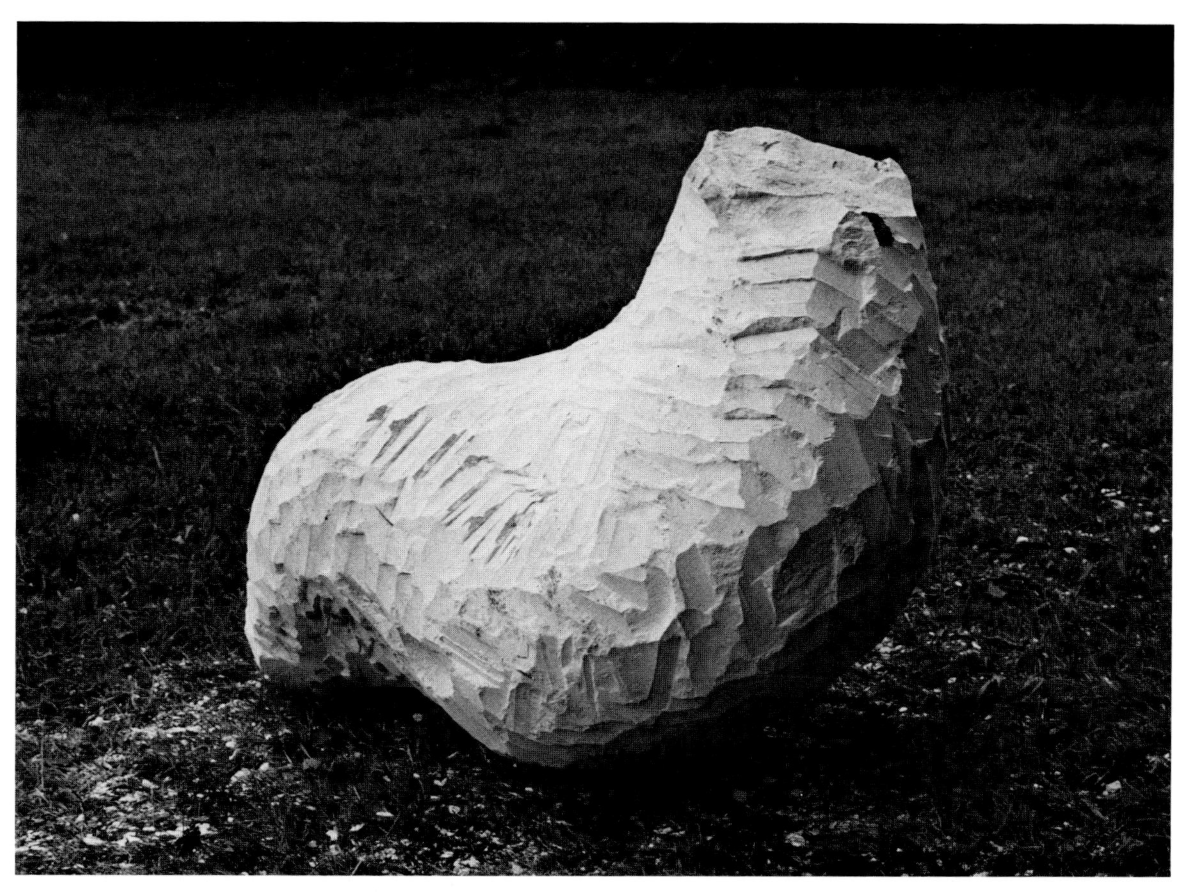

91.
Curved White Lump. Summer 1979
Chalk, 37 ″ high
Courtesy Anthony Stokes Gallery, London

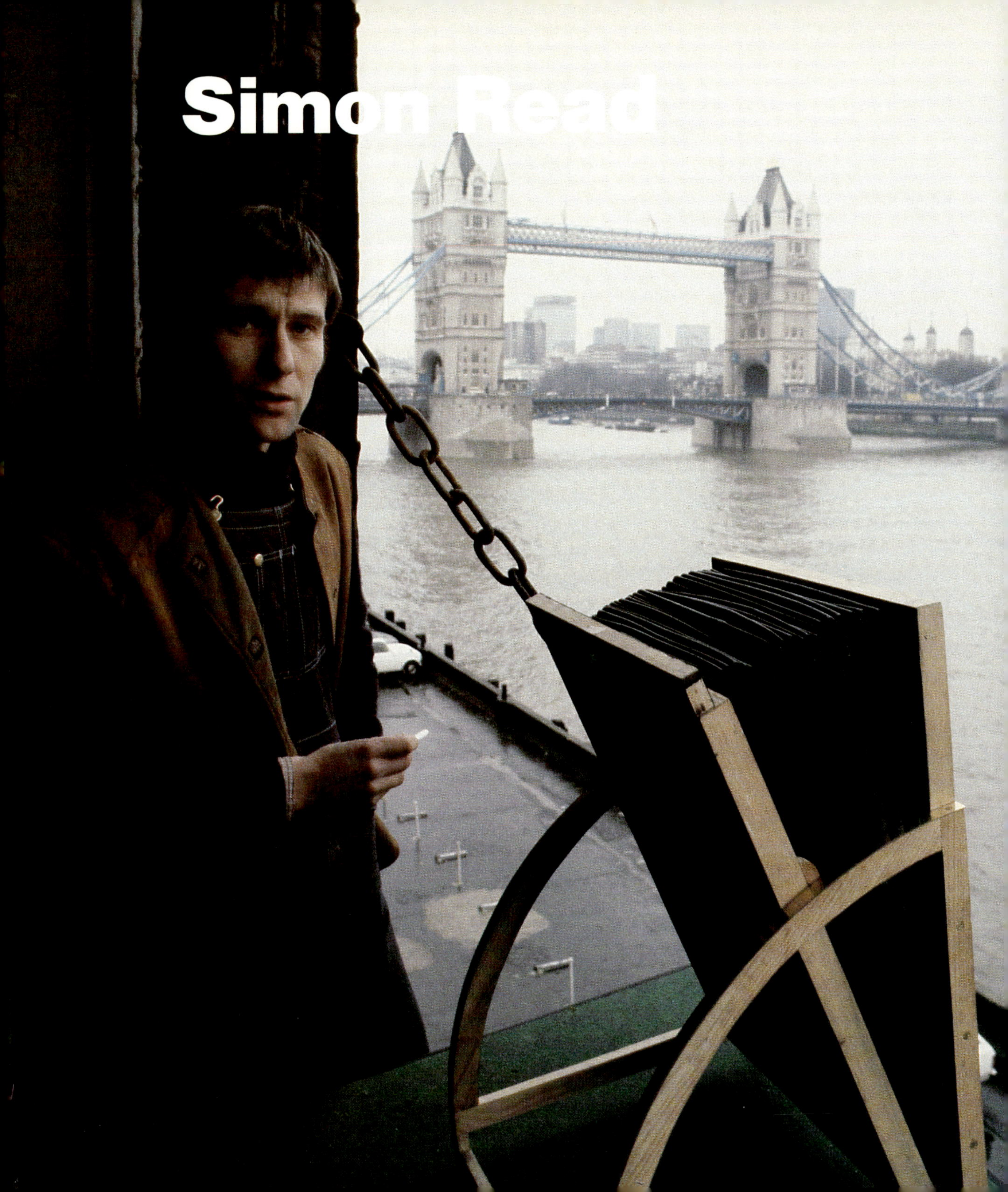

Simon Read

Simon Read lives and works in a cold damp warehouse along the Thames, east of Tower Bridge. He more or less camps out in a roughly partitioned corner of his studio, the only heated space in an otherwise unheated loft. Mean by New York standards, it is very cheap and large enough to accommodate the massive cameras that he has invented and built.

Read has modeled his cameras on the camera obscura, which he has adapted and adjusted to his own needs. The traditional camera obscura is a darkened enclosure into which light enters through an aperture, usually fitted with a lens, projecting the image of exterior subject onto the interior rear wall of the camera. Read's cameras are based upon this principle, with several significant differences. Read has varied the size of the traditional pinhole from a microscopic dot to a sizeable slash to allow different amounts of light to enter the camera. He never uses a lens, an optical device which conveys conventional perspective, but relies instead upon direct transmission of the subject through the aperture of the camera. The inverted image projected upon the rear wall of the camera obscura is Read's initial point of departure. It gives him the opportunity to convert an iconography rooted in fact but detached from natural phenomena into a new vision of reality. Building upon these images, Read has created a prolific vocabulary of profligate characters for his Dickensian fantasies.

He constructs special cameras (cat. nos. 97 and 100) for his strange images; before he photographs, Read plots the path the camera will take with a series of diagrams, notations and drawings (cat. no. 93). As he photographs, he changes the size and shape of the aperture for each shot. The resulting images were therefore enormously varied, and the most notable features of the studio interior, its pillars, lost their sense of mass and definition. The columns that supported the loft seemed no more than a series of discrete calligraphic marks. When he showed these black and white photographs, titled *A Taste of Honey makes the Bee change her Tune,* 1977 (cat. no. 94), Read arranged them to coincide with the route of the camera as it

documented the studio. In a series of photographs which recorded one reality but produced another, a bleak setting is transformed into a strikingly varied and exquisite group of abstract images resembling those in an Oriental scroll.

Recently, Read produced two groups of photographic portraits (cat. nos. 96, 98), using a single camera with two different apertures, one long, one round. As the camera was rotated 360 degrees, each aperture recorded the face of the sitter, producing stretched and undistorted images. Read mounted the photographs in two separate circles to echo the rotation of the camera and the order in which the pictures were taken. Read's images are based on the concept of anamorphic portraiture. His model is an anamorphic portrait of *Edward VI* by an unknown artist after a painting of the same subject by Holbein, illustrated in Gombrich's *Art and Illusion* (fig. 1). In anamorphic portraiture the image is extremely distorted when viewed frontally; when seen from the side, however, the deformation is corrected, at least in terms of conventional perspective.

Read is currently at work on yet another project, called *The Virtue of a Glancing Blow and a Sidelong Glance,* 1978-79 (cat. no. 101), in which the extended aperture of the camera distorts the subject even further. In these pictures Read combines the earlier stretched and undistorted subject into a single composite image. His curiously unreal portraits can be read as a revival of an old tradition, for they recall numerous earlier prototypes. Yet their modernity strikes us even as we remember these early paintings because we recognize the sitters as our contemporaries. Moreover, no attempt has been made to disguise the technological, if unconventional, means by which these images were captured. And the garish Warhol-like colors of the larger circle of photographs make us forcefully aware of their twentieth-century origins.

Working with portrait photography Read can convey a more loaded image than he could hope to achieve with the more anonymous subject of his studio. The artist has said that he wanted to work with the face because of its many associations. He feels that a face (whether known or unknown), because it is instantly recognizable, is the most appropriate vehicle for his ideas. The camera is Read's ideal tool, for it directly records a measurable relationship in space. Even more significantly, it allows the artist to conceptualize his subject in the manner of Duchamp, whom he very much admires. But unlike Duchamp or younger artists like Jan Dibbets and Ger van Elk, Read invests his imagery with the mystery of poetic metaphor.

At present Read is engaged in an extremely complex photographic project, entitled *Sweet Thames Run Softly till I End my Song,* which involves an exposure lasting from four and a half to nine hours. He wants it to run continuously for two and a half years. The title comes from a Tennyson poem. The river is what he sees from his studio window; the "End my Song" means that the piece will be completed when he is kicked out of his studio.[1] Many of his other titles involve similarly eclectic references to change. *A Taste of Honey makes the Bee change her Tune,* for example, originated with Read's love of The Beatles. He has said that he likes titles that send the viewer off on a tangent and here "The title has to do with making or having an idea and then not making it but using it to literally 'taste' the idea and as it is tasted so to change it. In other words, the process of change by sampling—changing happens anyway by something as simple as tasting." He would like to make a series of landscape images and has begun his experiments by taking long vertical color pictures of Tower Bridge (cat. nos. 104, 105, 106) with the same camera he used for *The Virtue of a Glancing Blow and a Sidelong Glance.* These pictures combine clarity and softness in a manner no conventional camera with a lens can produce. Now that the Tower Bridge piece is well underway, Read is considering a temporary move to the countryside around Cumberland, where he can explore the rural counterpart to his London landscape.

Read is a portraitist in the truest sense but he has chosen to record his subjects in a highly unconventional, even bizarre fashion. By reinvestigating the scientific dimension of his art and reinventing the camera, he has been able to produce images which challenge the Renaissance concept of ideal beauty. In testing the ambiguities of the third dimension and challenging the concept of orthodox perspective, Read has created an inordinately compelling set of images which force us to question the very nature of reality and our perception of that reality.

1. As this catalogue went to press, Read's Studio was destroyed by a fire. *Sweet Thames* . . . thus ended prematurely, but Read hopes to reconstruct the piece elsewhere.

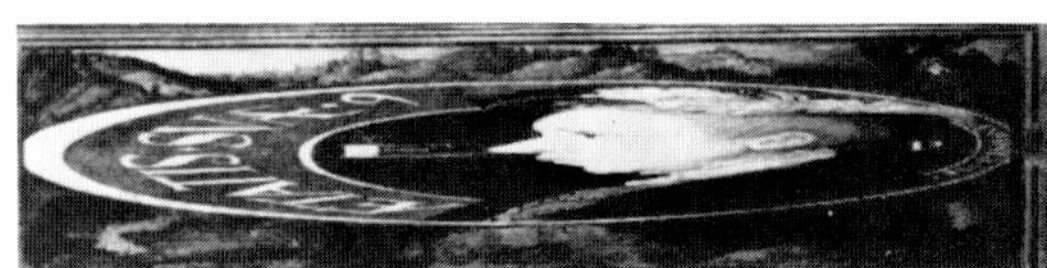

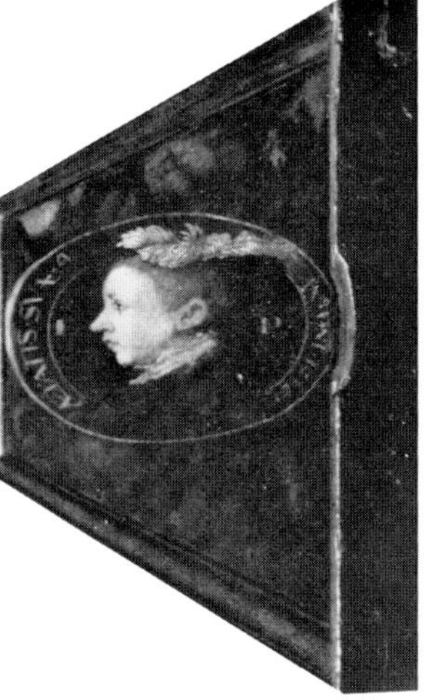

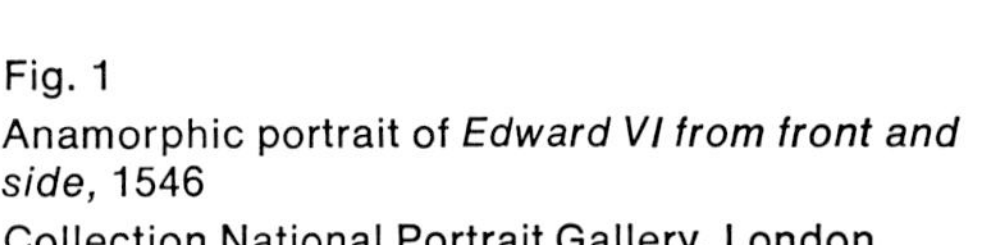

Fig. 1
Anamorphic portrait of *Edward VI from front and side,* 1546
Collection National Portrait Gallery, London

Simon Read

Born in Bristol, 1949

Somerset College of Art, 1968-69

University of Leeds, 1969-73

Chelsea School of Art, London, 1973-75

Arts Council Major Award, 1978

Teaches at Middlesex Polytechnic, London

Visiting Lecturer at Slade School of Fine Art, London; Chelsea School of Art, London; North East London Polytechnic; Reading University; Bath Academy of Art, Corsham

Studio fire, Butler's Wharf, 1979

Lives in London

Selected Group Exhibitions

Whitechapel Art Gallery, London, *Whitechapel Open Exhibition,* August 1977

ARC II, Musée d'Art Moderne de la Ville de Paris, *Un Certain art anglais . . .,* January-March 1979. Catalogue with text by Fenella Crichton

Palais des Beaux-Arts, Brussels, *JP II,* March-April 1979. Catalogue with text by Fenella Crichton

Fitzwilliam Museum, Cambridge, *Tolly Cobbold/ Eastern Arts 2nd National Exhibition,* from April 1979. Traveled to The Castle Museum, Norwich; Christchurch Mansion, Ipswich; Camden Arts Centre, London; Graves Art Gallery, Sheffield

Selected One-Man Exhibitions

Acme Gallery, London, *Twelve Stern Presences,* August 1976

Park Square Gallery, Leeds, *Entente,* April 1977

Wakefield Art Gallery, *Trajectory,* April-May 1977

Anthony Stokes Gallery, London, *An Imposition at Anthony Stokes,* November 1977

Roundhouse Gallery, London, *Faltering Steps— Staggering Feat,* July 1978

Galerie Swart, Amsterdam, August 1979

Selected Bibliography

Richard Cork, "When a One-Man show Clicks . . .," *Evening Standard,* August 26, 1976

Sarah Kent, "Twelve Stern Presences," *Time Out,* August 1976, p. 47

Mike Hazzledine, "Simon Read," *Studio International,* vol. 193, January-February 1977, pp. 47-48

Bill Oliver, "Park Square Gallery Leeds," *Yorkshire Evening Post,* April 15, 1977

Stephen Chaplin, "Stephen Chaplin looks at . . . work of Simon Read in Leeds and Wakefield," *April in Yorkshire, Yorkshire Arts Association Magazine,* April 1977, pp. 12-13

Bill Oliver, "Trajectory," *Yorkshire Evening Post,* May 5, 1977

Sarah Kent, "An imposition at Anthony Stokes' Gallery," *Time Out,* November 2, 1977, p. 47

Lynda Talbot, "Lenseless Exercise," *Hampstead & Highgate Express News,* July 14, 1978

Ian Banks, "A Camera Obscurer," *Photography Magazine,* vol. 13, October 1978, p. 715

Andrea Hill, "Simon Read at the Roundhouse," *Artscribe,* no. 14, October 1978, pp. 56-57

"The Biggest Pinhole Camera in the World," *Photographic Technique,* vol. 6, December 1978, p. 27

William Packer, "Un Certain Art Anglais," *Financial Times,* January 23, 1979, p. 17

Suzanne Page, "Un certain art anglais . . . à l'ARC," *L'Oeil,* no. 282-283, January-February 1979, pp. 64-65

France Huser, "Calligraphies et graffitis," *Le Nouvel Observateur,* January 29, 1979, pp. 69-70

Genevieve Breerette, "Jeunes anglais à l'ARC," *Le Monde,* February 10, 1979, p. 28

Pierre Cabanne, "Un certain art anglais à l'ARC: au-delà du regard," *Le Matin de Paris,* February 13, 1979, p. 25

Paul Overy, "A Certain Kind," *The Listener,* February 22, 1979, pp. 298-293

Lewis Biggs, "Un certain art anglais," *Aspects,* no. 6, Spring 1979

Terence Maloon, "English Uncertainty in Paris," *Artscribe,* no. 17, April 1979, pp. 48-49

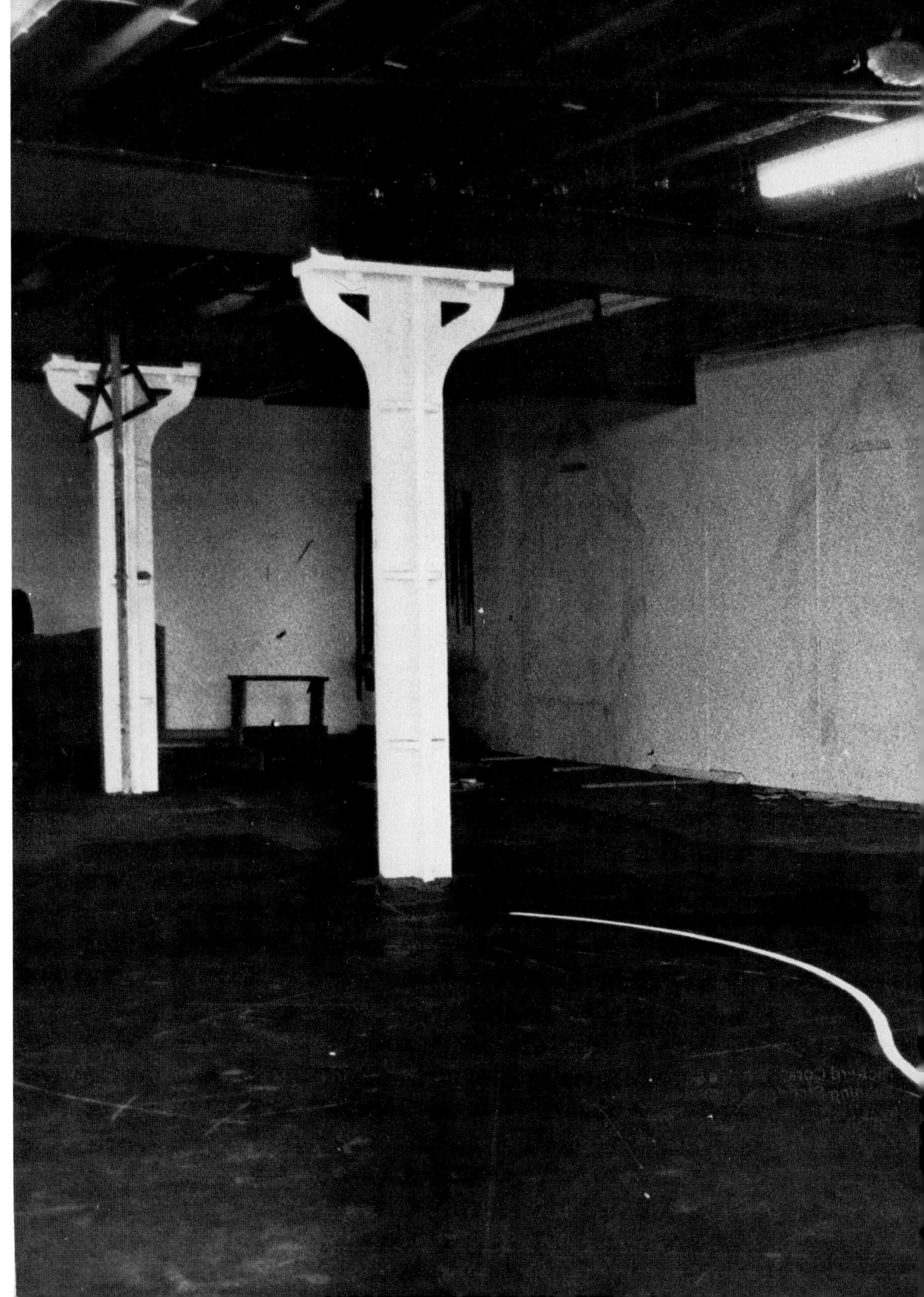

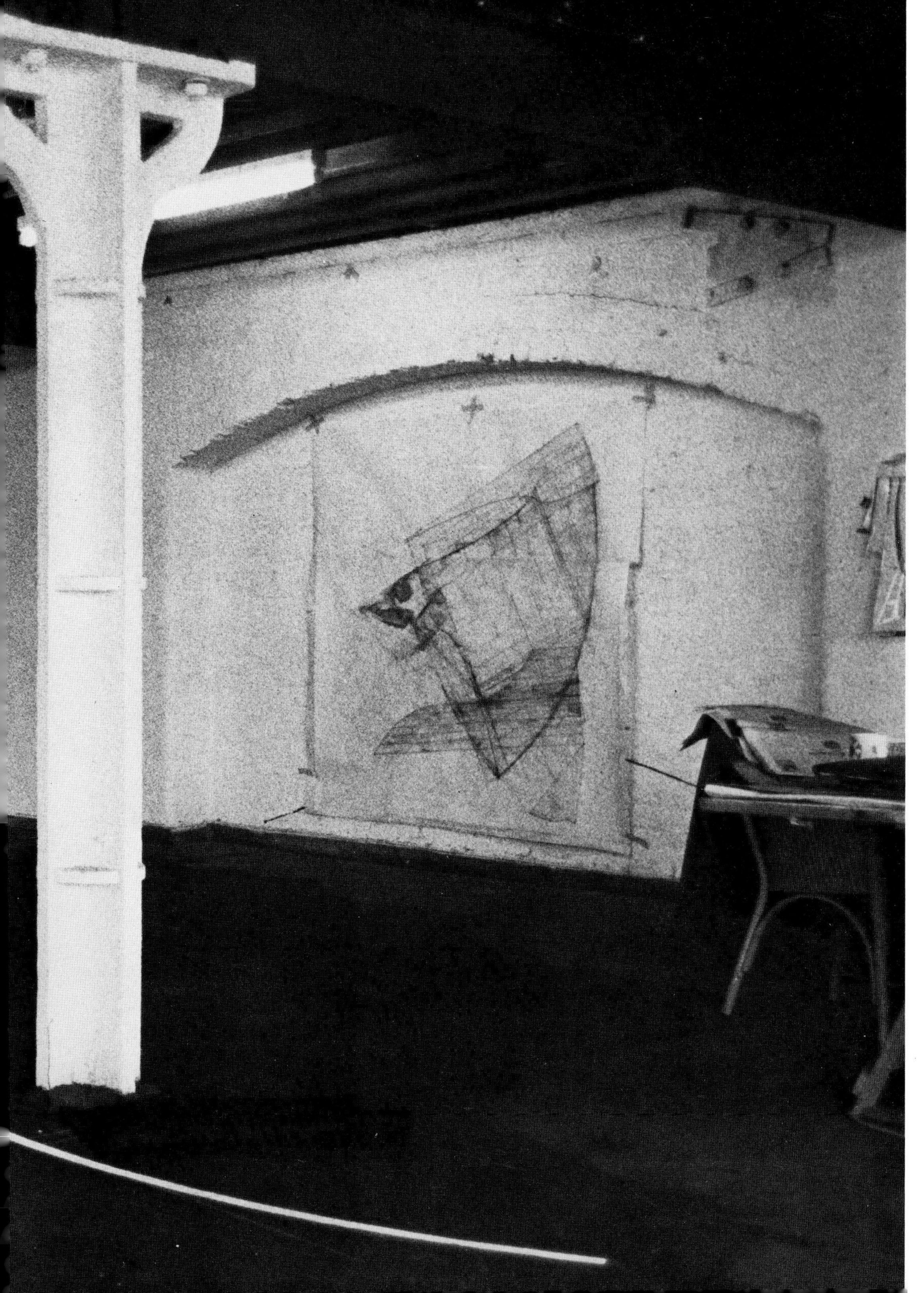

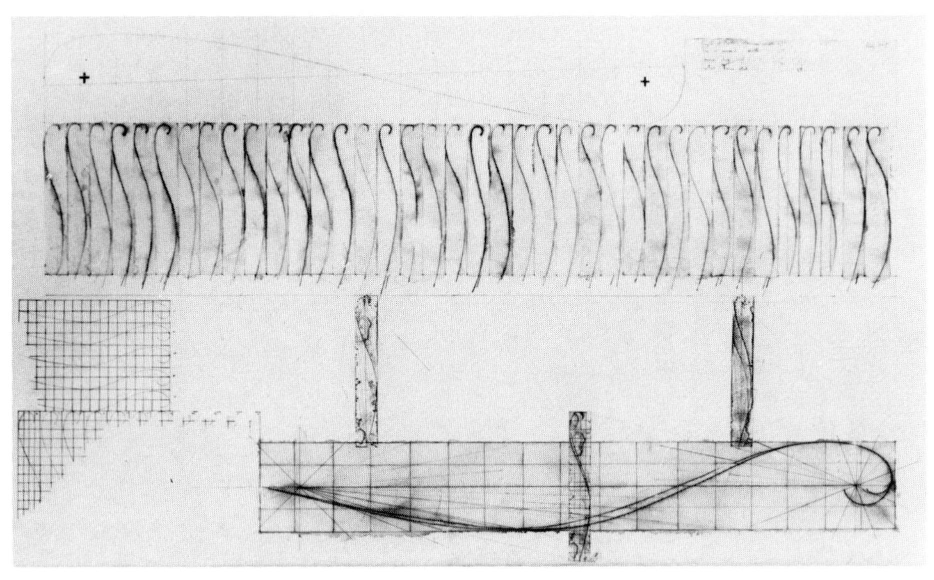

92. p. 138
A Taste of Honey makes the Bee change her Tune
in progress in Simon Read's studio

93.
Trims Stick. 1977
Ink, pencil and xerox on paper, 33 x 53″
Courtesy Anthony Stokes Gallery, London

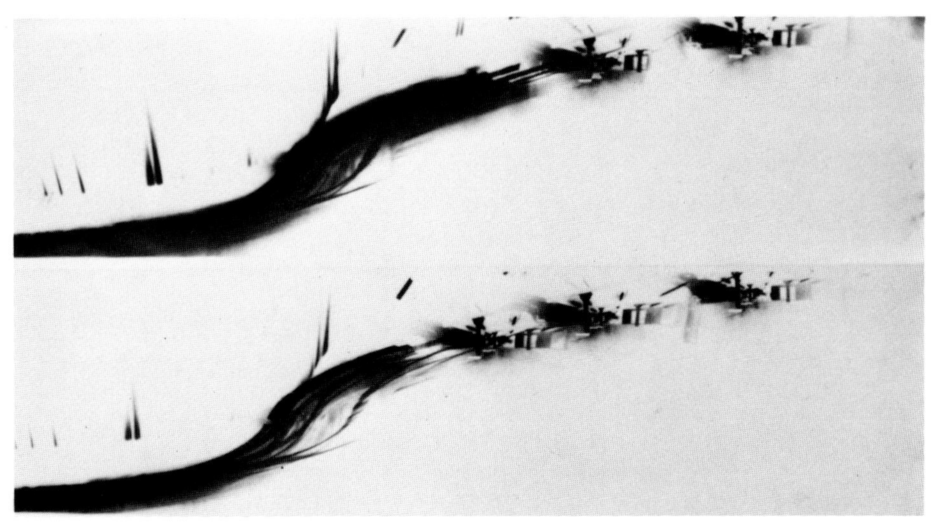

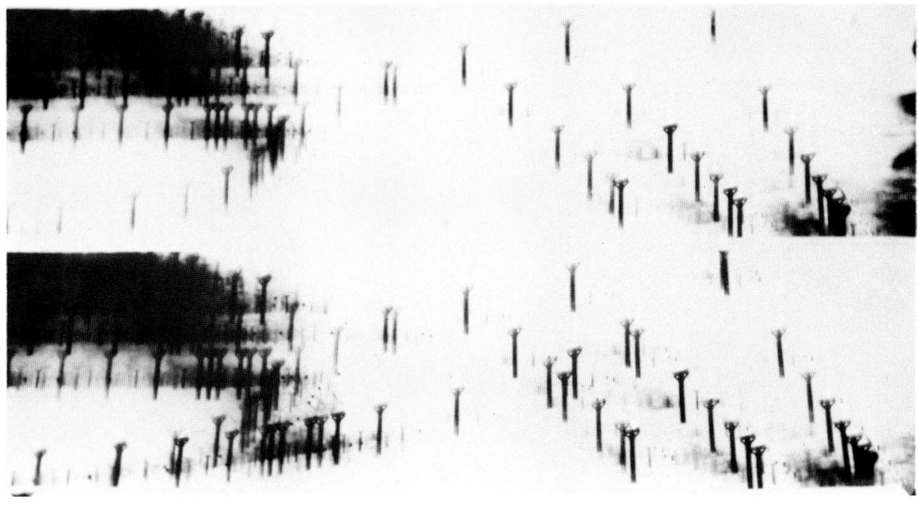

94.
Two-page sequence from *A Taste of Honey makes
the Bee change her Tune.* 1977
53 black and white photographic prints bound in
book form, 20 x 72"
Collection Leeds City Art Galleries

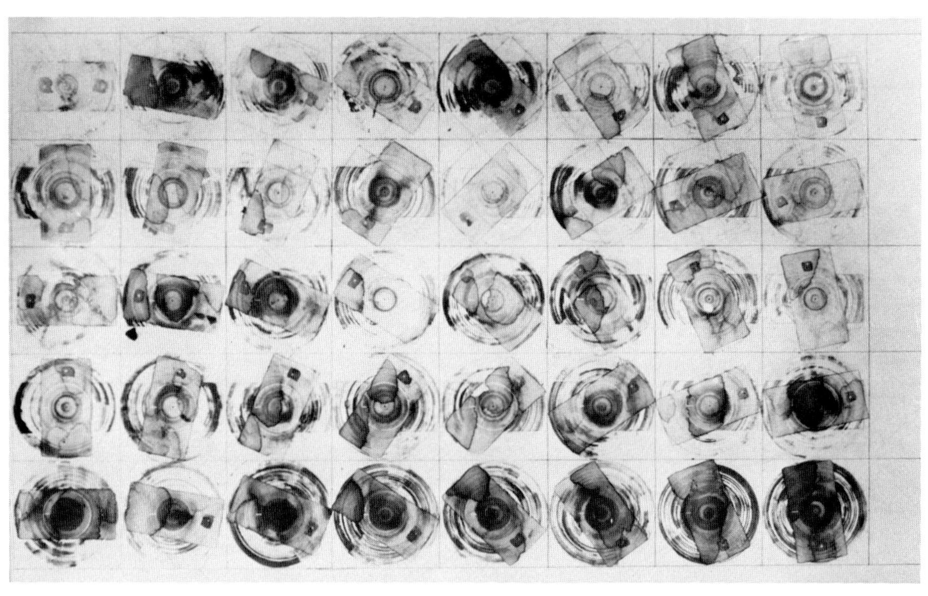

95.
Drawing Towards Uncertain Portrait. 1978
Ink, pencil and gouache on paper, 34 x 53″
Courtesy Anthony Stokes Gallery, London

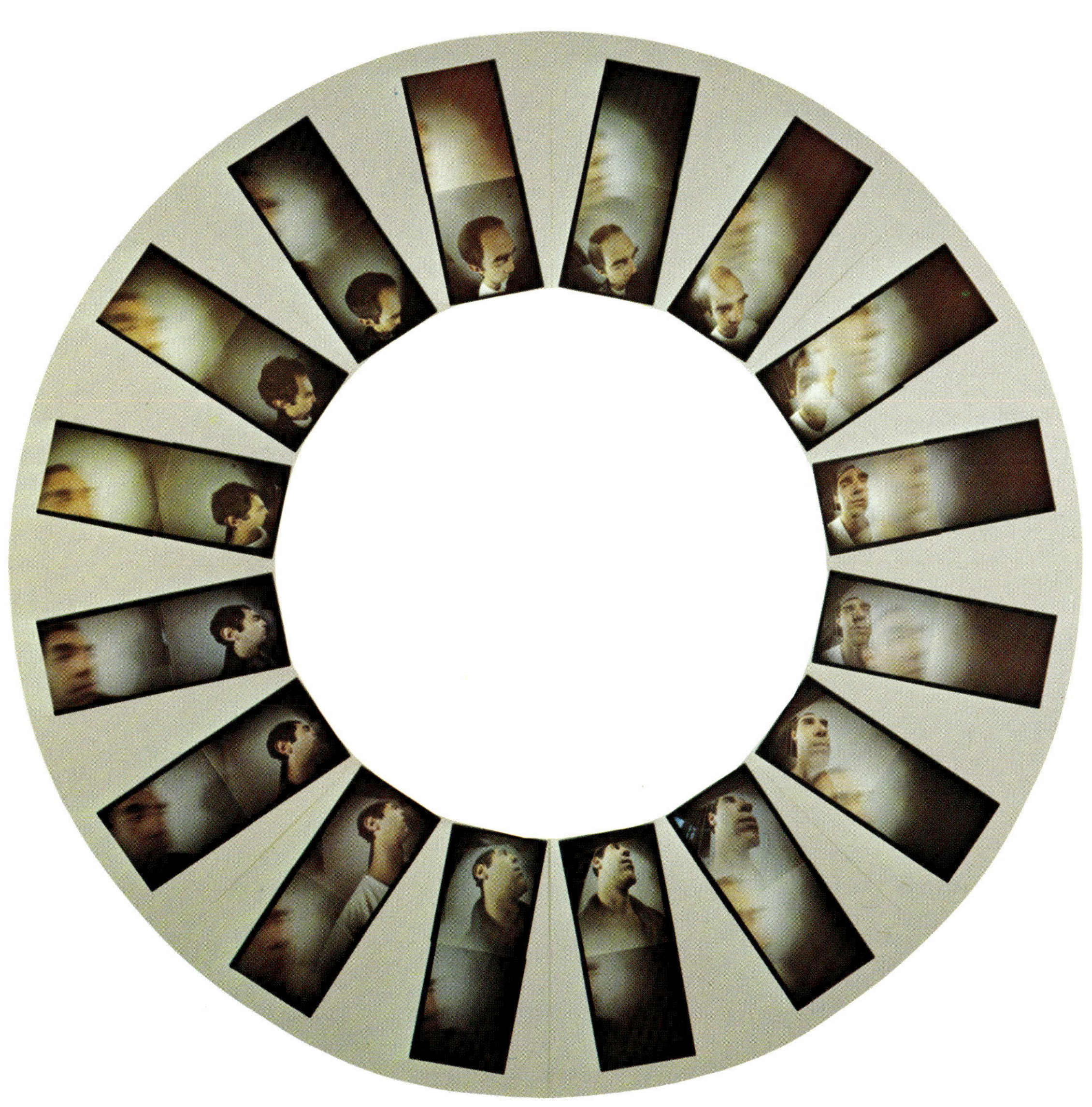

96.
Uncertain Portrait. 1978
16 pairs of color bromide photographs, each 8 x
10″, mounted in circular frame, 84″ diameter
Collection The British Council, London

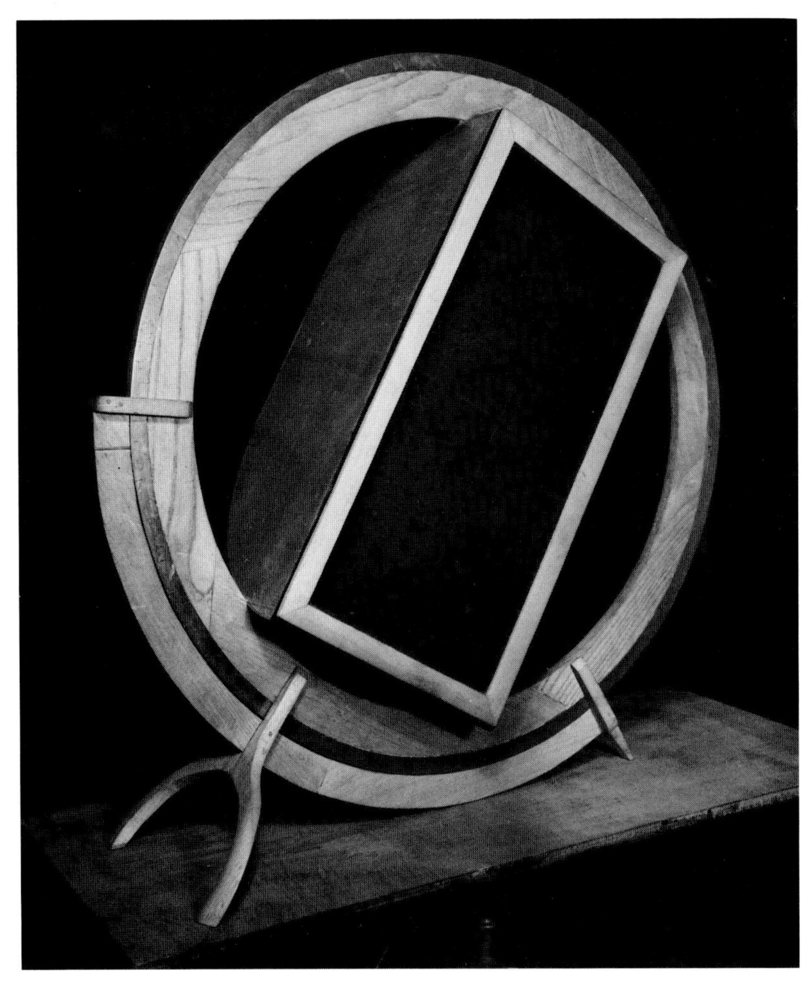

97.
Camera for *Uncertain Portrait, Neither to run with the hare, nor hunt with the hounds* and *Non-Sequitur I*

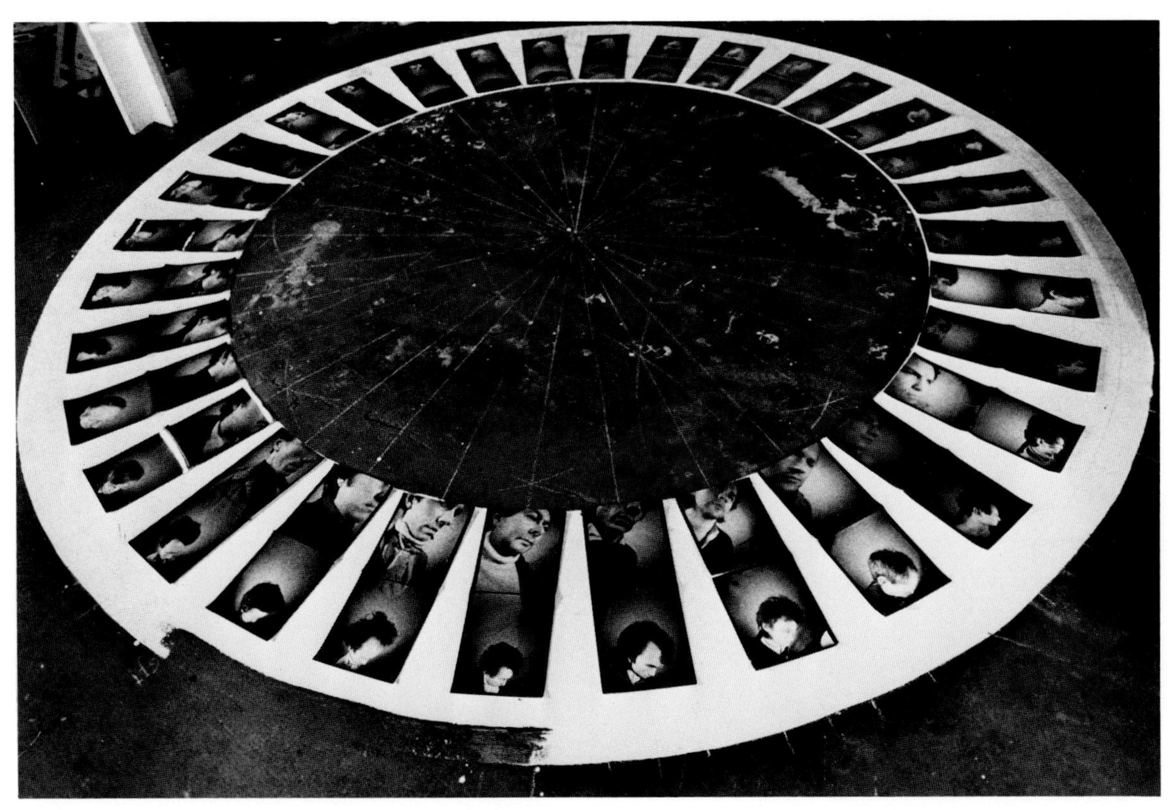

98.

*Neither to run with the hare, nor hunt with the
hounds* in progress in Simon Read's studio. 1978
32 pairs of color bromide photographs, each 8 x
10″, mounted in circular frame, 144″ diameter
Courtesy Anthony Stokes Gallery, London

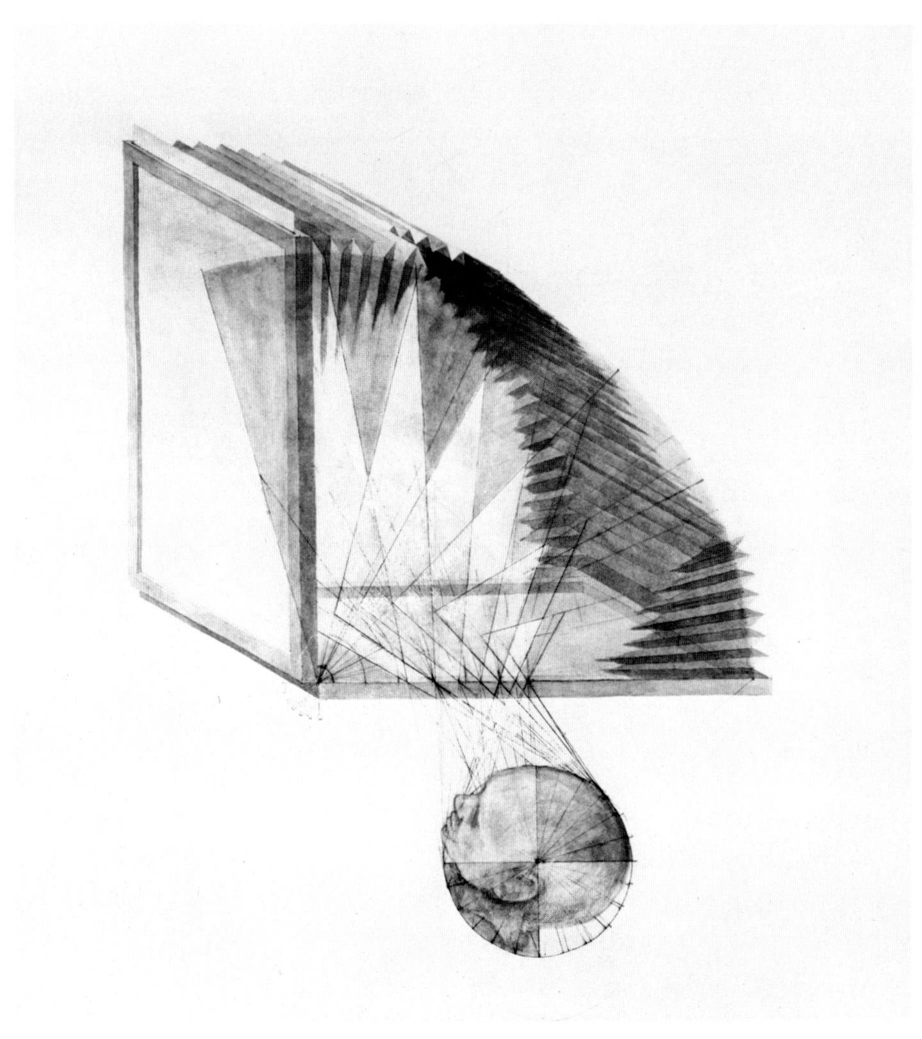

99.
Drawing towards a sidelong glance. 1978-79
Ink and pencil on paper, 53 x 53″
Courtesy Anthony Stokes Gallery, London

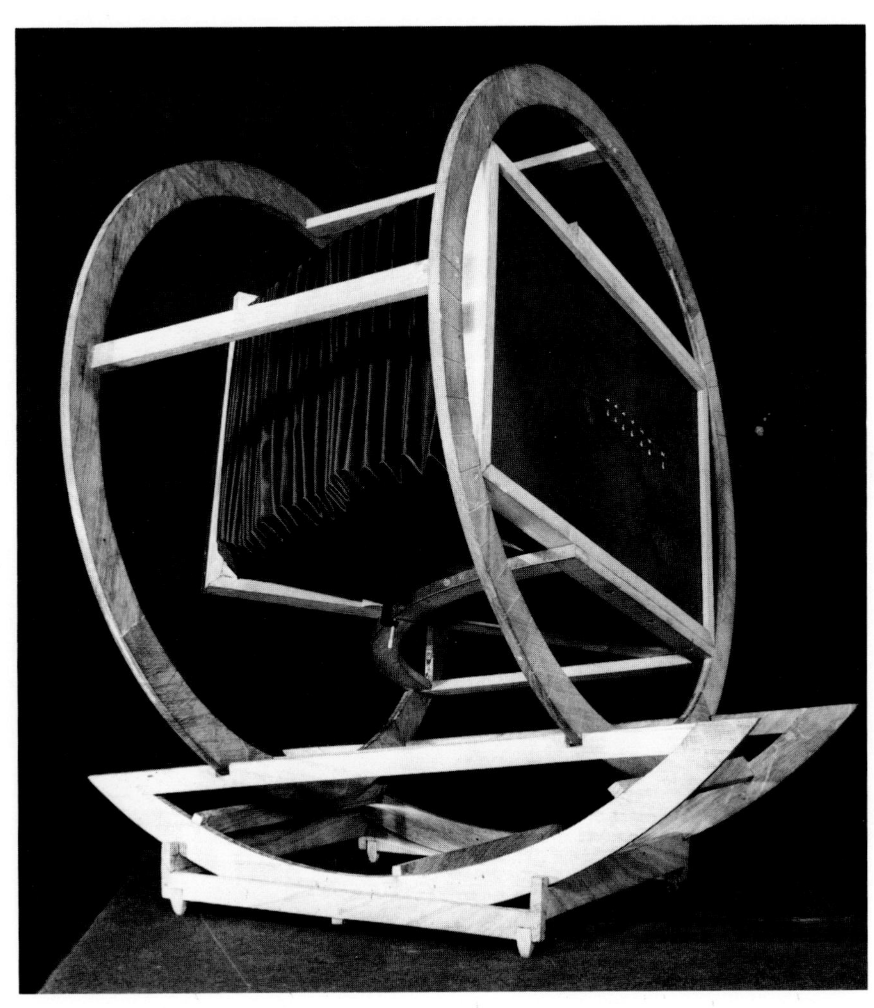

100.
Camera for *The Virtue of a Glancing Blow and a Sidelong Glance, Bugger Alberti, Bugger Alberti II, Concerning Alberti* and *Pyrrhic Victory*

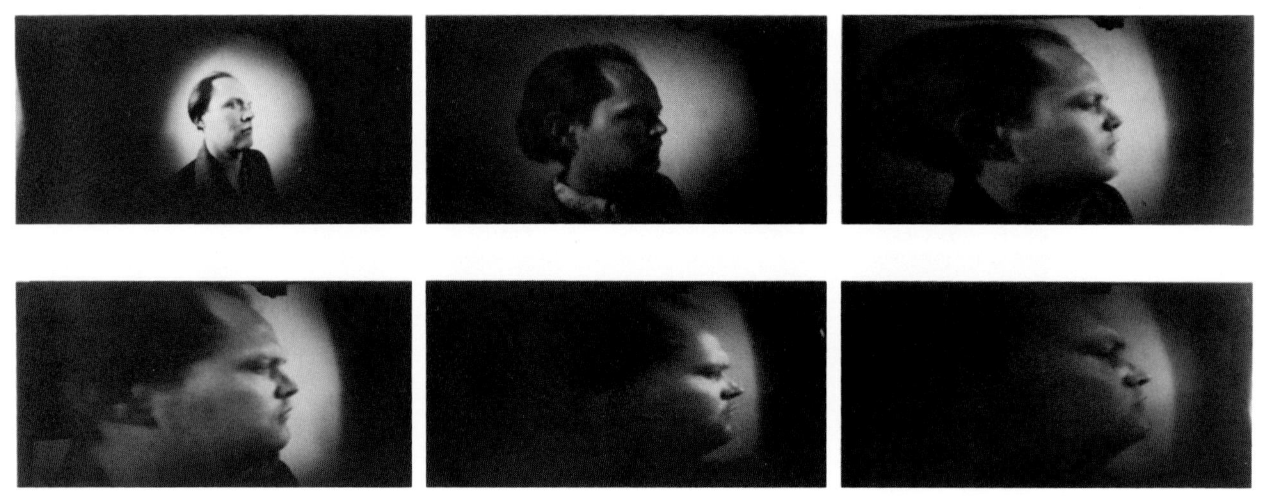

101.
The Virtue of a Glancing Blow and a Sidelong Glance. 1978-79
6 color bromide photographs, each 10½ x 20″, mounted in individual frames, each 11 x 24″
Courtesy Anthony Stokes Gallery, London

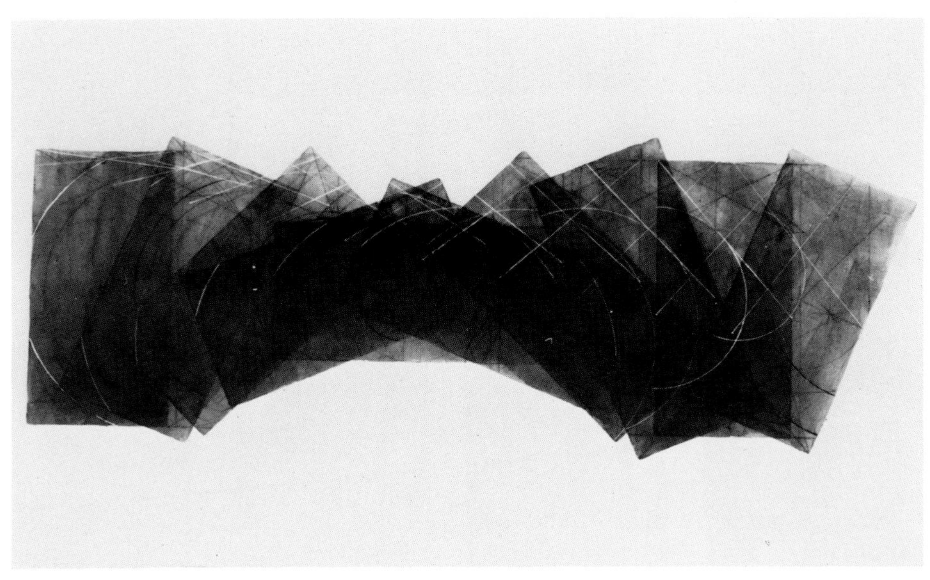

102.
Drawn Towards Non-Sequitur. 1978
Ink and pencil on paper, one of a pair, each 33 x 53″
Courtesy Anthony Stokes Gallery, London

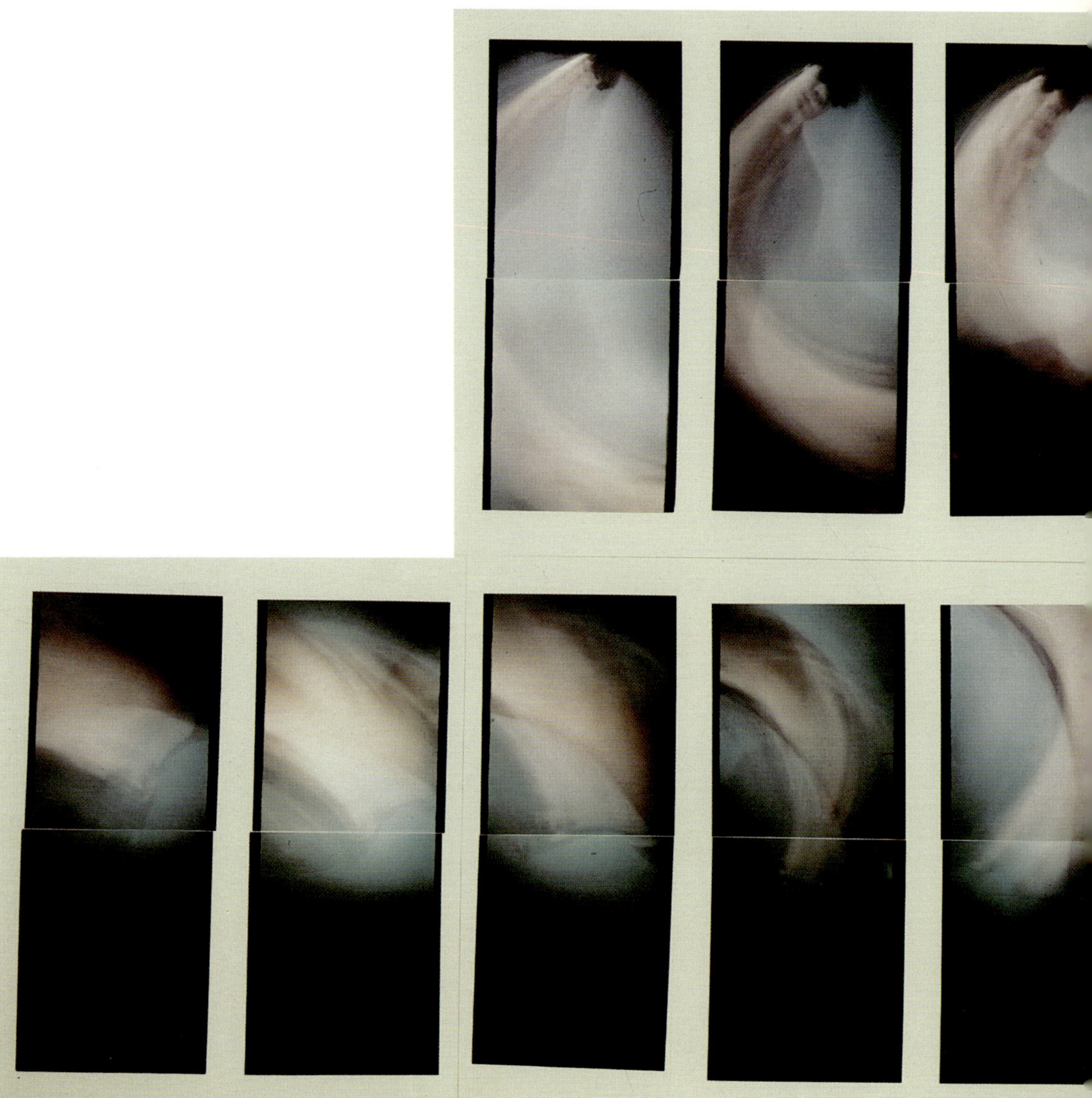

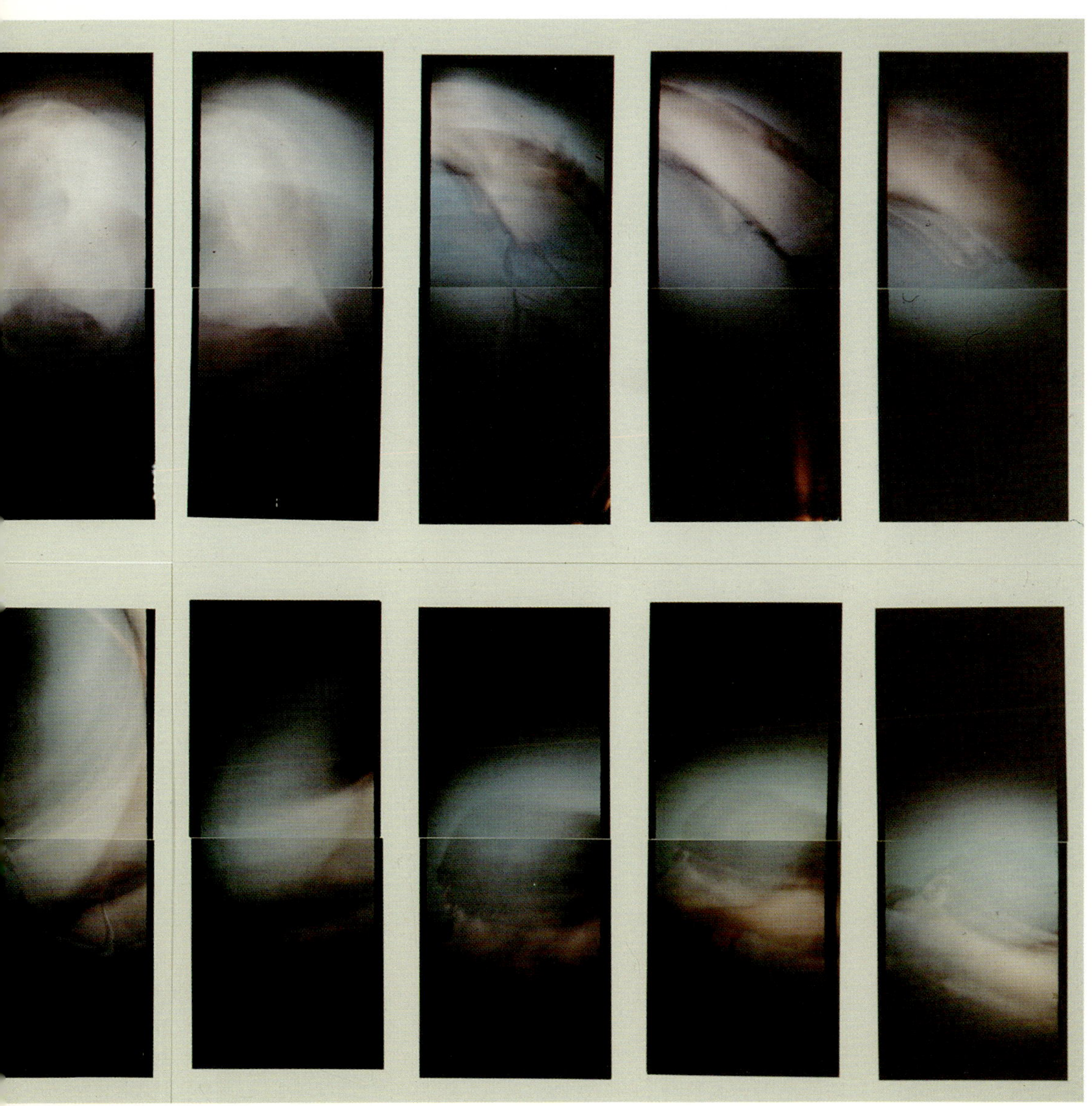

103.
Non-Sequitur I. 1978
18 pairs of color bromide photographs, each 8 x
10″, mounted in three frames, 24 x 120″, 24 x 96″,
24 x 23″
Courtesy Anthony Stokes Gallery, London

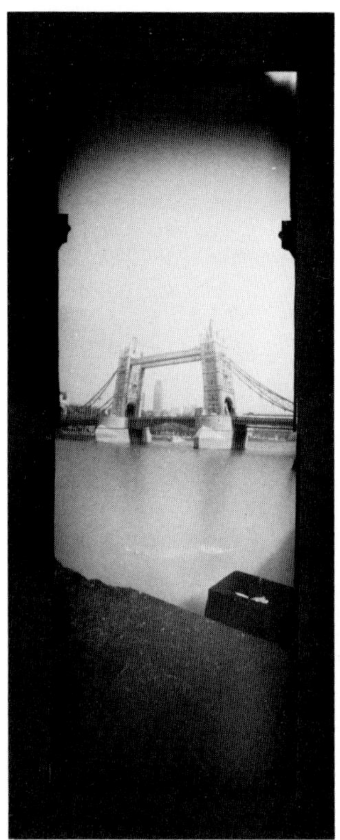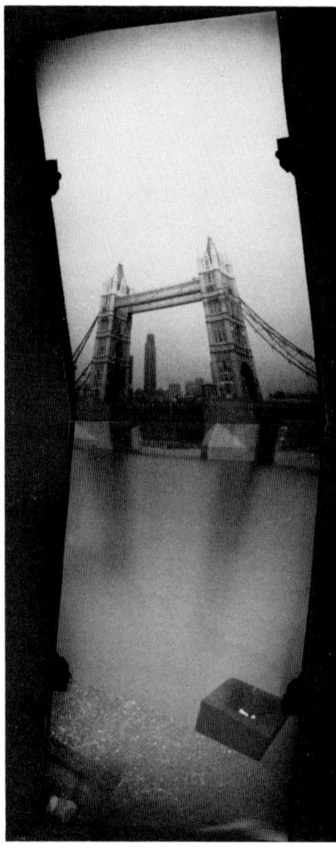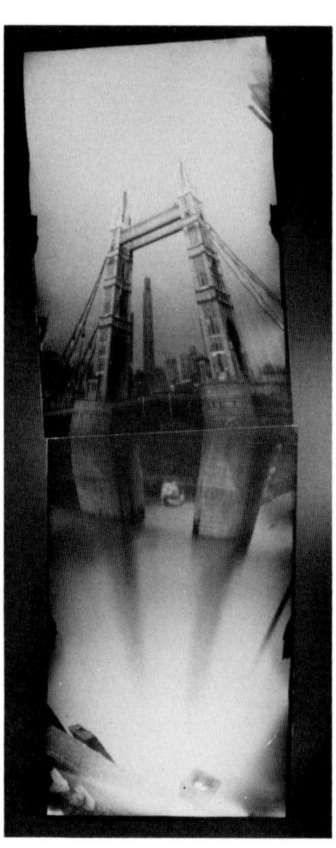

104.
Concerning Alberti. 1979
3 color bromide photographs, each 35 x 10½ ″
Courtesy Anthony Stokes Gallery, London

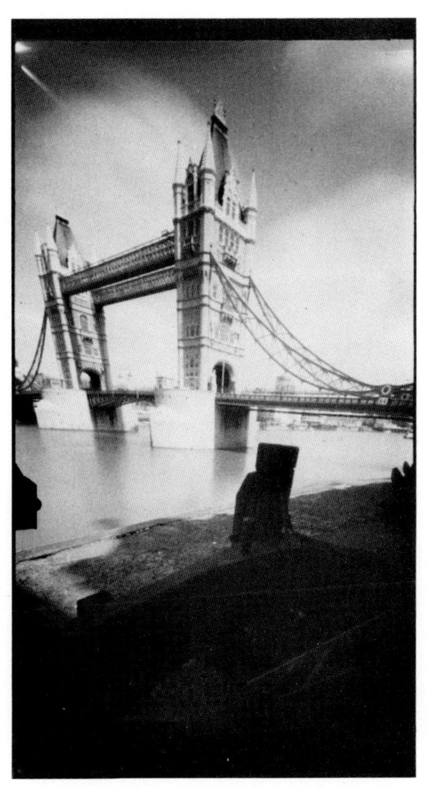

105.
Bugger Alberti II. 1979
Color bromide photograph, 20 x 10½″
Courtesy Anthony Stokes Gallery, London

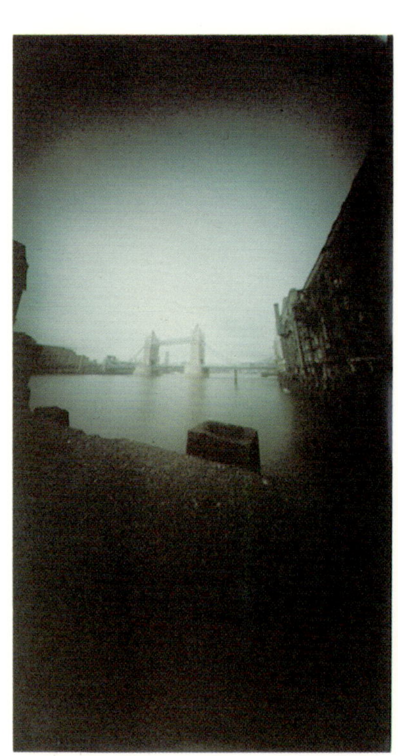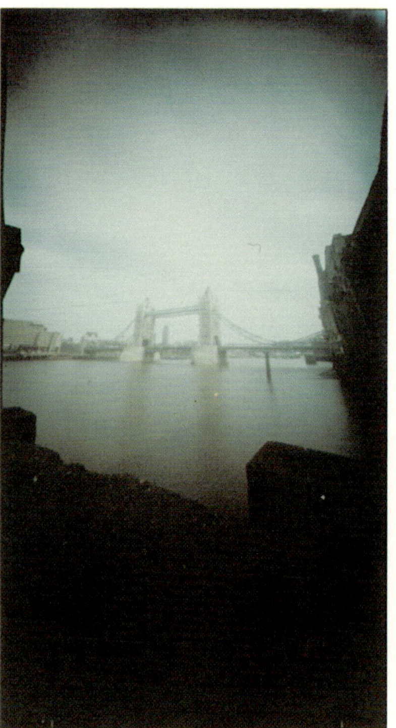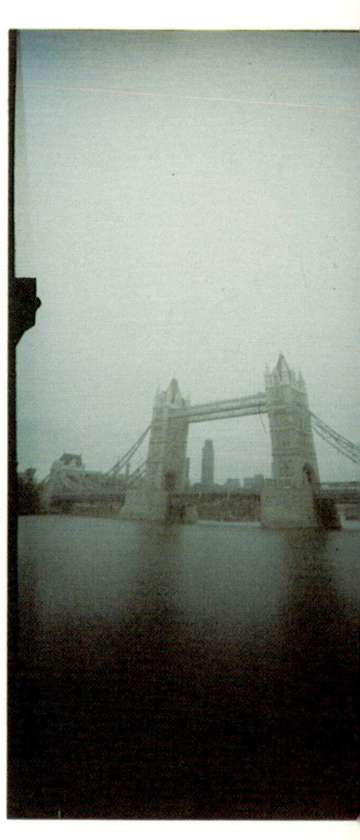

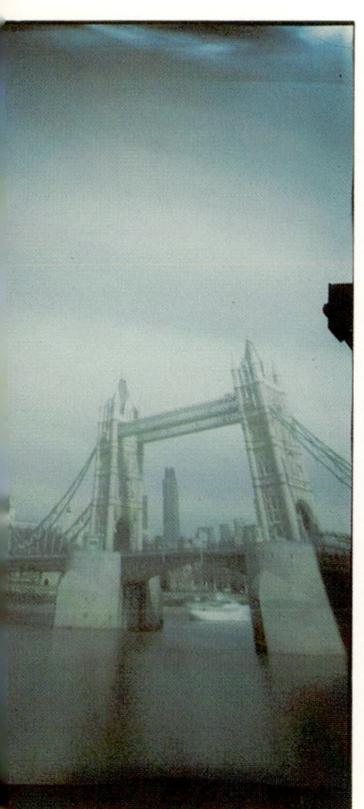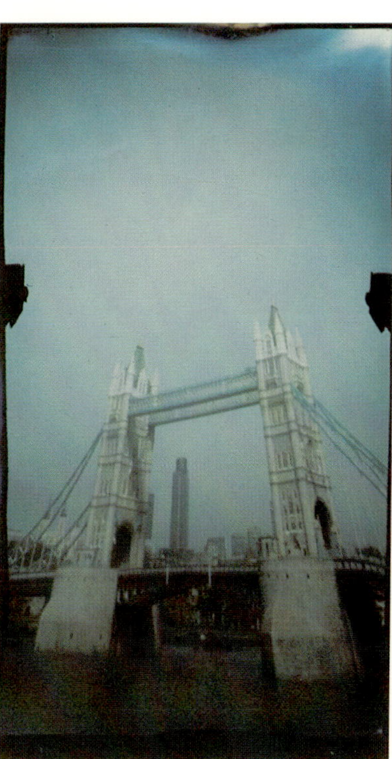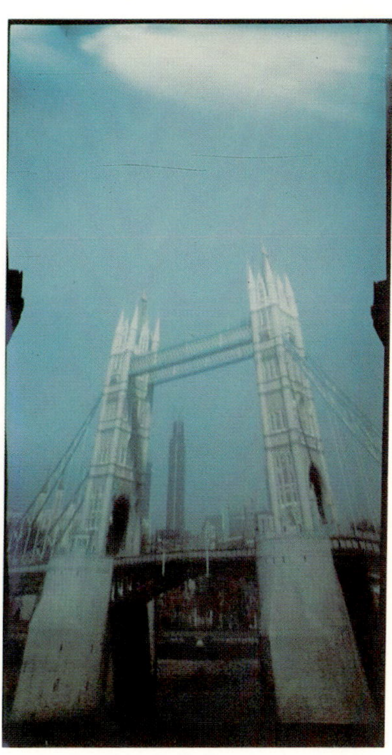

106.

Bugger Alberti. 1979
6 color bromide photographs, each 20 x 10½ ″,
mounted in individual frames, each 24 x 14½ ″
Courtesy Anthony Stokes Gallery, London

Photographic Credits

Color
Clive Adams: cat. no. 26
Chris Davies: cat. no. 32
John Goldblatt: cat. nos. 42, 44, 47
Courtesy Anthony Howarth, London: pp. 100, 134;
cat. no. 49
Geoffrey Shackerly, Photographic Records Limited:
cat. nos. 20, 88, 89, 96, 103, 106
Rodney Todd-White and Sons: cat. nos. 16, 19, 23
John Webb: cat. nos. 3, 7, 11, 71, 74
Sue Wells: cat. nos. 52, 63, 64

Black and White
Jonathan Bayer: pp. 10, 14
Janet Bonehill: p. 118
Commune di Milano: cat. no. 29
Courtauld Institute, London: cat. no. 52
Chris Davies: p. 44; cat. nos. 24, 25, 27, 28, 30,
31, 33
eeva-inkeri, New York: cat. no. 37
Tom Evans: cat. nos. 66, 68-70, 72, 73, 75-79
John Goldblatt: p. 62; cat. nos. 41, 43, 45, 46, 48
Alan Green: cat. nos. 14, 15, 17, 18, 21
June Green: pp. 26, 31
John Hunnex: cat. nos. 12, 13
National Portrait Gallery, London: p. 136
Photo Studios Ltd.: cat. no. 38
Photographic Records Limited: cat. no. 101
Nicholas Pope: cat. nos. 83, 91
Simon Read: cat. nos. 93-95, 97, 99, 100, 102, 104, 105
Tore Røyneland: cat. no. 34
Heini Scheebeli: cat. nos. 39, 40
Courtesy Sydney Biennale: cat. no. 35
Anthony Stokes: cat. nos. 80-82, 84-87, 90, 98
Tate Gallery, London: cat. no. 36
Rodney Todd-White and Sons: cat. no. 22
John Webb: cat. nos. 1, 2, 4-6, 8-10, 67
Sue Wells: p. 83; cat. nos. 50, 51, 53-62, 65

Exhibition 80/2

8,500 copies of this catalogue, designed by
Malcolm Grear Designers, typeset by
Dumar Typesetting, Inc., have been printed by
The Falcon Press in December 1979
for the Trustees of The Solomon R. Guggenheim
Foundation on the occasion of the

**British Art Now: An American Perspective
1980 Exxon International Exhibition**

Cover design courtesy Exxon Corporation